Teachers and Teaching:
From Classroom to Reflection

For LaVerne and Nancy

Teachers and Teaching:
From Classroom to Reflection

Edited by

Tom Russell and Hugh Munby

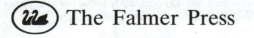

The Falmer Press

(A member of the Taylor & Francis Group)

London • New York • Philadelphia

UK   The Falmer Press, 4 John St, London WC1N 2ET
USA   The Falmer Press, Taylor & Francis Inc., 1900 Frost Road, Suite 101,
       Bristol, PA 19007

First published 1992

A catalogue record for this book is available from this British Library

Library of Congress Cataloging-in-Publication Data are available on request

Jacket design by Caroline Archer

ISBN 0 75070 020 3 Cases
     0 75070 021 1 Paperback

Set in 10/12 pt Times
by Graphicraft Typesetters Ltd., Hong Kong

Printed in Great Britain by Burgess Science Press, Basingstoke on paper which has a specified pH value on final paper manufacture of not less than 7.5 and is therefore 'acid free'.

Table of Contents

Acknowledgments

Jan Carrick, our secretary at Queen's University, made countless contributions that included complete retyping of several chapters, valuable editorial suggestions and encouragement when the task seemed overwhelming. Phyllis Johnston, who has been part of our research activities for more than five years, has contributed in many ways to our efforts to understand reflection in the context of teaching. Paul Park, Dean of the Faculty of Education at Queen's, has actively and enthusiastically encouraged our research and publication activities.

Since 1984, several research grants from the Social Sciences and Humanities Research Council of Canada have enabled us to contribute to the study of teachers' professional knowledge. The School of Graduate Studies and Research at Queen's University has made modest contributions to our research activities and conference travel that have helped us assemble this international collection of perspectives on teachers and teaching. The University of York provided office space and computing services while Tom Russell was on sabbatical leave in England for the 1990–91 academic year. These facilities supported the final editing of the various authors' contributions and permitted communication with many of the contributors.

The chapter by Jean Rudduck originally appeared in *Westminster Studies in Education*, **12**, 1989, pages 61–72 and is reprinted here with the kind permission of the editor.

Tom Russell
Hugh Munby
September 1991

1   Frames of Reflection: An Introduction

Hugh Munby and Tom Russell

The work collected in this book is intended to recognize the place of professional practice itself in the realm of research on teaching. Practice, we believe, precedes research just as practice is the realm in which we think efforts to improve research are most likely to be successful. As with other types of professional practice, teaching has not been accorded the status some believe it deserves, yet the status cannot be raised simply by assertion. The contributors to this book respect and take seriously the work of teachers and the challenges of teaching. The chapters in this volume speak clearly to the fact that teaching can be taken seriously, in schools and in programs of teacher education. To take teaching seriously is, at least in part, to seek new ways of bringing together the practice of teaching and research on teaching.

The Return of Research to Teaching Itself

The title of this collection, *Teachers and Teaching: From Classroom to Reflection*, signals our growing understanding of a shift in research on teaching, teachers, and teacher education. We joined the ranks of these researchers some twenty years ago when the process-product model had achieved prominence. For us, it has been important to understand that the process-product model for research on teaching embodied assumptions about two very different spheres of professional activity: research and teacher education. For research to be valid and publishable, it seemed that it had somehow to mirror the 'scientific' paradigm. The research assumption spilled into a conception of teacher education: the professional preparation of teachers implicitly became viewed as an enterprise in which beginning teachers were told authoritatively how they should teach. The occasional indication of problems with this research assumption (Russell, 1980) was unlikely to turn the tide.

Of course, the view that one can learn to teach by being told was not a novelty brought to teacher education by the process-product model. Yet the model appeared to endorse it. Neither would we argue that there is nothing valuable to be learned from the on-campus components of teacher preparation programs. But the endorsement of the view that we can prepare teachers by telling seems to have predisposed us not to ask which elements of the activities of teaching *cannot* be learned by telling.

Research on teaching published between 1980 and 1990 shows a marked shift in these assumptions. At one level the assumption about what yields valid research information is enlarged to admit ethnographic and qualitative approaches. At the same time, and possibly as a consequence of this, researchers have become increasingly interested in what teachers themselves think and know. Beneath this change we see researchers becoming more respectful of the experience of teaching itself, of the actors, and of their contexts. These movements in research approaches and foci have provoked and accompanied a change in the significance attached to the experience of learning to teach in practicum settings. The customary and lively attention to the curriculum for on-campus teacher preparation is being matched by attention to questions about how beginning and experienced teachers can and do profit from their professional experiences. When Schön (1983) described a 'crisis of confidence' in society's attitudes to professionals, he went on to argue that the connections between research and practice had to be addressed directly within research. We are encouraged to see research on teaching and teacher education moving in that direction, and the contributors to this collection are among those who have recognized and accepted the challenge of understanding how teachers develop practical professional knowledge.

The contents of this book reveal our enthusiasm for these changes, and in part the contents signal the journey that the idea of a science of education has recently taken. There are ironies in these changes, for it appears that the apparatus of educational research has begun to align itself with Dewey's view of the centrality of teaching experience. The science of education, in a sense, has come full circle so that it begins with practice, where Dewey argued that it should. The deeper irony is that a large portion of current research on learning to teach and improving teaching invokes the idea of reflection, and often with reference to Dewey.

The Faces of Reflection

Schön's (1983) distinction between technical rationality and the knowledge of practice has drawn our attention to the significance of the knowledge that teachers acquire from their own experience. His work has reminded us of Polanyi's statement that one's knowledge is far more extensive than what can be put into words, just as it has forced us once again to acknowledge that there is far more to teaching than can ever be learned from the on-campus classes in teacher education programs. Our own research (Russell,

Munby, Johnston and Spafford, 1988) has been prompted largely by this acknowledgement and by the realization that we seem to understand little of how teachers acquire this knowledge from their experience. Put another way, the slogan 'teachers learn from experience' masks questions that assume a special importance in the light of Schön's work. Examples of these questions are:

1 What particular elements of experience prompt teachers to learn from them?
2 What are the differences between the teaching of those who have learned from experience and the teaching of those who have not?
3 Are some teachers more disposed to learn from their experiences than others, and is such a disposition relevant to those for whom learning to teach is a long, slow and confusing experience?
4 Is it possible to arrange programs of teacher education so that learning from experience is encouraged explicitly?

Questions such as these are addressed in the chapters of this book, which have been arranged so that they instantiate facets of reflection as a central approach to the acquisition of professional knowledge. In this way, the book testifies to the progress made in what we prefer to think of as the science of teaching, where 'science' is understood in Dewey's sense of inquiry — the point at which Schön's work with 'knowing-in-action' begins.

Schön's epistemology of action, knowing-in-action, begins with the view that the knowledge resides in performance and so is non-propositional, representing more than can be put into words. Something of this type of knowledge is revealed in the chapter by Oberg and Artz, whose conversation can be read as an attempt to explain in text what they 'know-in-action' as teachers. Schön's epistemology continues with two different accounts of how the knowledge of action is acquired: reflection-on-action and reflection-in-action. Reflection-*on*-action refers to the systematic and deliberate thinking back over one's actions that characterizes much of what we do when we pause after an action and attend to what we believe has occurred. This form of reflection is parallel to what seems to be intended in a considerable amount of the literature on reflective teaching and reflective teacher education. As Richert puts it, the goal of the enterprise is to develop a cadre of teachers who are thoughtful about their work.

Reflection-*in*-action is Schön's term for those interactions with experience that result in the often sudden and unanticipated ways in which we come to *see experience differently*. The heart of this, for Schön, is reframing, a term that we have explained in the following way:

Reflection-in-action is a process with nonlogical features, a process that is prompted by experience and over which we have limited control. Teachers at every level of education are familiar with the circumstance of being unable to get a point across to a whole class. Success may come suddenly and unexpectedly, through the teacher's somehow hearing what the students say in a quite different way. For us, the essence of reflection-in-action is this 'hearing' differently or 'seeing differently', a process that Schön calls 'reframing'. Importantly, the form of reflection that involves reframing is very different from the more familiar form, which Schön terms 'reflection-on-action'. This refers to the ordered, deliberate, and systematic application of logic to a problem in order to resolve it; the process is very much within our control. The sort of thinking characterized by reflection-on-action involves careful consideration of familiar data. In contrast, reflection-*in*-action presents the data quite differently, so that they appear in a novel frame. What control we can exercise comes through reflection *on* reflection-in-action, when we think systematically about the freshly framed data. (Russell and Munby, 1991, pp. 164–165)

Frames, for Schön, function importantly in the epistemology of knowing-in-action. If problem solving is the essence of technological rationality, then framing or problem setting is the essence of knowing-in-action. How we come to frame experience establishes how the puzzles of experience are set and is thus the crucial first step in problem solving. This brings us directly to describing the contents of this book, for we can now speak to the chapters in terms of the puzzles of experience addressed in each and the particular frames that the authors have adopted for seeing these puzzles and then addressing them. The twelve chapters in this collection are organized into five sections.

Setting the Stage

The chapter by Douglas Barnes is unique in several respects: It is the longest chapter in the collection, it takes a broad perspective on teachers' work, and it takes advantage of long-term views across a range of curriculum development activities. Accordingly, this chapter leads off, introducing the topic of teachers' frames for reflecting on their work. Barnes draws on his own experiences with the London Association for the Teaching of English, with the introduction of 'oracy' into the secondary English curriculum, and with the Language Across the Curriculum movement to illustrate his broad points about the significance of teachers' frames for interpreting the settings in which they work. He emphasizes that personal commitments and professional experience exist in interaction with each other. Barnes concludes that teaching can change only when teachers' frames change, and these are in turn dependent on 'subtle and sensitive' changes in schools that will not easily be achieved.

Reflection in Teaching

John Baird, author of Chapter 3, describes two unique projects in Australia in which reflection and enquiry into classroom events are carried out by teachers (and others) in collaboration with one another with a view to improving teaching. Three 'guiding principles' are developed: to converge processes and outcomes, to support change adequately, and to base improvement on reflection. Four illustrations are provided from one of the projects, and each is described in terms of procedures and resulting issues. Baird concludes by using the concept of 'challenge' to summarize this research into ways to improve teaching and learning.

In Chapter 4, Hilda Borko, Mary Louise Bellamy and Linda Sanders report their study of teachers' plans for and reflections on their teaching, with specific reference to science teaching, and guided by a contrast between 'expert' and 'novice' teachers. They view teaching as a complex cognitive skill, and their vignettes of four teachers are rich with quotations from the teachers' reflections on their planning and teaching. The contrast between beginning and experienced teachers is particularly effective in illustrating the value of a cognitive skill perspective, as the experienced teachers revealed more appropriate and more developed schemata for interpreting and thus responding to the events of teaching. These schemata help to explain the experts' greater ability to interpret and respond to students' signals about how well they were understanding their lessons.

Reflection in Cases of Teaching

Brent Kilbourn specializes in detailed analysis of teaching and in Chapter 5 uses an instance of history teaching, by a teacher attempting to change, to illustrate that 'elegant practice in teaching requires the integration of philosophical, subject matter and classroom understandings'. After introducing each of the three types of understanding, one history lesson at the Grade 7 level is examined closely. The analysis provides valuable illustration of the nature of each of the three types of understanding while also achieving valuable insights into the challenges that are inevitable when one seeks to change one's teaching. Kilbourn's skillful presentation and interpretation of 'Bill Lander' at work in the classroom reveals the complexities that emerge when reflection rooted in one aspect of a teacher's understanding is returned to the action of the classroom where it inevitably encounters other aspects of professional understanding.

In our personal contribution to this collection, Chapter 6, we shift from our editorial roles to a recent case in our accumulating collection of cases about metaphor and reflection in the development of teachers' professional knowledge. We present the case of 'Debra', a beginning teacher of chemistry with a graduate degree and extensive experience as a research technician in chemistry. When Debra agreed to be observed and interviewed at intervals, she was experiencing difficulty with classroom interactions while achieving considerable success in laboratory activities. This chapter describes a number of patterns in Debra's teaching and in her thought about her work. Among the suggestions that emerge is the possibility that developing the necessary pedagogical knowledge of her subject of chemistry is complicated and constrained by her highly integrated view of her subject acquired in years of laboratory research.

In Chapter 7, Kathy Carter addresses an important recent development in teacher education: the possibility of developing the knowledge of teachers with case studies of teachers' work. Case studies for educational purposes pose the issue of whether teaching can be captured in written form in ways that will nurture the reflections of both beginning and experienced teachers. Carter's argument begins by considering the emerging understanding that teachers' knowledge is practical and contextualized, personal, task-specific and event-structured and rooted in recurring experiences of the classroom. The substance, the shape and the size of cases prepared for teacher education purposes are considered from this perspective of new understandings of teachers' knowledge. Carter's discussion concludes with important points about the nature of learning to teach and its significance for using cases for teaching purposes.

Narrative in Reflection

Jean Clandinin introduces in Chapter 8 the perspective of narrative and story in teacher education, building on the use of narrative inquiry in research that she has conducted with Michael Connelly. Teachers' 'personal practical knowledge' is taken to be narratively constructed, and an account is given of a specific narrative inquiry into teacher education. The illustrative case emphasizes the collaboration between teacher and researcher, as the stories of both are played out in interaction. Thus this chapter considers research methodology as well as the content of individuals' stories. Clandinin stresses the power of narrative and story in fostering reflection on teaching but readily acknowledges that the 'storying process' can be a hazardous as well as a constructive medium. Broad issues for teacher education are raised, and illustrated by the story of 'Julie' learning to teach.

Antoinette Oberg and Sibylle Artz provide a narrative account of their reflections about how they try to be reflective in their teaching. In Chapter 9 they direct our attention to questions such as 'What is it to teach reflectively?' and 'What is it to be a reflective teacher?', and the results are intriguing. Their conversation provides an unusual and indirect account, but in some ways it offers greater insights than replies structured in more familiar 'analytic' formats. For example, the doubts and uncertainties of teaching are much more apparent than would be the case in another format. They address in several ways the issue of 'subjectivity' in teaching, an issue that often arises in conjunction with efforts to be more reflective *in* one's work.

Reflection in Teacher Education

Jean Rudduck urges teacher education situated within universities to raise its level of intellectual challenge through 'some form of reflective classroom-based research or, more ambitiously, critical action research'. Chapter 10 begins with a clear account of the recent challenges to teacher education in the UK, showing that the very familiar criteria set out by the new Council for the Accreditation of Teacher Education are actually problematic for those who would encourage 'a habit of critical reflection on practice'. Rudduck moves on to argue that fostering critical reflection requires specific structures within initial teacher education, and she illustrates by describing recent developments at Sheffield. Rather than abandoning teacher education to an in-school apprenticeship model, a case is made for the greater value of school-university partnership.

In Chapter 11, Anna Richert provides data about how different structures for facilitating reflection *within* one teacher education program can make a difference to those learning to teach. She analyzes the content of reflections by twelve student teachers who reflected under two of four conditions involving presence or absence of a 'partner' with whom to reflect and a 'portfolio' of recent teaching materials about which to reflect. Those with neither partner nor portfolio showed the highest level of 'personal' reflections, while those with both partner and portfolio showed the highest level of attention to 'content specific pedagogy'. Richert's findings are plausible, and their value is in demonstrating that different structures *do make a difference*. Reflection under each of the four conditions is illustrated with quotations from the beginning teachers.

The chapter by Allan MacKinnon and Gaalen Erickson is a unique extension of their research into reflective practice by science teachers and the student teachers whom they help to learn to teach. In Chapter 12 they take a broad look at the structure of teacher education, considering the implications of a 'reflective practice' perspective for the place of 'foundations' courses in a teacher education program. They begin with an account of Dewey and then trace the evolution of Dewey's perspective to its recent interpretation by Schön. They suggest that teacher educators have tended to view foundation courses as sources of knowledge held separate from practice, and thus distant from beginners' experiences of learning to teach. To illustrate their view that teacher education should nurture 'particular dispositions for inquiry', they describe the constructivist perspective taken in their research and present data from the practicum experiences of 'Rosie' and 'Kevin'. They show how a 'reflective practice' perspective leads to the question, 'Can these forms of foundational knowledge actually be learned in a meaningful way independent of experience in classrooms?'.

From Classroom to Reflection

For us, the interaction between teachers and those who study and write about teachers and teaching has long been problematic, often sliding too easily into the familiar mode of one person telling another how to improve practice. The chapters of this collection consistently avoid and deny that mode, working instead to show teachers and teacher educators that fresh frames are possible and deserve serious consideration. In doing this, the chapters introduce various meanings of the term 'reflection'. Despite the risk, we find the term productive: it encourages us to think deliberately about our work and to search for productive frames, while echoing Dewey's significant thinking. The different meanings apparent in these chapters permit each author to contribute to our growing appreciation of the potential of novel frames for understanding teachers and teaching.

References

RUSSELL, T.L. (1980) 'Teacher education research and the problem of change', in MUNBY, H., ORPWOOD, G. and RUSSELL, T. (Eds) *Seeing Curriculum in a New Light: Essays from Science Education*, Lanham, MD, University Press of America, pp. 114–125.

RUSSELL, T. and MUNBY, H. (1991) 'Reframing: The role of experience in developing teachers' professional knowledge', in SCHÖN, D.A. (Ed.) *The Reflective Turn: Case Studies In and On Educational Practice*, New York, Teachers College Press, pp. 164–187.

RUSSELL, T., MUNBY, H., JOHNSTON, P. and SPAFFORD, C. (1988) 'Learning the professional knowledge of teaching: Metaphors, puzzles and the theory-practice relationship', in GRIMMETT, P.P. and ERICKSON, G.L. (Eds) *Reflection in Teacher Education*, New York, Teachers College Press, and Vancouver, Pacific Press, pp. 67–90.

SCHÖN, D.A. (1983) *The Reflective Practitioner: How Professionals Think in Action*, New York, Basic Books.

2 The Significance of Teachers' Frames for Teaching

Douglas Barnes

Teachers and Change

A characteristic recent statement about the conditions under which teachers can be expected to engage in professional and curriculum development runs thus:

> If classrooms are to become communities of active enquiring learners, the teachers who provide the leadership and guidance in such classrooms must themselves have professional development opportunities that are also enquiry-oriented and collaborative. This means, first, that they should be encouraged to become researchers in their own classrooms, carrying out inquiries about student learning and the conditions and practices which most effectively support it. And, secondly, there must be institutional conditions which enable them to share the results of their inquiries with their colleagues in an ongoing attempt to create a better curriculum guided by collaboratively determined goals. (Wells, 1989, p. 15)

In writing this, Gordon Wells cites Fullan's work (1982) but he might equally have called upon the support of other writers. Stenhouse (1975), for example, argued strongly that all teachers should be researchers, not by adding new activities to their role as teachers but by treating everything they undertake as hypotheses to be tested. Earlier still, Hoyle (1975) had invented the concept of the 'extended professional' who is interested in the principles underlying the teacher's role, and not merely devoted to carrying out current school policies. I am not wishing to question these admirably liberal views; indeed, I have elsewhere expressed similar ones. What I am interested in exploring is the reason why teachers who fit this pattern are comparatively rare.

Teachers' constructions of their professional roles can be said to include models of pupils, of subject matter, of how learning takes place, and of how lessons are conducted. These models are not just descriptive frames which specify what can be expected in a lesson but constitute dynamic scenarios, for at the centre must be not an observer but a teacher who has to act, often rapidly and upon minimal evidence. I have written elsewhere:

> Teaching is a highly skilled activity which requires of the teacher an immediate response to events as they develop. He or she must attend not only to long-term goals but also to the urgent details of individual pupils' participation in the lesson. The teacher must judge instantly whether the moment requires a suggestion, an invitation to explain, a discouraging glance, an anecdote, a joke, a reprimand, or the setting of a new task. These immediate decisions depend necessarily upon intuitive judgment.... (Barnes, Britton, and Torbe, 1990, p. 8)

In lessons, the teacher is necessarily establishing priorities, unconsciously balancing possible successes and costs, responding to a diverse range of pressures from within and without the school, some of which may be contradictory.

Some of these concerns will be more salient than others. John Olson (1982) has written of the 'classroom dilemmas' that all teachers must solve in order to survive: in a particular lesson the management of the pupils may be the first need, or the achievement of examination results, or the safe handling of breakable or dangerous equipment, and so on. Whatever 'dilemmas' are of first concern to teachers will strongly constrain their ability to act upon injunctions from other people to change what they do in the classroom. When we call upon teachers to be collaborative investigators, our voices will be heard — if they are heard at all — by teachers operating within this complex of considerations: it is this that determines who will hear or fail to hear the call for change. When we talk of 'teachers as researchers' we are not thinking of the production of theorized descriptions but of *principled action*. If teachers regard what they do in lessons as a series of partly explicit hypotheses to be tested, they are likely to become much more consciously aware of the principles and priorities upon which their teaching is based. Teaching depends necessarily upon intuitive judgment, but the intuitions can be reflected upon, sharpened, and related more precisely to long-term goals and values.

Some of these concerns and priorities are very different from those of academic educationists, whether they are writing theory or carrying out empirical research. In this chapter, the concept of 'frame', which refers to the underlying assumptions that influence teachers' actions in the classroom, is used to explore the implications of such differences of perspective. This includes considering how teachers generate frames in the course of interacting with the people they work with and aspects of the institutions in which they work, so that the resulting perspectives are neither entirely determined by the context nor entirely chosen by the teacher. The overall argument is that, in order to institute change, administrators and curriculum developers need to attend carefully to the ways in which teachers affected 'frame' crucial aspects of the schools they work in; without changes in the institutions themselves, many innovations are likely to fail. The argument is illustrated by two first-hand accounts of relevant examples, in the sections immediately following. Then the concept of teachers' interpretive frames is presented and discussed from several perspectives. A third first-hand account provides further illustration before the argument is drawn to a close.

Involving Teachers in Self-development: The Example of LATE

There are teachers who engage in critical reflection upon their own work: this must be acknowledged lest the picture appear too dark. As a teacher during the 1950s and 1960s I recollect taking part during evenings and weekends in the activities of the London Association for the Teaching of English (LATE). Apart from conventional meetings with speakers, we engaged in a range of professional activities. For example, we designed alternative examination syllabuses and persuaded an examination board to adopt them; we edited and published books of materials for classroom use; we collected material on such topics as students' writing and the criteria of assessing students' scripts and found a publisher for them; we set up working parties to consider aspects of our teaching; and we organized conferences on new topics in teaching. I am turning back in this anecdotal way in order to draw from these successes — and I have listed only a few of them — the conditions that made them possible.

LATE had no status in the official administrative hierarchy, and no financial support from it. It had originally been set up by a university academic, Percival Gurrey, and during the 1950s and 1960s the association benefitted greatly from the intellectual leadership of academics, particularly James Britton, Nancy Martin and Harold Rosen. However, the activities were planned and carried out by a committee of teachers, and although the academics played a crucial part, it was so unobtrusive that we had no sense of being directed. They established a style of participation that was crucial to the success of LATE. It is important to note, however, that of the tens of thousands of English teachers and primary school teachers in London and its suburbs, only perhaps sixty or seventy were active members of LATE. Could it be that the very large constituency provided by the conurbation was a necessary part of its success? If I ask myself why I was willing to travel after a day's hard work in school to spend evenings talking, listening, planning or writing, my answers would have to include the phrase 'intellectual excitement'. It was highly rewarding to meet a group of people who shared my dissatisfaction with much of schooling as it then was, and who could discuss principled alternatives — as well as policies to effect change — that were new and stimulating to a young teacher. Later, I became more deeply involved in the running of the association, and this provided its own dynamic. The publication in 1982 of a book called *Becoming Our Own Experts* (Eyers and Richmond) shows that LATE has continued to provide such opportunities for those teachers who wish to take part. The title also implies that the association has succeeded partly because it has strengthened teachers' sense that they can enquire and understand for themselves.

The LATE meetings and working parties provided a forum to which I could take my current teaching activities and problems; they helped me to see what assumptions I was making and allowed me to meet teachers who were thinking in unfamiliar ways about the possibilities of schooling. That is, the activities of the association offered me alternative ways of understanding without denying the reality of my day-to-day experiences as a teacher. I dwell on these recollections because they lead me to ask how it might be possible to provide such experiences for all teachers. How would schools and teaching have to change for most teachers to find similar intellectual excitement in discussing with other teachers their classroom strategies, successes and failures?

The Perspectives of Teachers and Developers: An Oracy Example

It is a commonplace of the literature on curriculum development (MacDonald and Walker, 1976; Fullan, 1982) that the differences of perspective and emphasis between teachers on the one hand and administrators, curriculum developers or researchers on the other, play a major role in determining the successes and failures of development projects. Such differences became visible during a small feasibility study of the teaching and assessment of oral English that my wife, Dorothy Barnes, and I carried out in 1983–4 for the Northern Universities Joint Matriculation Board in England. (I am indebted to her notes for this comparison.) It should be understood that spoken English ('oracy' in current jargon) has not previously been a compulsory part of the secondary school English syllabus in England and Wales. Though some English teachers had introduced oral activities into their lessons, there was no sign of a consensus about what oracy might consist. The proposed extension to the English curriculum therefore presented most English teachers with a challenge that caused them some anxiety. The secondary school teachers who took part in the study did so voluntarily, however; many had previously taken part in the development of an experimental syllabus in which oracy had a part. They were thus not a typical sample since they might have been expected to respond flexibly and inventively to the new requirements. This proved not always to be the case, so that there were instructive differences between even their perceptions of the new demands and those of the investigators, as the following lists illustrate.

Many of the teachers perceived the following to be pertinent aspects of the situation:

1   In spite of their previous experience and their willingness to join the project, some teachers appeared to be convinced that the problems of introducing oral English would be insurmountable. One head of department said, 'In this school we haven't done much', and laid down a set of constraints: the work could be done only with a low-ability group, no tasks could be set to be done out of lesson time, and there had to be a clear outcome.

2   Teachers had preconceptions about the resources needed for oral work in class. These resources varied from extra hardware ('Will the [examination board] provide us with tape recorders?') to teaching assistance. In some cases the size of classes was seen as a major obstacle: some teachers appeared to believe that small group work would not be possible without more adults in the classroom. One teacher said, 'Group work just isn't possible without extra assistance'.

3   Other constraints upon oral work were thought to arise from the characteristics of some students. Those thought to be 'of low ability' were often seen as lacking communicative abilities. Differences in cultural norms were seen as linguistic deficits: 'These children can't talk even to each other; they just shout and shove', said one experienced teacher, ignoring the competitive struggle for the attention of teacher and class that some lessons impose upon students.

4   Other teachers who had previously introduced oral work into their lessons often had quite different views of what aspects of speech should or could be taught. For example, one school had a tradition of success in a city-wide competition in public speaking; other schools saw oracy as part of effective learning in all subjects, and fiercely rejected the view that public speaking could play any part in it. Such differences could even divide teachers in the same school.

5   Many teachers were concerned about non-standard varieties of spoken English, and wondered whether they should 'correct' dialect forms or non-standard pronunciation.

The small group of academics and educational advisory staff who were leading the feasibility study had a different set of preconceptions:

1   The investigators believed that some, at least, of the teachers' perceptions had been generated as part of a familiar syndrome of resistance to classroom changes. Teachers had become familiar with the requirements of the existing English syllabus and had developed methods for fulfilling them. The researchers believed that the need to respond to new requirements, because it challenged the teachers'

sense of competence, had caused them to perceive insurmountable difficulties, rather than changes to be implemented. Some of the difficulties mentioned by them were felt to be somewhat oblique to the very real problems involved in the changes.

2   The teachers taking part were in many cases judged to have limited awareness of their own speech behaviour in lessons, for example, dominating class discussions and expecting female pupils to listen passively. Nor were they thought to be aware of the effects of this behaviour upon their students, since they assumed that the students' speech was a function of their 'oral abilities' alone, rather than a reflection of the social contexts in which they found themselves.

3   The steering group believed that even those teachers who had for some time taken oracy to be part of their responsibilities in English teaching did not have a clear conception of 'oracy', what its aims were, what aspects of speech needed to be taught (in one sense or another), or what methods were appropriate.

4   It was also thought that the teachers valued oral work in lessons when it provided a positive social milieu, that is, when students were interested and joined willingly in activities. The teachers were thought to take little account of criteria other than the social, such as the quality and relevance of the oral work or its contribution to curricular learning.

It is possible to see from these lists how the diverse priorities of teachers and researchers generated different perceptions of the curricular task in hand. The developers perceived resistance to change, whereas the teachers saw problems that were arising from trying to set up new practices without sufficient resources. Like other teachers, they attributed abilities to their pupils on the basis of their classroom behaviour. The researchers, from their more detached viewpoints, believed that the teachers' own behaviour was involved in producing that of their students. The researchers believed that the teachers lacked a clear view of what they were trying to do, but many of the teachers were devoted to quite particular views of the kind of spoken language that they should be encouraging. This included the valuing of students' interested participation in a way that the observers found excessive, and holding views about such matters as discouraging non-standard forms.

It is not difficult to account for these differences of perspective. Teachers have to maintain classroom order, and so are made anxious by any changes that threaten their repertoire of strategies. They often work in less than ideal circumstances, and yet are routinely judged by senior colleagues on their success. This often leads them, when extra demands are being made, to stress the difficulties, including the shortage of resources. Assessment is a normal and everyday part of the teacher's role, so it is natural for them to treat students' classroom behaviour as 'evidence' of ability or success in learning, thus ignoring the significance of the social context provided in the classroom (Cazden, 1970), a context which is largely of the teacher's making. Teachers have to respond immediately to whatever their students say or do, and from this arises their concern for such questions as whether to 'correct' low-status forms of speech when students use them.

The teachers taking part in the oracy project showed another characteristic: they commonly read tacit meanings into the requirements of the project. For example, in spite of explicit denials, some assumed that the steering group were advocating one particular classroom method (small group work) because some members of the group were known to have had an interest in this. This assumption seems to have arisen from their lack of control over the activities of the project, which was being led by the non-teaching group. Because of their relative powerlessness, the teachers were tempted to attribute hidden purposes to the members of the steering group and to shape some of their teaching upon the basis of these assumptions. This reaction may also occur outside the confines of a development project, for example in teachers' relationships with administrators at various levels.

The interpretive frameworks that guide teachers' choices of teaching strategies are not inferior to those of curriculum developers or administrators, but represent responses to different concerns and priorities. The possibility of principled change in teaching strategies, and therefore in what is learnt by students, depends upon teachers' frames. For this reason we now turn to the nature and formation of these frames.

Teachers' Interpretive Frames

Teachers cannot easily afford the luxury of a detached viewpoint: they have to teach, to make choices, whether or not they have a clear view of where they are heading. Experienced teachers develop repertoires of strategies for dealing with the multifarious signs and signals that demand immediate attention in the course of a normal lesson: teaching is in its very essence interactive. Reflection on teaching can only come later, in whatever tranquillity a busy life affords. Thus when teachers theorize — and not all do so — the theories are not always closely related to their actual behaviour in lessons. This is not because they wish to deceive but because they are often acting upon a set of priorities of which they are not fully aware. Moreover, what a teacher tells a curriculum developer is always partly a justification of strategies already adopted for coping with dilemmas, and thus not necessarily relevant to the developers' concerns. That is why, in the oracy project, the teachers' picture of the situation was so different from that of the academics and advisers. But how are these perceptions, and these sets of longer-term and shorter-term goals, organized?

The concept of 'frame' (Minsky, 1975; Schön, 1983; Wyer and Srull,

1984) can be used to consider the ways in which teachers perceive and execute their professional tasks. The term 'frame' is used to refer to the clustered set of standard expectations through which all adults organize, not only their knowledge of the world but their behaviour in it. We might call them 'the default settings of our daily lives'. When we enter a schoolroom, an office or a bar, we take with us a set of interconnected expectations about what we shall find there. These will include not only the equipment but the persons and their activities. A 'normal' schoolroom will be furnished with desks or tables, and there will be students sitting at them, and one adult interacting with them. If we find typewriters or computers on the tables, this will cause us to switch to a modified frame: we are perhaps in the context of Business Studies or Information Technology. What we would not find it easy to cope with would be the presence of a bar in the room, with an attendant serving drinks. To interpret this we would have to make a leap to an unlikely frame: perhaps we are observing a work simulation, or an unusually realistic modern language lesson. These examples serve merely to show how the frames that we bring to any context allow us both to categorize what we see and to attempt to interpret what is going on there, including unexpected features and events. We also use the frame to supply, sometimes misleadingly, those aspects of the context that we did not consciously notice. Shibutani (1955, quoted in Ball and Goodson, 1985) neatly defines a frame as 'an outline scheme which, running ahead of experience, defines and guides it'.

Teachers' professional frames are a good deal more subtle than these examples would suggest, however. Experienced teachers would rapidly determine whether the teacher was recapitulating previous material, eliciting suggestions, presenting new ideas, supporting his or her students while they worked individually or in small groups, or carrying out another of the procedures that constitute 'teaching'. They would quickly know whether the teacher was on good terms with the students, and whether they were genuinely engaged with the tasks before them. They would probably be able to suggest alternative strategies that could be used if they thought that all was not well. To take a more concrete example, where one teacher sees a group of students who are too lazy to study their history books, another teacher may see an opportunity for the students to investigate aspects of history that have affected their own neighbourhood, and then go on to help them to contrast this with comparable events elsewhere in the world.

The frame that experienced teachers take to a lesson enables them not only to recognize what is happening but also to consider the action that they would take if they were playing the teacher's role. Though the frames appear to be made up of information about teaching, they incorporate an equally complex system of values and priorities, along with strategies which would enable them to be put into effect. To describe the frames as 'teachers' knowledge' is potentially misleading, unless 'knowledge' is seen as value-laden and dynamic.

Donald Schön (1983) has applied the idea of alternative 'frames' to the understanding of teachers' choices in the classroom.

> As [teachers] frame the problem of the situation, they determine the features to which they will attend, the order they will attempt to impose on the situation, the directions in which they will try to change it. In this process they identify both the ends to be sought and the means to be employed. (p. 165)

Teachers who can only 'frame' in one way what happens in their classes can therefore only see one set of possibilities for teaching. If such teachers are asked what they would wish to change in their work, they often mention only such external concerns as the time or the technical resources available. For them, the social context and its demands, the kinds of learning expected, the constraints of examinations and syllabuses, and the power structure of the school are taken for granted as part of the conditions of teaching that must be coped with. This is particularly true of beginning teachers: the first kind of learning they achieve is likely to be adjustment to the situation in school and classroom as they initially perceive it.

In contrast, it can be hypothesized that the most effective teachers will have other interpretive frames available which will free them to see alternatives and to make informed choices. The importance of Schön's thinking for curriculum development is that it explains why teachers are often unable to make use of advice, since they can often interpret it only in terms of an inappropriate frame. To achieve change, teachers need to discover that their existing frame for understanding what happens in their classes is only one of several possible ones, and this, according to Schön, is likely to be achieved only when the teachers themselves reflect critically upon what they do and its results (Day, 1979).

The Shaping of Teachers' Frames

Teachers' professional frames have both an individual history of development and a relationship to the conditions and history of teaching as a profession. They are generated during the interaction with persons, events and constraints that constitute teachers' work context, and represent the teacher's interpretation of the roles and strategies available to him or her within the particular situation. Professional frames may be generated as individual solutions to practical problems or to value dilemmas, but at the same time they are interpretive hypotheses that may have to be negotiated with colleagues and shared so that the teachers reinforce one another. The frames are not easily open to change for they are sometimes maintained by what is arguably the teachers' most significant reference group, the colleagues with whom they collaborate day by day. A teacher's frame can also be invalidated by a particularly uncooperative group of pupils who refuse to collaborate in activities that the teacher conceives to be appropriate (Riseborough, 1985).

We must not make the mistake of thinking of teachers' frames and their consequent teaching strategies either as solely individual commitments to what teachers sometimes call their 'philosophy' or as simply determined by their objective conditions of work. Commitments indeed there are, which are often based upon deep-seated assumptions about people and society and thus closely related to political and religious attitudes. These are, however, likely to have been modified by the experience of teaching in particular schools (Ball and Goodson, 1985; Ball, 1987; Lacey, 1977). However, 'experience of teaching' is itself shaped by the expectations and values — the commitments — that the young teacher brings to them. Neither the commitments nor the experience can exist separately, and the two together create the frames that shape a teacher's strategies. Frames are created 'from inside outwards' as much as 'from outside inwards'.

Insofar as schools are alike, we can expect common elements in different teachers' frames, but they are certainly not strictly determined by the context. All teachers construct their frames for themselves, beginning at the time when they were themselves playing the role of school student and (sometimes critically) observing their teachers. This foundation is built upon during their university courses and particularly during the short periods when they are experiencing school placements as interns. But probably the most important shaping of teachers' frames occurs during the first year or two of teaching, when they must interact with their students and with their more experienced colleagues. Even though the conditions of the classroom and school play a large part in how teachers perceive their work, these do not determine what frames are available: a teacher's perceptions are as much his or hers as they are the creation of the situation.

Teachers' Construction of their Professional Roles

Freema Elbaz (1983), in an analysis of one teacher's thinking, chooses to use five categories as a basis for her analysis of the knowledge on which such thinking rests: knowledge of self, knowledge of the milieu of teaching, knowledge of subject matter, knowledge of curriculum development and knowledge of instruction. It is strange that she omits from this list 'knowledge of students' (though she discusses it briefly later in the book), since a teacher's understanding of the tasks that particular students will be able to learn from is both central to the ability to teach and separate from more general understanding of methods of presentation and management in the classroom. However, she points out that teachers' thinking operates at three levels of generality: rules of practice (specific directives for action), practical principles (at an intermediate level) and images (broad metaphoric statements). Every teacher imposes on the situation of teaching a prescriptive framework that in part determines what he or she sees as possible, so that Elbaz's use of the word 'knowledge' seems slightly misleading in some of the contexts in which it appears. It is more useful to consider teachers' construction of their work in terms of models or frames they impose on the situation that faces them, since 'frames', unlike 'knowledge', are value-laden and dynamic. What then are the most significant frames likely to be? I suggest the following:

1 preconceptions, often implicit, about the nature of what they are teaching, and — for secondary specialists — about the subject they teach and how to interpret it;
2 preconceptions about learning and how it takes place, though modified by a view of what can be achieved in the classroom;
3 preconceptions about students (in general, and about the particular group being taught) that place limits upon what is thought to be useful or possible;
4 beliefs about priorities and constraints inherent in the professional and institutional context;
5 the nature of his or her overall commitment to teaching — 'vocational', 'professional', 'career-continuance' (Woods, 1981, pp. 291–292).

All of these are value-laden: policy choices that include implicit preferences. From one point of view the values concern the kind of life for which the teacher believes that he or she is preparing the pupils; equally, though, they are choices of the behaviours that will be valued in that teacher's lessons.

The reader may already be wondering whether these sets of preconceptions are to be identified with what I have called frames. It is better to see each of them as made up of a repertoire of frames. For example, an elementary school teacher will have an array of possible frames available for thinking about the content of what he or she teaches. There will be frames that deal with bodies of knowledge, perhaps in history, that may be presented to the students for them to 'learn'; but there will also be sets of skills and procedures that in other contexts may guide the teacher's thinking about what he or she is teaching. In other cases, the teacher's planning may be guided by ideas of suitable activities, such as persuading the student to collect and organize botanical material, or ways of interesting them in reading stories for themselves. These frames that organize thinking about 'content' are not distinct but influence and even interpenetrate one another. Moreover, as we shall see, a frame that specifies a particular conception of knowledge may also imply a particular way of thinking about what learning activities are appropriate. Frames are not discrete entities but patterns that help us to organize and understand the complex events in which we take part.

It has already been suggested that these preconceptions and commitments are mainly constructed during the earlier years of a teacher's experience. They are the outcome of an interplay between the young teacher's value commitments and his or her developing conception of the opportunities and constraints inherent in the organization of a particular school. These two are discussed in turn.

Teachers' Personal Conceptions of Learning and Knowledge

Of central importance is the teacher's conception of what constitutes learning, which normally includes an implicit epistemology. Some teachers conceive of knowledge as existing independently of persons who know it; it can thus be transferred from teacher or textbook to pupil through straightforward methods of communication. The pupil merely has to rehearse and 'practice' in order to 'consolidate' the knowledge. We can contrast with this the constructivist view that the learner needs to be engaged in the purposive reconstruction of the knowledge offered. Lying behind this is the idea that the learner can only make sense of new information, instruction, and experiences by interpreting them in the light of what he or she 'knows' already. We can use the concept of 'frame' again here, but this time in relation to the students: in order to 'understand', the learner has to construct a frame that will encompass the new knowledge but can only do so with the aid of an old frame, which may assimilate the new or conflict with it. If the new ideas or experiences challenge the learner's existing frame, then that frame will need to be revised, thus accommodating the unfamiliar: the world will never appear quite the same again. (The terms 'assimilation' and 'accommodation' derive from Piaget.) However, as all teachers are aware, there are many occasions when pupils find it easier to ignore the unfamiliar experience, not allowing it to influence their picture of the world. If they then remember it at all, it is as 'school knowledge', not as the kind of knowledge that might affect how they live and act in their daily lives.

No doubt few teachers hold either of these conceptions of learning in a pure form: most will teach as if both have some partial truth. Nevertheless, whichever model of learning is dominant in a teacher's thinking in a lesson will have a profound influence upon the kinds of tasks set to students, the ways in which students are spoken to, as well as listened to, and the extent to which information is transmitted and tested. That is, the patterns of teaching that can be observed in a teacher's normal behaviour are based upon implicit models of what knowledge is and how it is learnt.

The teacher's conception of what knowledge is and of how it is gained may come from training in a specialist subject or from courses in education, but for secondary teachers the very subject taught can be shown to have a considerable effect. This is of necessity closely related to the teacher's view of what learning is, for upon this must depend his or her conception of what should be done to advance learning. Both of these will inevitably shape the teacher's ability to respond inventively to new challenges, including the challenge to put a new teaching policy into effect.

In a study of secondary teachers' statements about the role of written work in students' learning (Barnes and Shemilt, 1974) a colleague and I found teachers' views of teaching to be closely associated with the subject that each taught. The teachers were asked about the role that written work played in their teaching; their responses were differentiated according to whether they saw written work as an opportunity for the learner to make sense of his or her learning or as a mechanism for rehearsing or recording information. Thus, amongst other things, the measures indicated teachers' tacit pictures of learning, from constructivism on the one extreme to transmission of information on the other, as well as various intermediate positions. We called the two extremes 'Interpretation' and 'Transmission' views of teaching.

The secondary school teachers' specialist subjects proved to be highly predictive of the place of their views on the Interpretation-Transmission dimension. Teachers of English and Religious Education tended to cluster at the Interpretation end of the scale, though a minority appeared elsewhere, including one or two at the Transmission end. In contrast, teachers of technical subjects and science were predominantly clustered at the Transmission end. Teachers of history tended to be near the centre of the scale, and teachers of geography were relatively widely distributed, perhaps because of competing humanistic and scientific versions of the subject. Our statistical analysis showed that approximately half of the teachers' statements could have been predicted from the subject taught. No doubt the remainder of the variance was only partly random: as has already been pointed out, personal value-systems and previous experiences in training and in teaching must play an important part. Nor are teachers necessarily consistent in their thinking: a frame partly based upon a Transmission view of knowledge can sometimes co-exist (perhaps uncomfortably) with elements of constructivist thinking that influence the planning of learning activities.

These elements in the frame with which a teacher approaches his or her work have an incalculable effect upon the way in which he or she responds to demands for change — for example in relation to a curriculum development project. Teachers who, knowingly or not, are locked into a Transmission view of teaching and learning will make little sense of teaching materials that accord a more active role to the learners. Indeed, they are likely to reinterpret the project's model of teaching and learning into procedures with which they themselves are comfortable, thus changing the project into something different. No doubt any project survives through a compromise between an idealized conception and the practicalities of putting it into effect, but too wide a gap between intention and performance will destroy any hope of productive change. The phrase 'innovation without change' was devised to refer to occasions when this occurred.

The Effect of the Institutional Context upon Teachers' Frames

It is important for all those concerned with curriculum development, whether in schools or in wider supervisory roles, to realize the extent to which the institutions of schooling influence teachers' frames and therefore their ability to accept change and take a creative part in it. Teachers are not free agents, able to work out in some neutral milieu the implications of an abstract conception of education. They are participants in institutions and cultural traditions that antedate their assumption of the role of teacher, and which have close relationships with powerful forces outside schooling. Teachers may not be free agents, but neither are they merely creatures of the schools they serve. They develop at one and the same time their teaching strategies and the account that they give of their purposes, and do so in interaction with the influences from the specific situations in which they find themselves. I therefore now turn to schools as contexts for teachers' work, in order to identify some of the conditions that influence teachers' constructions of their tasks.

Aside from the insistence by teachers' unions (no doubt for reasons of status) that teaching is a profession, there has been serious discussion by sociologists about the appropriateness of describing teachers either as professionals or as bureaucratic functionaries (Joyce, 1971; Johnson, 1972; Hoyle, 1975; Ball, 1987). Bureaucratic organizations are those that display characteristics such as the choice of goals by someone other than the person who is to pursue them, the definition of employees' roles in such a way that individuals can easily be replaced, and the evaluation of the work by persons not of their number, often in order to move up the steps of a predetermined hierarchy. Professionals, in contrast, have more control over the range of tasks that they undertake; they determine their goals and evaluate their own and others' work collaboratively. Ball and Goodson (1985) point out that during the last decade in the UK there has been a greater division of labour in schools and an increase in the amount of form-filling and record-keeping, whilst school policies are increasingly defined by senior management with little reference to the views of rank and file staff. The new National Curriculum for England and Wales certainly implies that the goals of teaching are being defined outside the classroom. In spite of all this, in a later book Ball (1987) resists the call to consider teaching a bureaucratic employment. He defines three kinds of institutional control (professional, hierarchical, and membership-controlled) and insists that schools in the UK display elements of all three.

The influence of these control patterns upon teachers' concepts of their tasks must be considerable. The stronger the hierarchical elements in the control of a school, the more likely it is that teachers will pursue a minimalist policy, defending themselves against the possibility of criticism by working very close to guidelines and avoiding individual experimentation. Insofar as a school is 'membership-controlled', this will encourage those teachers who wish to risk experiment and innovation, but leave some teachers free to maintain their existing practices. The professional element in school control reminds us how important support from other teachers is: when change is in question, a supportive anecdote from another practitioner carries more weight than the opinions of any university professor, local authority adviser or curriculum consultant. The possibility of substantial change in the subculture of teaching depends upon the mutual trust that can be developed in a professionally controlled institution (Fullan, 1982; Lacey, 1977).

In addition to location of control, we must also consider the characteristics of the teachers themselves. In spite of the strength of staffroom opinion, it cannot be assumed that all teachers see their work in the same way. Their attitudes and strategies are likely to differ according to age, (or perhaps according to the career stage that has been reached), to gender, and to the level of specialism. Thus teachers in primary schools are likely to perceive their tasks very differently from most of those in secondary schools; within the latter, there are differences that can be attributed to the subjects taught by that teacher. Secondary schools are powerfully divided not only by subject specialisms but by the differences between teachers who have taken on 'pastoral' responsibilities and those whose prime concern is academic. These are not merely interest groups but the source of alternative frames for interpreting whatever is going on in the school, 'contrasting definitions of the school, and competing systems of legitimation', as Beynon (1985) phrases it. Grace (1978) referred also to differences in social origin; in his view, the London teaching profession was 'now more differentiated in terms of the social and cultural origins of its members'. One result of this was that teachers differed in 'the contexts and contents of their socialization and the principles which they are attempting to realize in their teaching activity'. The very differences between teachers may relate quite closely to the institutional contexts in which they work or have worked.

One outcome of this lack of agreement about goals is that the common ground on which effective school organization rests has to be negotiated and perpetually renewed, through various forms of controlled conflict. Even strong school principals have to 'manage' the opinions and attitudes of their colleagues. The typical result of this negotiation, especially in secondary schools, is a struggle to achieve a partial autonomy for certain activities, since departments and other groups need to collaborate even though their goals may partly conflict. Discussing 'the individualist nature of the profession', Jennifer Nias (1985) wrote:

Teachers' reference groups result in and reinforce multiple realities which give individuals a false sense of having achieved within their schools agreement over ends and means. In short, teachers neither wish nor are able to talk to one another. They are not able to because outside their reference groups they lack a shared language by which to attach meanings to their common experience. They do not want to because the process of creating such a language would threaten the social context which sustains and defends their substantial selves. (p. 116)

Of course, 'language' here is not just a matter of words but of the common understandings that I am calling 'frames'. In spite of this lack of common frames, practical collaboration is unavoidable. The success of a school staff in achieving practical agreement, or obtaining elbow-room by vertical division between different aspects of the school's work, will have a marked effect upon the teachers' view of what is possible and therefore upon their participation in curricular and other forms of innovation. In understanding teachers' frames it is necessary to take into consideration not only 'school ethos' (the shared priorities, practices and values that characterize a school) but also the sub-group norms that differentiate particular groups of teachers within it.

In the pursuit of consensus, teachers often seek to shape others' perceptions. It is not at all unknown for a new teacher in a school staffroom to be buttonholed by a member of staff who will 'tell them about the school' and its students, and thereby attempt to provide the probationer with the staff's standard interpretive frame. It is almost as if the more experienced teacher were saying: 'If you want to belong here you will have to see things as we do'. But of course not all young teachers are entirely compliant when faced with this demand. Hammersley (1984, p. 210) has pointed out, however, that staffroom talk is not to be interpreted as a literal transcript of teachers' attitudes but as a shared perspective that has been constructed to answer the particular needs of informal staffroom talk. When interviewed alone, teachers express other priorities, sometimes appearing considerably more enlightened and liberal, but go on to explain why these priorities cannot be achieved in that school.

Some teachers have reference groups outside the school: these may be trade unions, subject associations (such as the National Association for the Teaching of English) or political groups. The possibility of discussing policy in a supportive context outside the school may have one of two contrasting effects. It may make the teacher a potent force in the school by supplying a repertoire of strategies for approaching current issues and arguments to support those strategies, or it may isolate him or her as an outsider whose loyalty is not to the school but to a wider constituency. When a teacher stands out strongly against some proposed new practice, this is often because of strength drawn from support by such a reference group.

Teachers almost always teach in isolation, and often preserve that isolation with some fierceness. The closed door is an essential element in teachers' culture: it is all the more noticeable in contrast when one comes across a school where team-teaching occurs. The presence of another adult in the classroom disturbs the teacher-class relationship by forcing the teacher to be aware of another audience, whose values and expectations may be very different from those that the teacher has established with some care in that group of students.

Lortie (1975) has suggested that some aspects of teachers' common professional culture can be attributed to the unclearness of goals and to lack of feedback on the success of their teaching. As a teacher, one has to 'work for protracted periods without sure knowledge that one is having any positive effect on students' (p. 83). Moreover, explicit recognition of good classroom work by a teacher's superiors is hard to find: as Grace (1978, p. 35) pointed out, it is more profitable to catch a head teacher's approval by busying oneself with more visible activities, for the effectiveness of teaching is largely invisible. Lortie believes that, as a result of this lack of feedback, teachers value the personal rewards of warm relationships with students more highly than the more doubtful rewards of children's cognitive development.

It has already been pointed out that teachers have limited control of the conditions of their work. One implication of this is that their satisfaction and security depend upon meeting simultaneously a bewildering range of requirements and concerns from different sources. Frequently, the demands laid upon teachers by their superiors, their students, and their students' parents are mutually contradictory, and create a conflict that causes many to have an intense desire for the privacy that can be obtained by wrapping the walls of the classroom tightly about them. Others suffer from anxiety generated by the inability to satisfy at once all three of the major groups that make demands of them. Moreover, teachers' work in its very nature leaves little time for thought, for success depends upon a rapid choice from a well-practiced repertoire.

The students, too, are active participants in the formation of a teacher's frame of reference; older students in particular are far from being merely passive receivers of whatever a teacher wishes. The students' attitudes to learning and willingness to take the curriculum seriously are a crucial element in what happens in the classroom, and this has a powerful effect upon the teacher's conception of what it is possible to teach and what activities are manageable in the classroom. 'The teacher may be taming the pupils, as they see it, but in their proactive strategies the pupils are profoundly shaping and directing the teacher's self-concept and moral career' (Ball and Goodson, 1985, summarizing the work of Riseborough). This should not be underestimated in any attempt to understand the formation of a teacher's construction of classroom realities.

One outcome of the conditions of teaching in the UK is that most teachers have an essentially practical view of their tasks. Listening to staff-room talk leaves one in no doubt of the scorn that many teachers have for theorizing about teaching. The suggestion by Jennifer Nias that the failure to communicate is a product of the diversity of interpretive frames has already been quoted, but the professional subculture of teachers seems to leave little room for detached discussion when immediate action is so often required. This probably accounts in part for the unacceptably negative picture of teachers in Jackson's study (1968) in which teachers were de-scribed as having an uncomplicated view of causality, an intuitive rather than rational approach to classroom events, an opinionated — as opposed to an open-minded — stance when confronted with alternative teaching prac-tices, and a narrowness in the working definitions assigned to abstract terms. In contrast, Riseborough (1985) rejects the picture of teachers as unreflect-ive and unable to think for themselves, and insists that, if they reject current innovations and the theory that underpins them, they do so for some good reason that derives from their current view of their work and its probable future. His view is that teachers, far from being irrational, are responding rationally to complex sets of demands that those outside the profession are hardly aware of. These demands are created by the institutional contexts in which they work.

Nor are there rewards for theorizing: as Grace (1978, p. 125) pointed out, the teacher who earns approval from his or her superiors is likely to display 'efficiency, punctuality and "busyness"', that is, being seen to be making things happen. Grace was writing about teachers in selected inner-city secondary schools. In one of them eight teachers were designated 'good teachers' by the administrators. Grace wrote of these teachers:

> All the teachers were characterised by what might be called immer-sion: a total involvement in the life of the school and concern for its pupils which made heavy demands upon their time and energy and which tended to produce a very school-centred consciousness which gave low salience to the wider structural location of the educational process or to its social and political correlates. (Grace, 1978, p. 135)

This sounds very like the 'restricted professional' described by Hoyle (1975). Their recognition as 'good teachers' often implies that they will soon move into middle management where they will be able to reinforce further the more conservative elements in the professional subculture. It is not the teacher who tries new teaching methods on the basis of principle who is rewarded by promotion. If administrators wish teachers to become more reflective and analytical, to consider their work in the light of alternative frames, they must provide both occasions and rewards for doing so.

This section serves to illustrate some of the elements in schools as institutions that may play a critical role in the development of the frames through which teachers conceptualize various aspects of their work. These include the effects of bureaucratic practices on the control of teaching; the effects of age, career goals, and specialism on individual teachers' frames; the presence of powerful sub-groups within the overall ethos of a school; the effects of diverse and unclear goals upon teaching practices; the influence of students' priorities and behaviour; and the forces that lead to an anti-theoretical bias in the profession. This analysis is intended to suggest that those who seek to change teachers' perspectives and practices take too little account of the conditions that have contributed to forming them and that continue to sustain them.

The 'Language Across the Curriculum' Movement

I now turn to the case of a nationwide movement in education that was intended to have a profound influence upon teachers' perspectives and practices but which failed to do so in spite of formal support from official bodies. My purpose is to understand why this movement had so little effect and to draw more general conclusions from the example.

In 1975 the Bullock Committee, set up by the British Government to look into the teaching of English and particularly of literacy, recommended in its report *A Language for Life* (DES, 1975) that every school should have a policy for language. The report made it clear that language should be valued as a means of learning that can be used by students in any subject 'across the curriculum', and not only as a goal. All teachers should take responsibility for the language used in their lessons since language significantly influenced what the students learnt there: the matter could not be left in the hands of specialist teachers of English. In spite of this official support, ten years later the movement had almost vanished in its country of origin, though it still showed some life in Canada and Australia. It is useful to consider why it is that this perspective on teaching, with its implication that all teachers should reflect critically on the talking and writing that went on in their lessons, was so ineffective in achieving substantial change.

The movement began in the London Association for the Teaching of English, a group of teachers who were successfully involved in critical reflection on their teaching. One of the outcomes of their reflection had been the realization that, when young people talk or write about their experiences, trying to make sense of them, they are engaged in the central activity of learning. At that time the term 'constructivism' was not in use, but theoretical support for this thinking was derived from diverse sources that included Piaget, Vygotsky, George Kelly and Bruner. The example and participation of James Britton was particularly important in achieving this synthesis, which became an important part of the dynamic that made LATE an intellectually challenging experience for its members. Of course, the ideas also required changes in classroom methods, and these were discussed at the association's meetings and conferences. As time went on, it became clear to members that it should not only be English teachers who were involved; if talking and writing were central activities in learning, this must be true throughout the subjects of the curriculum. Particularly significant in the development of this line of thought were two conferences organized by Harold Rosen in 1966 and 1968; in the second of these, the participants formulated a policy document on the role of language in learning that was addressed to all teachers. The slogan 'Language Across the Curriculum' was invented as a title for that document, which was then published (Barnes, Britton and Rosen, 1969).

Although in the succeeding years other professional associations joined in discussions about the policy document, 'Language Across the Curriculum' did not achieve wide publicity until the publication of the Bullock Report in 1975. Even then the movement had very restricted influence, especially among teachers in secondary schools, and it is the reasons for its lack of success in the secondary phase that merit further discussion. The policy had official support not only in the Bullock Report but from Her Majesty's Inspectorate who ran courses and endeavoured in other ways to interest teachers in looking critically at the learning tasks that they set for their students. At the centre of the movement was the idea that in certain kinds of talk and writing young people can advance their own learning by manipulating and reinterpreting their existing understanding in the light of new perspectives that have been presented to them. The book in which the ideas were first mooted was widely prescribed in colleges and university departments where teachers were trained, and has now gone to a fourth edition (Barnes, Britton and Torbe 1990). To put this policy into effect would, however, require many teachers to make radical changes in their classroom practices. In the event, little seems to have changed in secondary schools, even though similar messages were coming from elsewhere — the 'resource-based learning' movement, the emphasis in Nuffield Science on active problem-solving, the similar changes recommended in history and geography and, more recently, the movement for 'experiential learning' associated with the Technical and Vocational Education Initiative. The fact that so many well-argued recommendations were ignored deserves explanation.

The first point to be made is that any proposed change is interpreted by teachers through the existing frames that they have developed, usually in common with others, as ways of interpreting and dealing with the requirements of the school. That is, the frames are in effect stipulative definitions of the constraints and possibilities inherent in the situation in which each of them teaches. They are both responses to the institution and definitions of how best to cope with the demands and constraints that arise from its characteristics. In one sense every institution can be said to be made up of the frames constructed by its members, though the effects of these constructs are real indeed.

In one very obvious way, the failure of 'Language Across the

Curriculum' relates to the organization of the curriculum not only in schools but in universities and elsewhere. The separation of subjects into departments is important (as has already been suggested) as a means of allowing groups of teachers to pursue diverse subject-based priorities within an administrative whole. Nevertheless, a price has to be paid for such a divided institution, and one loss is the weakness of any project that is intended to cross departmental boundaries. One of Her Majesty's Inspectors who was much concerned with the Bullock report and its outcomes attributed the ineffectiveness of the 'Language Across the Curriculum' movement to 'subject chauvinism'. From the point of view of many teachers in secondary schools, language was by definition the responsibility of English specialists and therefore not of other departments.

This opposition was reinforced by many teachers' Transmission view of teaching; this in its turn was supported in secondary schools by public examinations that were more effective in testing students' recollection of taught material than their understanding of it. As already pointed out, teachers have to meet a variety of demands that may include the achievement of good examination results and the appearance of a tightly controlled classroom. To many teachers the injunctions of the 'Language Across the Curriculum' movement seemed to threaten both of these. The spoken and written language used by students in lessons was not seen by such teachers to contribute to learning, and was thus not considered a concern of teachers other than English specialists. This was reinforced by a tendency for school principals to give to senior English teachers the responsibility for recommending 'Language Across the Curriculum' ideas to their colleagues, with the predictable result that in many schools the movement was seen as an attempt at empire building by the English department, or at least an unacceptable interference with their colleagues' teaching. The fate of the movement was thus closely linked to structural characteristics of the educational system, including its tacit goals and values, as interpreted by teachers into priorities for teaching.

'Language Across the Curriculum' met a different fate in primary schools. It was more welcome there, both because most primary school teachers recognize that their students' language activities are amongst their responsibilities, and because many primary teachers had been trained in colleges that provided specific language courses, some of which dealt explicitly with the recommendations of 'Language Across the Curriculum'. It is not surprising, however, to find that over the years the ideas of the movement, which are centrally concerned with talking and writing as a means of learning, have been transmuted into a concern for the students' development of language skills. Primary school teaching can itself be seen as a special reference group within the culture of teaching as a whole, and this provides perspectives (frames) on teachers' responsibilities for advancing their students' language competencies. That is, because the new concerns were viewed by teachers through their existing frames they were transmuted into familiar concerns, a conversion strongly reinforced because these are recognized and approved by all primary school teachers.

It might further be hypothesized that the proposals of the movement for different kinds and functions of talking and writing in lessons challenged some of the well-established patterns of classroom activities that have earned a professional consensus in both primary and secondary schools because they enable teachers to cope economically with the manifold demands of classroom life. Many of the precepts of the movement implied that students should be given greater control over their own learning, and this was frequently perceived by teachers as unrealistic, especially in schools where students often refused to cooperate because they rejected school goals and values.

Although this example of a failed movement for changed classroom methods does not refer to all of the institutional characteristics discussed in the previous section, it illustrates that the forces that determine the outcomes of an innovation are not solely a matter of the free-standing priorities and preferences of teachers.

Planning for Change

This paper opens with the assertion that teachers who fit the pattern of the 'extended professional' are rare, that is, teachers who reflect critically upon the principles underlying their work and can switch from one interpretive frame to another in making decisions about teaching. It is now possible, using ideas from the previous two sections, to suggest why this is so. Teachers work in contexts not of their own choosing, and do so under pressure from reference groups who make contradictory demands upon them. Their rewards depend upon visibly meeting these demands: innovative behavior is as likely to earn criticism as praise. The hierarchical control common within schools discourages risk-taking; powerful definitions of curricular content, of students' capabilities, and of classroom order are reinforced by colleagues and students alike. The structure of schools, particularly high schools, favors the formation of departmental groups who are more disposed to defend territory than to join colleagues in critical thinking. Under such pressures it is remarkable how many teachers fit the alternative description of 'extended professional': they are likely to be those who have found reference groups outside the school which support them in reflective and critical thinking about their work, but these outside sources of support make it very likely that many of them will eventually move to careers that are in education but not in the classroom. This situation is unlikely to change unless it becomes possible to find rewards, including career routes within schools, that will encourage more teachers to become 'researchers' in Stenhouse's sense.

The general point that underlies this is that teachers' interpretations of their teaching tasks (their current frames, that is) are likely to be based on a strategy for dealing with what they see as institutional imperatives, a strategy all the more powerful because it is shared. If changes in teaching are to take place, the teachers' frames must change. Though this implies reflection and learning on their part, this is unlikely to take place without changes in the institutions as well, and this must include changes in the demands (both explicit and implicit) made upon teachers by administrators and parents. Any cultural frames that govern the interaction and communication between people are complex and difficult to change. The analysis presented in this chapter is not intended to be a counsel of despair but a warning that changes in curriculum and instruction have all the complexity and uncertainty of all deliberate attempts to engineer cultural change. They require subtle and sensitive management; there are no simple recipes.

References

BALL, S.J. (1987) *The Micro-Politics of the School*, London, Methuen.

BALL, S.J. and GOODSON, I.F. (Eds) (1985) *Teachers' Lives and Careers*, London, Falmer Press.

BARNES, D., BRITTON, J. and ROSEN, H. (1969) *Language, the Learner and the School*, Harmondsworth, Penguin Books.

BARNES, D., BRITTON, J. and TORBE, M. (1990) *Language, the Learner and the School*, 4th ed., Portsmouth, NH, Boynton-Cook/Heinemann.

BARNES, D. and SHEMILT, D. (1974) 'Transmission and interpretation', *Educational Review*, **26**, 3, pp. 213–228.

BEYNON, J. (1985) 'Institutional change and career histories in a comprehensive school', in BALL, S.J. and GOODSON, I.F. (Eds) *Teachers' Lives and Careers*, London, Falmer Press, pp. 158–179.

CAZDEN, C.B. (1970) 'The neglected situation in child language research and education', in WILLIAMS, F. (Ed.) *Language and Poverty*, Waco, TX, Markham Press, pp. 81–101.

DAY, C.W. (1979) *Classroom-based In-service Education: The Development and Evaluation of a Client-Centred Model*, unpublished DPhil thesis, University of Sussex.

DEPARTMENT OF EDUCATION AND SCIENCE (1975) *A Language for Life* (The Bullock Report), London, HMSO.

ELBAZ, F. (1983) *Teacher Thinking: A Study of Practical Knowledge*, London, Croom Helm.

EYERS, S. and RICHMOND, J. (Eds) (1982) *Becoming Our Own Experts*, London, ILEA England Centre.

FULLAN, M. (1982) *The Meaning of Educational Change*, Toronto, OISE Press.

GRACE, G. (1978) *Teachers, Ideology and Control*, London, Routledge and Kegan Paul.

HAMMERSLEY, M. (1984) 'Staffroom news', in HARGREAVES, A. and WOODS, P. (Eds) *Classrooms and Staffrooms*, Milton Keynes, Open University Press, pp. 203–214.

HOYLE, E. (1975) 'The creativity of the school in Britain', in HARRIS, A., LAWN, M. and PRESCOTT, W. (Eds) *Curriculum Innovation*, Milton Keynes, Croom Helm, pp. 329–346.

JACKSON, P.W. (1968) *Life in Classrooms*, New York, Holt, Rinehart and Winston.

JOHNSON, T.J. (1972) *Professions and Power*, London, Macmillan.

JOYCE, B.R. (1971) 'The curriculum worker of the future', in McCLURE, R.M. (Ed.) *The Curriculum: Retrospect and Prospect*, 70th NSSE Yearbook, Part 1, Chicago, University of Chicago Press, pp. 307–355.

LACEY, C. (1977) *The Socialization of Teachers*, London, Methuen.

LORTIE, D. (1975) *School-Teacher: A Sociological Study*, Chicago, University of Chicago Press.

MACDONALD, B. and WALKER, R. (1976) *Changing the Curriculum*, London, Open Books.

MINSKY, M. (1975) 'A framework for representing knowledge', in WINSTON, P. (Ed.) *The Psychology of Computer Vision*, New York, McGraw-Hill, pp. 211–277.

NIAS, J. (1985) 'Reference groups in primary teaching: Talking, listening and identity', in BALL, S.J. and GOODSON, I.F. (Eds) *Teachers' Lives and Careers*, London, Falmer Press, pp. 105–119.

OLSON, J. (Ed.) (1982) *Innovation in the Science Curriculum*, London, Croom Helm.

RISEBOROUGH, G.F. (1985) 'Pupils, teachers' careers, and schooling: An empirical study', in BALL, S.J. and GOODSON, I.F. (Eds) *Teachers' Lives and Careers*, London, Falmer Press, pp. 202–265.

SCHÖN, D.A. (1983) *The Reflective Practitioner*, London, Temple Smith.

SHIBUTANI, T. (1955) 'Reference groups as perspective', in MANIS, J. and MELTZER, B. (Eds) *Symbolic Interaction*, 2nd ed., 1972, Boston, Allyn and Bacon; *cited in* BALL, S.J. and GOODSON, I.F. (Eds) *Teachers' Lives and Careers*, London, Falmer Press, p. 107.

STENHOUSE, L. (1975) *An Introduction to Curriculum Research and Development*, London, Heinemann.

WELLS, G. (1989) 'Educational change and school improvement', *Let's Talk*, Newsletter 2:1 of the Talk Project, Mississauga, Ontario, Peel Board of Education.

WOODS, P.E. (1981) 'Strategies, commitment and identity: Making and breaking the teacher', in BARTON, L. and WALKER, S. (Eds) *Schools, Teachers and Teaching*, London, Falmer Press, pp. 283–302.

WYER, R.S. and SRULL, T.K. (Eds) (1984) *Handbook of Social Cognition*, Vol. 1, Hillsdale, NJ, Erlbaum.

3   Collaborative Reflection, Systematic Enquiry, Better Teaching

John R. Baird

Introduction

The chapter title captures my beliefs about how to improve the quality of teaching. The meaning of each of the three terms requires clarification, as does the nature of the relations among them. My purpose in this chapter is to achieve such clarification. By better teaching, I mean that the teacher *knows* more about what teaching is and how it best works for him or her, is more *aware* of what is happening in the classroom as he or she teaches, and is more purposeful in the pedagogical *decisions* that he or she makes. These three aspects — knowledge, awareness and control — may be subsumed within the general term *metacognition*. On this view, better teaching requires enhanced metacognition regarding teaching. But better teaching is more than this, for it is affective as well as metacognitive. It is having more positive attitudes to yourself and what you do. It is caring more, being more committed, and having greater self-confidence and self-assurance. Because of this, improving one's teaching is not just learning better teaching techniques. It is undergoing fundamental change in one's attitudes, perceptions, conceptions, beliefs, abilities and behaviors.

The complexity of such change is only now being fully appreciated. Increased understandings of learning have arisen from different focuses and methods of educational research. There has been a trend in educational research, particularly over the last two decades, away from a positivist, psychometric perspective towards one which is more interpretive and naturalistic. This trend has resulted in increased attention being paid to the interdependence of an individual's thoughts and actions during learning, and the importance of the teaching-learning context in influencing these thoughts and actions.

Because of its complexity, personal change is a demanding and often unsettling process. The constraints to change are many and varied; some constraints are generated within the individual, others without. In order that these constraints to change are surmounted, certain exacting conditions must apply. The findings in this chapter suggest that better teaching requires that teachers reflect on themselves and their practice, that this reflection should be set within a process of systematic enquiry, and that both reflection and enquiry should proceed by collaboration among members of a group. In sum, the findings indicate that we can and should think differently about improving teaching, and that when we do, improvement results.

In the analysis that follows, I do not cite widely from the research literature in such diverse areas as reflection, teachers' thoughts and attributions, constructivism, teacher change and school improvement, and meta-cognition. Rather, I base my argument largely on findings from two recent research projects with which I have been associated. I then leave it to the reader to judge the relevance and validity of the assertions I make to his or her own experience and professional context. I do this because of my commitment to the belief that productive pedagogical theory must be grounded firmly on particulars of personal practice.

Data are drawn from two research projects with which I have been involved over the last five years. From the experiences of these projects I develop three 'guiding principles' by which collaborative enquiry and systematic reflection lead to better teaching. Then four episodes are described to give substance and detail to the guiding principles. Throughout the chapter, I return to one aspect of theory which, in different ways, seems to underpin effective change. It is the importance of striking a *balance* between apparently contrasting elements. Success in improving teaching seems to be generated by seeking balance between teaching and research, cognition and affect, reflection and action, individual development and group endeavour, challenge and reward. The chapter concludes with a discussion of the concept of 'challenge' as it emerged from the many experiences of the two research projects.

The Basis of the Argument: Two Research Projects

The first project is entitled the *Project for Enhancing Effective Learning* (PEEL); the second, *Teaching and Learning Science in Schools* (TLSS). Both projects may be distinguished from much other research into classroom teaching and learning on the bases of the duration of the project, the number of voluntary participants, and the extent of active and protracted collaboration among teachers, 'consultants' (tertiary academics) and, particularly, school students in grades 7–12. In addition, PEEL is unusual in the extent of cross-faculty collaboration among the participating teachers.

PEEL involves three types of participant (teacher, student, consultant) researching together ways by which students can take more responsibility and control over their learning. The project is now in its sixth year. In its first year, 1985, ten teachers and more than 120 students in a Melbourne secondary school participated in PEEL. The students were in grades 7–10 in five classes; project activities were carried out in six subject areas (English, History, Geography, Integrated Studies, Commerce, Science). By 1990, PEEL has grown to the stage where it involves more than seventy teachers in eight Victorian city and country schools, and well over 1,000 students in grades 7–12, across all faculties.

The TLSS project ran for three years, from 1987–89. It was directed to enhancing understanding and practice of secondary science teaching and learning, through a similar process of group-based collaboration and action. Twenty science teachers and more than 1,000 students in grades 7–11 from five schools participated for periods ranging from several months to the entire three years. Additionally, in 1987, thirteen science teacher trainees, two of their teacher educators, and I participated in a case study of pre-service science teacher education.

Large quantities of data, of various types, arose from different facets of these projects. For example, different procedures undertaken by the partici-pants (long-term group-based collaborative action research; shorter term (1–6 months) intensive one-to-one collaboration between a teacher or stu-dent and a consultant; repeated class-based surveys, questionnaires, and written evaluations; periodic individual and group discussions; individual diaries) provided a thorough blend of quantitative and qualitative informa-tion. In Miller and Lieberman's (1988) terms, information ranging from group-based survey data to intensive personal perspectives provided both 'nuance and numbers'; individual perspectives arising from close, personal collaboration were grounded within a broader teacher group, class, or whole-school context.

Details of the two projects are described more fully elsewhere (e.g., Baird and Mitchell, 1986; Baird, Fensham, Gunstone and White, 1989, 1991; Gunstone, Slattery and Baird, 1989; White, Baird, Mitchell, Fensham and Gunstone, 1989). Here, I present aspects of the projects in terms of three guiding principles for practice to improve teaching. The first principle is a stance that guided the design and implementation of the projects; the second and third principles comprise significant general findings. Each prin-ciple underlines, in a different way, the importance of balance for personal and professional development.

Three Guiding Principles for Better Teaching Through Collaborative Enquiry and Systematic Reflection

Guiding Principle 1: Converge Processes and Outcomes in Teaching, Learning, and Research

The bankruptcy of the dictum 'Good teaching results in good learning' has been recognized for most or all of the twentieth century. However, the seeds planted by those such as Dewey, that responsibility for learning process and outcome centers firmly on the learner, have taken a long time to germinate and bear fruit. One reason for this delay may be that, until perhaps the middle 1960s, surprisingly little was known of the process by which people learn. At about this time, rejection of behaviorism and the emergence of cognitive psychology were the forerunners of the currently common view of learning as active and generative, rather than reactive and receptive. Elsewhere, I have argued that learning is made more effective and productive by training students to direct *active enquiry* — comprising evaluation, reflection, and action — in a way which enhances metacognition regarding their own learning (Baird, in press). Indeed, such beliefs underpinned both PEEL and TLSS. The challenge remains to incorporate these processes within everyday classroom activities in order to foster systematically the desired product of school: the person who takes responsibility and control over his or her own learning throughout life.

This active view of learning has fundamental implications for what is considered to be good teaching practice. If one holds a constructivist view of learning, in which the learner actively constructs meaning according to what he or she already knows and believes, it follows that good teaching must itself involve learning through active enquiry. The teacher must ascertain the needs, concerns and abilities of the learners, and select teaching approaches and strategies accordingly. These activities are part of the more general orientation towards better teaching through enhanced metacognition outlined at the start of the chapter.

School contexts often fail to encourage teachers to enquire actively and systematically into their work. At the same time, university research traditionally has separated research from practice. These two forces contribute to separating two activities that have much in common. To make active enquiry more routine requires practice; to make it more systematic requires research. Here, I am arguing that we should converge, and bring into balance, the two complementary pairs: teaching and research, and process and outcome. Research is systematic enquiry; so is good teaching. In order to improve teaching, the teacher must reconceptualize the meaning of educational research. Educational research into teaching and learning is not just something done by educational researchers *on* teachers and learners. It can also be something done *by* teachers and learners *as* educational researchers. Teaching, learning and research share common processes. Each is directed towards enhanced metacognition to inform and direct practice, and the quality of each can be described in terms of the extent to which practice *is* informed and directed by personal metacognition. Guiding principles 2 and 3 concern making classroom enquiry more systematic, and the importance of basing such enquiry on personal and professional reflection.

In summary, the essence of guiding principle 1 is that teachers and students have an important part to play in research into teaching, learning and individual development, for two reasons. First, research into each of these areas requires consideration of the cognitive *and* the affective, the content *and* the context, the overt *and* the covert, behaviors *and* their mechanisms, effects *and* their causes, observations *and* explanations. No one is in a better position to protect the validity of findings from errors of interpretation or inference. Second, findings from the PEEL and TLSS projects indicate that, by engaging in such research, teachers and students will practice doing better what they do.

Guiding Principle 2: Support Change by Providing Adequate and Appropriate Time, Opportunity, Guidance, and Support

Two features of the normal teaching context often preclude desirable teacher development. The first feature is the isolationist nature of teaching where teachers, while working alongside others, normally operate independently. What happens in another teacher's classroom is largely unknown, but considered sacrosanct nevertheless. Peer enquiry into, much less appraisal of, one's teaching is a disquieting notion for many teachers. The second feature, which Griffin (1987) describes as the 'dailiness' of teaching (p. 35), relates to the myriad short-term duties, demands and deadlines which often overwhelm teachers' thoughts and actions.

Personal development is difficult and demanding; it requires concerted and protracted effort, time and opportunity. The findings from many studies of teacher change, including PEEL and TLSS, indicate that the time needed for durable, substantive change is often of the order of months or years, rather than days or weeks. It seems that one essential factor which helps teachers to surmount the two limitations to change above is to undergo personal change as part of a group endeavour. As I discuss next, the group facilitates change by providing two crucial requirements: support and guidance.

Both PEEL and TLSS were based on collaborative group-based research (Baird, Mitchell and Northfield, 1987). At each school, a group of teachers met regularly (weekly or bi-weekly) to identify problems, discuss issues, share information and determine appropriate action. Usually, one or more tertiary academics (consultants) were active members of the group. The two types of participant (teachers, consultants) brought to the group different perspectives and expertise. Through regular discussion, group members shared in generating tentative principles of theory and practice that seemed valid from both perspectives.

In order that collaborative research endures, group members must accept various responsibilities for dealing with the different needs which arise. Four major types of responsibility were found to be crucial:

1 *Organization and Administration*
   Someone has to arrange and organize meeting times and agenda and provide necessary materials. If, say, a questionnaire is administered, someone has to process and collate the data.

2 *Conceptual Guidance*

Goals must be set and plans must be made. Appropriate methods and techniques must be determined for classroom activities and collection of data. Often, information on appropriate techniques and theoretical perspectives must be provided. Once obtained, data must be interpreted and evaluated. Patterns of results may need to be organized within a conceptual framework for understanding and action.

3 *Sharing Perspectives on Classroom Practice*

Different perspectives regarding the 'What', 'Why', 'How', and 'How Well' of classroom practice need to be shared.

4 *Support*

Support must be given: uncertainties shared; effort acknowledged; failures commiserated with; successes rewarded.

Two points regarding these responsibilities need to be stressed. First, we have often found that, for up to a year, the non-teaching consultants carried responsibilities for organization and conceptual guidance. Had this not been done, we believe that the project would have languished. Conceptual guidance is demanding, as it requires experience in professional reflection and in classroom research. Conceptual guidance is directed to helping the group to focus the dialogue, to clarify direction and, particularly, to structure and systematize the craft-based knowledge of teachers. The extent to which these two responsibilities were carried by the consultants during this time highlights the advantage of having external input into the group. In terms of conceptual guidance, the consultants introduced different expertise and an external perspective against which teachers could contrast their perceptions and beliefs. Regarding organization and administration, one of the most significant constraints to progress, in the eyes of teachers, is the lack of time available to them to take on these responsibilities. The numerous teaching-related, pastoral and administrative duties of teachers mean that even attending regular meetings is a significant extra challenge to effective time management. Apart from self-perceived lack of expertise (a significant factor early in the project but less so later) time pressure was the major reason why teachers were reluctant to take responsibility for such things as organizing meetings or processing data. For at least one year in both PEEL and TLSS, most teachers participated willingly, but in a reactive rather than in an active fashion. The second point relates to shift in responsibility. With experience, with observation of the consultants carrying out responsibilities 1 and 2 and with the confidence that came from sharing responsibilities 3 and 4, the teachers gradually took on more, and all responsibilities came to be shared more equally. At the same time the consultants learned about how to meet these responsibilities more effectively.

Some of the groups in PEEL have never had an external consultant as a regular participant. For these groups, external input has been achieved by having at least one member of the school group in regular contact with tertiary consultants, either through formal study at Monash University or through meeting with the PEEL Reference Group, a group made up of teachers in PEEL groups at other schools and six staff members at the University. The PEEL Reference Group meets at monthly intervals throughout the year. It is important to note that, in each of these cases, the teacher who makes this external contact is often the group leader and is always an 'idea champion' (Miller and Lieberman, 1988), a person with sufficient motivation, commitment and, above all, energy, to shoulder the bulk of responsibilities 1 and 2 and to inspire the other teachers. We have noticed that when such a person is not present the group soon breaks down. Similarly, in groups which lack a school-based idea champion, the withdrawal of the outside consultant from active input into the group usually signals the group's decline, even when the group has been together for up to two years. The momentum for change is soon dissipated by the other pressures which demand teachers' attention.

The importance of the group and, particularly, of a colleague who acts as an idea champion indicates the importance of *affect* for change. To maintain progress, new knowledge and understandings must be accompanied by positive attitudes and feelings. I return to the importance of affect when I discuss the concept of challenge.

Apart from group-based collaboration, another type of collaboration was found to be critically important for teacher development. This collaboration involves intensive on-going one-to-one interaction between a teacher and a consultant or a teaching colleague. It is collaboration of the sort that Rudduck (1987) calls partnership supervision. Using her term, a 'focused professional dialogue' (p. 129) is established. This focused professional dialogue is related to a specific pedagogical problem or issue of importance to both individuals. The pair work closely together towards understanding and resolving the problem or issue, each member of the pair deriving benefit from the endeavour. Later, when I illustrate the guiding principles with particular episodes, I present three different examples of this type of one-to-one collaboration.

Guiding Principle 3: Base Personal and Professional Improvement on Reflection

If learning is a constructivist process by which the learner generates meaning according to what he or she already knows and believes, it follows that reflection is a cornerstone of learning and of personal and professional development. The word reflection is used in many different ways; here I use it to mean a conscious, thoughtful, purpose-related process. Reflective processes such as asking evaluative questions, selecting procedures to answer these questions, evaluating the results and making appropriate decisions may lead to enhanced cognitive understanding and metacognitive awareness and control (Baird, in press).

The subject of reflection about teaching may vary: particulars of classroom practice, perspectives or regularities (theory) guiding practice, or even what it is to be a teacher. The latter subject differs from the first two in that it is more phenomenological, directed more to better understanding of personal lived experience, in contrast to the more explanatory focus of the reflections on practice. The two research studies indicated that personal and professional development derives from an increase in the frequency and systematic nature of reflection. Initially, many teachers were unaccustomed to careful, thorough and purposeful reflection on themselves or their teaching. Indeed, it seems likely that much teacher knowledge is gained through experience as the 'knowing-in-action' which accrues by non-purposeful, largely subconscious reaction to unforeseen events (Schön, 1983). While this process, and the knowledge so gained, is of undoubted importance in the development of a teacher's expertise, it is not the focus of this chapter. My interest lies with the improvement that derives from increased attention to conscious, purposeful reflection before, during, or after the teaching event.

The results of both PEEL and TLSS indicate that, in the process towards improvement, initial reflection should link strongly to particulars of practice. Specific classroom problems should be identified, issues related to these problems considered and appropriate action decided upon. As teachers practice these processes, the focus of reflection gradually turns towards more generalizable issues that become workplace pedagogical theory. This theory is predictive; it serves to inform and guide future practice.

Findings from the TLSS project indicate that, for some teachers, reflection that is less tied to specifics of classroom content and context can also foster development. This is a phenomenological type of reflection, where the person seeks to understand more about teaching and being a teacher by drawing out from personal lived experience the essences by which they seem to be characterized. Large numbers of teachers and students were involved in such reflection. In the next section, I describe four episodes illustrating how reflection can contribute to improved teaching and learning outcomes. These episodes also indicate the importance of the two earlier guiding principles for generating improvement.

Four Episodes Exemplifying the Guiding Principles

Four episodes from the TLSS project exemplify guiding principles 1, 2 and 3. Each episode centers on a particular research procedure; for further detail, see Baird *et al.*, 1991, and White *et al.*, 1989). For each episode, I summarize the research procedure and identify an issue that emerged from the findings. As the project proceeded, issues such as these led to the development of the concept of *challenge*, to be discussed later.

Episode 1: Initial Trialling of Reflection on Practice Using Teacher-Consultant Collaboration

The procedure

Initially, each teacher and I collaborated on a trial of three lessons in order to increase the teacher's expertise in reflecting on classroom practice. The teacher prepared and taught the first of the three lessons in the usual way. I observed the lesson and, soon afterwards, the teacher and I wrote answers to a series of questions concerning the what, why, how and how well of the lesson (e.g., 'What was the topic?', 'Why were you doing it?', 'How did you go about teaching it?', 'How well did the lesson go?, 'Was it successful?, 'Did the students understand the work?', 'Was it enjoyable for them?'). We then discussed and compared our perceptions. The same procedure was followed in the second lesson, with the addition that each student in the class wrote answers to a similar set of questions. After this lesson, I collated the responses of the teacher and all the students and returned the collated material to the teacher. We then considered the meaning and significance of the findings. There was one further procedure for the third lesson. Beforehand, the teacher predicted the outcomes by writing answers to the same questions. Our post-lesson discussion took into account the teacher's prospective and retrospective perceptions, together with my own and those of the students recorded after the lesson.

The experience proved rather unsettling for the teachers. Many students seemed to have little idea of the answers to such questions are 'Why were you doing the topic?', and their ratings of the success of the lesson were often lower than that of the teacher. However, all the teachers valued the experience. They believed that it had helped them to reflect more deeply about their practices, and that this enhanced reflection had resulted in positive changes in their classroom attitudes, awareness, and outcomes.

An emergent issue

The trials involved me in close observation of twenty-seven lessons with students from grades 7 to 11. In these observations, I noticed a clear trend across year levels: the higher the grade, the less the students appeared to contribute actively in lessons. Although this trend was recognized by the teachers in a rather vague, ill-defined way, the collaborative procedure highlighted the trend by providing a structure and a different perspective. Teachers decided to study this finding in order to determine possible causes for it.

Individual and group reflection led the teachers to propose forty-four possible causes for this drop-off in students' motivation and application. Of these forty-four causes, eleven were rated by the teachers as both 'worth-while' and 'researchable'. These included some with a teacher-centered focus, (insufficient variation in teaching technique; teaching not challenging some students, but going over the heads of others; teacher dominance of classroom activities and behaviors) and others with a student-centered focus (interests more polarized, through specialization; peer group influence to not work; changes in interests and needs).

Teachers, individually or in pairs, then selected one or more of these causes for further research, which was based on student questionnaires and in-class discussions between teachers and students. This research illuminated various aspects of students' views regarding cognitive demand, interest in and enjoyment of work done, and personal control over one's learning (Baird et al., 1989).

Episode 2: Joint Lesson Evaluation by Teacher and Consultant

The procedure

Here the procedure was a more thorough and intensive version of the classroom-based one-to-one collaboration described in Episode 1. It involved my working with each of four teachers from one school to examine a sequence of six lessons, 'taking each lesson to pieces'. After each lesson, the teacher and I completed a form that required detailed identification and analysis of each teacher and student activity. Teacher and student behaviors and outcomes were then evaluated according to the espoused aims and objectives of a new curriculum that the teachers were attempting to implement. Thus the focus for the dialogue upon which the collaboration was based was the incidence and effectiveness of implementation of this curriculum. After each lesson, the teacher and I compared and discussed our written responses and tried to clarify any emerging issues of importance to the teacher. We then worked together on these issues in order to improve the quality of teaching and learning.

An emergent issue

One issue arising from this procedure concerned the extent to which good teaching is a balance between cognitive and affective elements. We found that we could interpret shortcomings in classroom teaching and learning in terms of lack of attention to, or lack of balance between, cognition and affect. For example, one question on the form required teachers to select from a list of thirty-six terms all of those that they believed applied to their teaching behaviors during the lesson. In this list, essentially cognitive terms (e.g., accurate, logical, well-structured, thorough) were intermingled with terms having a significant affective component (e.g., stimulating, inspiring, caring, perceptive). When we reviewed their selections at the end of the six lessons, it was clear that several teachers had consistently selected many of the cognitive terms but few of the affective ones. Through the ensuing discussion, these teachers came to the realization that they were down-playing, both consciously and subconsciously, potentially productive affect-ive interactions between them and their students. Equally, they came to realize that increasing the affective dimension of their teaching by providing for more perceptive, sensitive and motivating interactions would require considerable commitment and effort. Some (but not all) of the teachers were prepared to invest this effort, and subsequently attempted to change the manner of their interactions with students.

Episode 3: Teacher-Students-Consultant Agreement for Change

The procedure

In this procedure, students joined the teacher and me as researchers. The teachers wanted to involve the students more in lessons; they wanted also to improve their own performance. At my suggestion, they did this by discuss-ing with their students improvements that they and the students could make in classroom behaviors. From the numerous suggestions that were made, each class chose three improvements for the teacher and three for the students. These were set down as a contract — an agreement for change. For example, in one class the teacher was to use more variety in lessons, use simpler language and give clear instructions on what to do. For their part, the students were to ask more questions, be more supportive of each other and complete work set. At frequent intervals, the teacher and each student wrote an evaluation of the extent to which he or she and the other partner in the agreement had been achieving the promised changes during the previous week. Students also evaluated separately the extent to which changes made by the teacher and themselves had affected their level of enjoyment of, application to and understanding of the work done.

Twelve teachers and 316 students in grades 8 to 11 in fourteen classes participated in the agreements. Each class was involved for a period ranging between ten days and fourteen weeks. The findings were positive and encouraging. Over the duration of the agreements, students remembered the changes agreed to, they perceived that they and the teacher had made changes, and they often reported that enjoyment and understanding of science had increased because of the changes (Baird *et al.*, 1991; White *et al.*, 1989).

An emergent issue

The Agreement for Change procedure demonstrated to teachers and stu-dents that they can work together to research and improve the quality of classroom teaching and learning. More specifically, the agreements demons-trated the efficacy of changing the nature of the teacher-student relationship towards one which took greater account of students' needs and concerns, in a situation where there was shared accountability for making improvements.

Episode 4: Phenomenological Reflection Procedure

The procedure

Eleven teachers and seventy-five students in grades 8 to 11 participated voluntarily in a procedure requiring them to reflect carefully on what, from their own experience, constituted teaching and being a teacher (or learning and being a student). At roughly monthly intervals, they wrote answers to the same series of questions. For teachers, these questions included 'For me, what is it to be a science teacher?', 'For me, what is science teaching?', and 'What is the most important pay-off in science teaching?'. In addition, each participant met with a consultant at regular intervals in order to elaborate written responses and to clarify and develop personal views. This procedure extended from five to twenty-two months, depending on the person. It provided a means of obtaining more detailed and comprehensive information on attitudes, beliefs, and needs than was possible from such probes as questionnaires.

An emergent issue

Many teachers and students derived benefits from the opportunity to undergo extended, careful reflection on elements of personal experience. The stimulus for reflection provided by the task of responding to the questions, together with the guidance and support given by the consultant, led them to realize the importance of reflection for personal development. The nature of the procedure required them to draw back from the minutiae of problem-centered aspects of their practice and take a more fundamental, evaluative view of themselves and what they do.

Individuals differed widely in the extent to which they applied themselves to, and benefited from, this task. Some teachers found that the procedure had led them to a clearer idea of the thoughts and feelings that underpinned their behaviors and of the ways in which these behaviors were being constrained by the responsibilities and demands of teaching. This type of reflection is difficult, for it requires the person to extract from a mass of details those aspects that seem to characterize, or engender meaning for, personal experience. It is likely, therefore, that such reflection is best attempted only after prior practice at reflection on more specific, concrete aspects of practice.

Systematizing the Emergent Issues as Theory: The Concept of Challenge

Collectively, the different procedures undertaken in the two research projects provided an opportunity for balanced reflection on the nature and processes of teaching and learning. Balance was apparent in the synthesis of issues arising from qualitative, personal probes and quantitative, group-based data. One product of such synthesis is itself a matter of balance: the concept of *challenge* as a balance between cognitive and affective aspects of teaching and learning. I developed this concept from findings of episodes such as the four outlined above. It is theory based on the attitudes, beliefs, and behaviors of teachers and students and generated through processes of collaborative reflection operating as part of increasingly systematic enquiry. Thus this concept of challenge derives from a process of progressive abstraction from actual classroom practices. The concept of challenge is many things: a frame for generating meaning for the different findings; a focus for systematizing further enquiry (e.g., for diagnosing shortcomings in teaching and learning and for organizing remedial action); above all, it is a specific construction that assists in operationalizing the nature of good teaching. Some preliminary thoughts about the concept of challenge as derived from classroom research and practice are presented in the final section of the chapter.

Challenge in Teaching and Learning

Many of the factors identified as influencing the extent of effort, achievement and satisfaction, for teachers in their teaching and for learners in their learning, are interpretable in terms of *level of challenge*. As it emerged from the findings of the project, challenge has two main components: a cognitive-metacognitive *demand* component and an affective *interest* component. For an individual teacher or learner, the *balance* between these two components determines a particular level of challenge which in turn influences level of involvement and nature of outcome. Nine major perceived features of a teaching-learning event interact to influence the cognitive and affective components of challenge.

Amount of work
Difficulty of the work
Importance of the work
Relevance of the work to, and the opportunity the
work provides to extend, existing knowledge,
abilities and interests
Novelty or variety of the activities
Extent of individual control over the process
(which, for students, includes control over personal
learning and assessment)
Opportunity for active involvement (both physical
and mental) in the process
Interpersonal (teacher-student; student-student)
features of the teaching/learning context
Physical features of the teaching/learning context.

The same features can be applied analogously for teachers in determining level of personal challenge in teaching which, in turn, influences teaching attitudes, behaviors and outcomes. Balance between cognitive and affective aspects is central to the concept of challenge.

Boredom as Lack of Challenge

A common reason given by students for inadequate application to their work is that they find it 'boring'. This comment is usually taken to indicate lack of interest or enjoyment. While it does have this common sense meaning, the concept of challenge can also provide a more comprehensive perspective. Rather than a unitary lack of interest and enjoyment, boredom may arise from a more multi-faceted lack of challenge. Consider, for example, four different situations, all related to different levels of the cognitive and affective components of challenge. Let us propose that, for each situation, both (cognitive) demand and (affective) interest are at one of two levels: *High* (but not too high) or *Low*.

When both demand and interest are High, the cognitive and affective components assume a desirable balance and the student is challenged to become actively involved. When demand is High, but interest is Low, the challenge is less desirable; at best, the student submits to externally-derived pressure to comply. When demand is Low and interest is High, this situation lacks challenge and may be characterized by frustration and limited involvement. Finally, when both demand and interest are Low, challenge is absent and the student fails to engage in the task.

Discussion with students reveals that they may label each of the last three situations as 'boring', even though the word has a different underlying meaning in each case. In none of these three situations is the balance between cognition and affect sufficient to stimulate the student to invest a desirable level of effort. In each case, the outcomes would also be expected to be less than desired. Often, lack of (cognitive) achievement is associated with (affective) feelings of lack of accomplishment, self-assurance and fulfilment.

It may be that one route towards better teaching is to reflect on one's practice in terms of the extent to which it challenges students. The components of challenge may act as a basis for diagnosis and, if appropriate, remedy. Teachers and students could collaborate to evaluate lesson activities in terms of levels of challenge and then decide jointly to change in ways that, through manipulation of these components, provide the potential for enhanced challenge. By providing a focus for reflection and action, the concept of challenge may facilitate collaborative reflection and systematic enquiry. For example, the perspective of challenge may provide a means of revisiting issues that emerged in earlier research (e.g., those in episodes 1–4 above) and of framing questions that provide further illumination. Examples of such questions are:

> 'Is the observed drop in the level of students' contribution as they proceed through school related to a reduction in the level of challenge?'
> 'If so, what has changed, and what can be done about it, in order to match better the type of challenge to students' needs and interests?'
> 'To what extent are poor teaching practices interpretable in terms of an imbalance between cognitive and affective aspects of challenge?'
> 'How might the concept of challenge be applied so as to provide students with a more desirable balance between guidance and support, responsibility and accountability?'

A similar situation related to lack of challenge arises for many teachers in their teaching. Extensive anecdotal evidence exists to suggest that, over time, teachers commonly experience increasing demands but diminishing interest. In such a situation, coping strategies prevail, routine replaces innovation and boredom replaces challenge. Again, the concept of challenge may provide a useful focus for research on teaching and professional development. Questions analogous to the four student-centered ones above could guide this teacher-centered research and development.

Conclusion

The aims and practices of schooling are undergoing substantial changes. More than ever before, the desired aims of secondary schooling are being defined clearly in terms of developing students' willingness and abilities to act as informed, purposeful and independent learners. The practices of everyday schooling must match more closely, and train for, this desired product.

Teachers have a central role to play in orchestrating these changes. By engaging in educational research guided by the three principles above and proceeding through processes of collaborative reflection and systematic enquiry, teachers can work with their students and non-teaching colleagues to inform and improve their teaching. Results obtained, and issues arising from these results, will progressively become transmuted into theory; this theory can then be turned back to the classroom to be tested and refined.

In this chapter, I have demonstrated these processes by considering how challenge emerged from research as a perspective for improving teaching and learning. This concept, with its complex association of cognition and affect, is supported by a wide range of findings, and has the potential for guiding further classroom-based research. Research and professional development initiatives based on the three guiding principles above and focusing on exploring conditions for optimizing challenge in one's own teaching may generate the metacognitive and affective outcomes that characterize better teaching.

References

BAIRD, J.R. (in press) 'Individual and group reflection as a basis for teacher development', in HUGHES, P. (Ed.) *Teachers' Professional Development*, Hawthorn, Victoria, Australian Council for Educational Research.

BAIRD, J.R., FENSHAM, P.J., GUNSTONE, R.F. and WHITE, R.T. (1989) *Teaching and Learning Science in Schools: A Report of Research in Progress*, unpublished manuscript, Faculty of Education, Monash University.

BAIRD, J.R., FENSHAM, P.J., GUNSTONE, R.F. and WHITE, R.T. (1991) 'The importance of reflection in improving science teaching and learning', *Journal of Research in Science Teaching*, **28**, 2, pp. 163–182.

BAIRD, J.R. and MITCHELL, I.J. (Eds) (1986) *Improving the Quality of Teaching and Learning: An Australian Case Study — The PEEL Project*, Melbourne, Monash University Printery.

BAIRD, J.R., MITCHELL, I.J. and NORTHFIELD, J.R. (1987) 'Teachers as researchers: The rationale; the reality', *Research in Science Education*, **17**, pp. 129–138.

GRIFFIN, G.A. (1987) 'The school in society and the social organization of the school: Implications for school improvement', in WIDEEN, M.F. and ANDREWS, I. (Eds) *Staff Development for School Improvement: A Focus on the Teacher*, London, Falmer Press.

GUNSTONE, R.F. SLATTERY, M. and BAIRD, J.R. (1989) *Learning about Learning to Teach: A Case Study of Pre-service Teacher Education*, presented at the annual meeting of the American Educational Research Association, San Francisco, March.

MILLER, L. and LIEBERMAN, A. (1988) 'School improvement in the United States: Nuance and numbers', *International Journal of Qualitative Studies in Education*, **1**, 1, pp. 3–19.

RUDDUCK, J. (1987) 'Partnership supervision as a basis for the professional development of new and experienced teachers', in WIDEEN, M.F. and ANDREWS, I. (Eds) *Staff Development for School Improvement: A Focus on the Teacher*, London, Falmer Press.

SCHÖN, D.A. (1983) *The Reflective Practitioner: How Professionals Think in Action*, New York, Basic Books.

WHITE, R.T., BAIRD, J.R., MITCHELL, I.J., FENSHAM, P.J. and GUNSTONE, R.F. (1989) *Teaching and Learning Science in Schools: An Exploration of Process*, presented at the annual meeting of the American Educational Research Association, San Francisco, March.

4   A Cognitive Analysis of Patterns in Science Instruction by Expert and Novice Teachers

Hilda Borko, Mary Louise Bellamy and Linda Sanders

This study of the nature of pedagogical expertise examines the thinking and actions of a small number of expert and novice science teachers. We draw upon a conceptual framework that characterizes teaching as a complex cognitive skill determined in part by the nature of a teacher's knowledge system to explain patterns in participants' planning, teaching and post-lesson reflections. The chapter begins with a discussion of the conceptual framework and a description of the investigation and its findings. We then present abbreviated case descriptions of four teachers to illustrate patterns in the expert and novice teachers' thinking and actions. These patterns are examined in terms of the conceptual framework of teaching as a complex cognitive skill. Finally, we compare this investigation with a similar study of mathematics instruction and offer several suggestions for future research.

The Nature of Pedagogical Expertise

Research on cognitive skills in domains other than teaching has demonstrated that there are qualitative differences in the knowledge, thinking and actions of experts and novices. For example, experts and novices differ in the way they represent problems (Chi, Feltovich and Glaser, 1981) and in the strategies they employ to solve them (Fredericksen, 1984). Information which is useful for experts may hold little meaning for novices (deGroot, 1965). The growing body of literature on expert-novice distinctions in teaching suggests that characteristics of expertise in other complex cognitive domains apply to teaching as well. For example, expert teachers notice different aspects of classrooms than do novices, are more selective in their use of information during planning and interactive teaching, and make greater use of instructional and management routines. (See, for example, Berliner, 1987, 1988; Borko and Livingston, 1989; Borko and Shavelson,

1990; Calderhead, 1983; Carter, Cushing, Sabers, Stein and Berliner, 1988; Carter, Sabers, Cushing, Pinnegar and Berliner, 1987; Leinhardt and Greeno, 1986; Leinhardt and Smith, 1985; Peterson and Comeaux, 1987; Sabers, Cushing and Berliner, 1991).

It should be noted at the outset that the educational literature provides no shared definition of an 'expert teacher', and that the identification of experts continues to be a troublesome issue for researchers, practitioners and policy-makers alike (Berliner, 1986). In this study, we relied on nominations by teacher center coordinators who were responsible for placing university students with cooperating teachers for their student teaching experiences. During our observations of the four cooperating teachers, we agreed that all should be classified at least as 'proficient', the fourth stage in Berliner's (1988) five-stage model of pedagogical expertise. Proficient teachers share many characteristics with experts, including well-developed knowledge structures and thinking skills that enable fast, fluid and flexible behavior. Because of the difficulties in agreeing upon a definition of expertise and because of the similarities in the knowledge, thinking and actions of 'expert' and 'proficient' teachers, we concluded that it is reasonable to use the term 'expert' to describe the teachers with whom we worked in this study.

Schema, pedagogical reasoning and pedagogical content knowledge — three concepts central to the characterization of teaching as a complex cognitive skill — provide a framework for interpreting differences between expert and novice teachers. A 'schema' is an abstract knowledge structure that summarizes information about many particular cases and the relationships among them (Anderson, 1984). People store knowledge about objects and events in their experiences in schemata or knowledge structures representing these experiences.

'Pedagogical reasoning' is the process of transforming subject matter knowledge 'into forms that are pedagogically powerful and yet adaptive to the variations in ability and background presented by the students' (Shulman, 1987, p. 15). Pedagogical reasoning includes the identification and selection of strategies for representing key ideas in a lesson and the adaptation of these strategies to the characteristics of learners. This form of thinking is unique to the profession of teaching and is relatively undeveloped in novice teachers (Feiman-Nemser and Buchmann, 1986, 1987).

'Pedagogical content knowledge', or knowledge of subject matter for teaching, is also specific to the teaching profession. This domain of knowledge consists of an understanding of how to represent specific subject matter topics and issues in ways that are appropriate to the diverse abilities and interests of learners.

> [It includes] for the most regularly taught topics in one's subject area, the most useful forms of representation of those ideas, the most powerful analogies, illustrations, examples, explanations, and

demonstrations — in a word, the ways of representing the subject that make it comprehensible to others ... [It] also includes an understanding of what makes the learning of specific topics easy or difficult: the conceptions and preconceptions that students of different ages and backgrounds bring with them to learning. (Shulman, 1987, p. 9)

Schemata for pedagogical content knowledge seem to be virtually non-existent in novices' knowledge systems. Developing these knowledge structures and learning pedagogical reasoning skills are major components of learning to teach (Feiman-Nemser and Buchmann, 1986, 1987; Wilson, Shulman and Richert, 1987).

In an investigation of the thinking and actions of expert and novice mathematics teachers, Borko and Livingston (1989) analyzed participants' planning, teaching and post-lesson reflections using the characterization of teaching as a complex cognitive skill. When compared to experts, novices showed more time-consuming and less efficient planning, they encountered problems when attempts to be responsive to students led them away from scripted lesson plans, and they reported more varied, less selective post-lesson reflections. These differences were accounted for by the assumptions that novices' cognitive schemata, particularly their schemata for pedagogical content knowledge, are less elaborate, less interconnected and less easily accessible than those of experts, and that their pedagogical reasoning skills are less well-developed.

This study extends the program of research on pedagogical expertise to the content area of science by examining differences in the planning, teaching and post-lesson reflections of expert and novice science teachers. Although we anticipated differences in the patterns of thinking and actions of science teachers and mathematics teachers that are attributable to differences between the disciplines, we expected to be able to explain contrasts between expert and novice science teachers using the conceptual framework of teaching as a complex cognitive skill.

Data Collection and Analysis

The participants in this study were four student teachers in the secondary science education program at a large American university and the junior high school teachers with whom they were placed. Students in the program enroll in student teaching full time for one semester after completing their science and education coursework. The student teaching semester includes two eight-week placements, one in a junior high school and one in a high school. Typically it is the last semester of a four-year undergraduate teacher education program.

This study is part of a larger investigation that also included a planning simulation. The six student teachers who participated in the planning simulation were selected on the basis of their academic major, overall grade-point average, and enrollment in a secondary science methods course in the preceding semester. All six had grade-point averages above 3.0 on a 4-point scale. Three had majors in life sciences and three in physical sciences, one in physics and two in chemistry. Four of the student teachers were selected for the field study component on the basis of gender (two male and two female), science background (two majors in life sciences, one in physics and one in chemistry) and scheduling considerations. The student teachers were placed with cooperating teachers who were identified as 'experts' by teacher center coordinators in the two school systems in which the study was conducted, and who also expressed a willingness to participate in the study.

Data for the student teachers were collected at the end of their junior high student teaching placements. For the two student teachers whose first placements were in junior high schools, data were collected in March. For the two whose second placements were in junior high schools, data were collected in May. Data for the cooperating teachers were collected when the student teachers were not in their classrooms. Thus for two, data collection occurred in March or April, before their student teachers arrived; for the two others it occurred in May, after the student teaching placements.

The data collection plan for this study was modeled on the earlier investigation of expert and novice teachers' mathematics instruction (Borko and Livingston, 1989) with modifications designed to accommodate expected characteristics of junior high school science instruction (e.g., demonstrations and laboratory activities). Participants were observed teaching science during a single class period (approximately fifty minutes) over one full week of teaching. In all but one case, observations occurred on consecutive school days. Participants were interviewed prior to each observed lesson about their planning, and following the lesson about their reflections after teaching. The consecutive planning-observation-reflection cycles enabled us to trace the evolution of sequences of instruction and the influence of classroom events and participants' reflections on subsequent planning and teaching.

Our observations were guided by a set of general questions about the nature of instructional activities, classroom routines and teachers' instructional and management strategies. We wrote notes during the observations and we audiotaped the class sessions. The written notes and audiotapes were used to prepare detailed fieldnotes of each lesson we observed, and these fieldnotes were the primary data source for investigating teachers' actions while teaching.

An interview was conducted prior to the observation cycle to determine the nature of the lessons to be observed and the participant's long-range planning. Daily pre-observation interviews focused on instructional planning;

questions requested participants to discuss the nature of the lesson to be observed, how they planned for the lesson, what they thought about as they planned and what factors influenced their plans. Post-observation interviews examined participants' reflections after teaching; questions requested them to talk about prominent features of the lesson (what stands out), unexpected occurrences, changes from plans and reasons for those changes. A final interview asked participants to discuss their reflections about the entire observation cycle, changes in their knowledge or thinking as a result of their teaching and any effects of the research project.

All interviews were semi-structured. This format ensured that parallel information was collected from all participants while enabling the researchers to pursue unique lines of inquiry relevant to our research questions with individual teachers. Interviews were tape-recorded and later transcribed, and the transcripts served as the primary data source for investigating the teachers' planning and post-lesson reflections. Transcripts were supplemented by photocopies of planning documents such as texts, written plans, class handouts and content notes.

Interview and observation data were analyzed using ethnographic procedures designed specifically for the analysis of text-based qualitative data (Spradley, 1979, 1980). In the first step of the analysis, we identified categories of characteristics, thinking and action and sorted participants' statements, activities and behaviors into these categories. We based the category system on the earlier investigation of mathematics instruction, modifying it to include additional categories for teacher characteristics (e.g., science background, knowledge, beliefs) and for activities typical of science classrooms (e.g., laboratory exercises, demonstrations). As one example of the categorization process, we grouped statements about planning into a set of categories that included lesson agenda, goals and objectives, content, activities, organization and management, planning process and influences on planning. Statements in the category 'planning: activities' were further divided into subcategories that included demonstrations, explanations, laboratory exercises, 'timing, pacing and sequence' and evaluation. We then prepared a case description summarizing each participant's characteristics, thinking and actions, following an outline generated from the category system. In the final step of analysis, we examined these case descriptions for patterns of similarities and differences across participants.

In reporting our findings, we focus on patterns that emerged in the cross-case analysis of the thinking and actions of expert and novice science teachers. To illustrate these patterns, we include data from four participants, two experts ('Nina' and 'Jim') and two novices ('Shari' and 'Steve'). We first present abbreviated case descriptions of the two expert teachers' pedagogical knowledge and beliefs, planning, interactive thinking and post-lesson reflections, and we discuss the patterns apparent in the descriptions. We then turn to the student teachers and highlight aspects of their teaching that reveal their 'noviceness'. Finally, we compare characteristics of the experts' and novices' teaching in terms of the conceptual framework of teaching as a complex cognitive skill.

In general, we selected information that illustrates patterns across the entire set of teachers for inclusion in the abbreviated case descriptions. With respect to interactive teaching, our presentation focuses primarily on demonstrations and laboratory exercises. In addition to comprising central components of each teacher's science curriculum, these activity types illustrate the impact of participants' educational beliefs and knowledge systems on their teaching.

Patterns in the Experts' Science Teaching

Nina's Classroom Teaching

At the time of the study, Nina had taught at the junior high level (ages 12 to 14) for over fifteen years and had taught Grade 8 in the same school system for ten years. Although her educational background is in biology, our observations involved her teaching the first week of a unit on weather to a 'gifted and talented' Grade 8 earth science class. Although we did not ask the teachers directly about their educational philosophies, Nina, like the other expert teachers, shared her ideas about teaching junior high science during the course of our conversations. She saw junior high as a unique time in students' lives and had strong ideas about how science should be taught to these students. For example, Nina favored an 'inductive' approach to teaching. In describing an extended discussion of a laboratory assignment she explained:

> They didn't understand what I was talking about and I didn't want to move on until they got some idea. But I wanted them to tell me. I didn't want to have to tell them ... I prefer it that way, you know, to see if they can figure it out ... If they feel like they have figured it out, it just stays with them longer, and makes them feel good too.

Nina also believed that junior high students should be introduced to laboratory exercises. Such hands-on activities were a major component of her Grade 8 curriculum, despite her awareness that junior high students do not listen well to instructions and that, if they finish early:

> They are *never* going to sit there and check their results or re-do the lab or read up on what the lab was about ... I always try to do something after the lab that needs no instruction, so they can simply move from the lab to the other assignment.

Nina stated that instruction must be related to students' 'everyday experiences':

> I always try to think of some way that what we are studying is related to their lives and how it's fun too ... And so I usually try to introduce things so that they can see that there's some meaning in their lives.

Planning

Like all the expert teachers in this study, Nina engaged in both long-term and daily planning. Her planning was the most extensive and most routinized, which is not surprising given the priority she placed on this aspect of teaching.

> I'm a really firm believer in planning on a day-to-day basis. I'll sit down and do [plan out] exactly what I'm going to do each day ... I can't stand to come to school without my lessons for the next week done, you know, for Monday morning. It simply wrecks my entire life to come to school unprepared.

Over the years Nina had developed a planning routine that included yearly, unit, weekly and daily planning activities. She did almost all of her planning with Pam, the teacher next door who also taught Grade 8 earth science. Yearly planning included decisions about what units to teach and what major projects to include. This year, for example, they added a unit on glaciers and a small group project on computers, and they decided not to participate in science fair projects. Unit planning consisted of deciding 'what would be useful to know if you were never going to have another science course that would cover weather'. Unit planning also involved deciding what laboratory activities to perform.

> The next step, I guess, is deciding what lab activities do I want to be sure that I include, what demonstrations do I want to include, and what kinds of written activities do I want the kids to do, to reinforce the things that I want them to learn from the chapter.

After she and Pam thought about these issues independently, they met to make final decisions and to pull the needed materials from their activity files. Nina and Pam also worked together on weekly plans.

> Usually sixth period on Thursday we sit down and really seriously talk about what we've done for the week, what we've gotten done, what we think we should do next week. And sit down and write out the assignments for the next week ... and then take everything out that we need to run off.

Gathering and organizing materials was a major component of Nina's daily planning. She placed materials for demonstrations on the worktable in the front of the classroom and materials for lab exercises on a cart to be wheeled into the room.

> Just the logistics of teaching science is very time consuming. You couldn't do a lab any simpler than this lab [composition of the atmosphere]. And yet you've got to bring out five or six things, and get them on the cart, count them, get them ready. It just always takes time. No way around that, no matter whether you've been teaching five minutes or fifty years.

Nina also mentally reviewed demonstrations, explanations and laboratory exercises prior to class sessions.

> [I think about] only the idea that I want to get across. Not the exact words. I couldn't, I wouldn't be able to do something word for word, you know, like a script. I have to know what I'm talking about ... But I don't sit down and think the exact words that I'm going to use to say it.

For lab exercises, she also tried to remember problems that occurred in the past and thought about procedures and cautions to emphasize when introducing the lab, in order to avoid similar problems. For the lab on composition of the atmosphere, it was important

> to tell the kids to be sure to get the steel wool wet. The kids that didn't get it wet [in her classes the week before] didn't get good results.

She also typically planned additional activities for students who finished lab exercises before the end of class and for class sessions that might end early. Nina made most of her decisions about content presentation prior to class sessions.

> Now having taught for a long time I have a lot of materials already available. And so the problem generally is deciding what to omit rather than what to put in, because you're constantly finding new things that you want to try and there are some old things you just don't want to give up.

For the class in which she conducted a series of demonstrations on air pressure, she decided in advance which demonstrations she would use and the order in which she would use them. Her lesson followed that plan.

Interactive teaching

The week of observation in Nina's class was characterized by variety. Students participated in two laboratory exercises, a series of teacher demonstrations, a teacher-directed individual activity, student presentations of group computer projects, a film and a twenty-minute silent reading period (a school-wide policy). Here we focus primarily on her demonstrations and laboratory exercises.

Nina's demonstrations, like all other aspects of her interactive teaching, were accomplished without the assistance of notes, textbook or other written materials. She typically provided a verbal explanation of what she was doing as she conducted the demonstration. She then engaged students in a discussion of the phenomenon and its possible causes. She guided the discussion toward the scientific principle the demonstration was designed to illustrate by acknowledging some student responses but not others and by elaborating on some of those which she acknowledged. The following example illustrates these characteristics. It comes from a discussion following a 'collapsing can' demonstration in which an empty duplicating fluid can is filled with a small amount of water, heated until the water boils and steam escapes, and then capped. As the trapped steam cools, the pressure inside the can is reduced, causing the can to collapse due to the greater air pressure outside. The following excerpt from the field notes begins just after the demonstration was completed; Nina has drawn a diagram of the can on the board.

Nina: Let's go through this step by step, what we did. What's the first thing I did to the can, besides rinse it out?

Students call out that she put water in it.

Nina: Put water in it. Just a little bit of water down at the bottom. [She adds water to her diagram] Now, what did I wait for the water to do?

Most students who call out say 'boil'; several say 'evaporate'. Nina continues, drawing arrows to represent the air inside and outside the can as she talks.

Nina: Now, when we started out, there's air out here and air in here, and the can was just sitting there minding its own business, right? Air pressure was equal here and here. When I started to boil the water, what did it do?

Several students call out. Nina tells one that her answer is exactly right. She elaborates, drawing the arrows to represent air moving out as she talks.

Nina: The steam drove the air out, because steam is not the same thing as air, right. When the water boiled, the little molecules in here got so excited, they got so hot and so excited, they jumped out of the liquid and they became airborne. And so, pretty soon the whole can was filled with little molecules of water roaming around in the form of water vapor.

After explaining that the water vapor forced air molecules out of the can, Nina reminded the students that she had then removed the can from the heat and immediately capped it.

Nina: Now, as it cooled, what began to happen to the water vapor?

Several students call out. One suggests, 'It went back to a liquid'.

Nina: OK, it began to go back to being a liquid ... I had taken the heat away and so they [the water molecules] began to lose their energy and fall back down into the water again. What did that leave in here then? [Nina points to the can]

Several students call out 'Air'.

Nina: Air?

Several students suggest 'nothing'.

Nina: Nothing. What do you call a space where there is nothing?

Students call out several suggestions, including 'void' and 'space'.

Nina: There was at least a partial vacuum in there, meaning that there was nothing in there. [She writes 'vacuum' on the diagram, with a line pointing into the can.] Now, what did that do to the balance of air pressure?

Students call out several suggestions, including crushing the can.

Nina: Yes, the air crushed the poor little can, because the air pressure outside the can was greater than the air pressure inside. Air pressure is the most amazing thing. It is absolutely amazing how strong it can be.

The laboratory exercises observed in Nina's class were preceded by detailed procedural explanations and demonstrations and followed by whole class discussions of what happened and why. Nina's instructions, typically accompanied by warnings about where to be especially careful, illustrate her knowledge of content and of Grade 8 science students. The following illustration is from her introduction to a lab exercise on rusting and oxidation.

You have to wet the inside of the test tube, dump the water out. Dampen the steel wool. Not soaking, but wet. Just pull off a little chunk, like this. Nothing big. Put it in the test tube so that there's about one inch from the top. Believe me when I tell you that it should be about one inch from the top. Otherwise tomorrow when I explain how to get it out, yours will be stuck. Then take a beaker from here. Put fifty milliliters of water in it. That's to here. Put the test tube upside down. Write your initials on here with the wax pencils up there. And put it on the top shelf up here. Think you can do that in two minutes?

While students worked on laboratory exercises, Nina moved from group to group, monitoring, assisting and challenging students to think more carefully about what they were seeing. As she explained later:

> Most of the time you are just wandering around doing whatever's called for, either helping set up the lab or answering questions or giving little nudges or pushes to try to get them to go in the right direction. And trying not to act as an encyclopedia, which is hard because that's what they would like for you to do.

Reflections

The reflections that Nina shared with the researcher each day after teaching focused primarily on the students. On most days she commented about their understanding of the material and their participation or involvement in the lesson. In assessing student understanding she often compared her current students to those she taught in previous years. Nina expected most, but not all, students to pay attention and to participate in class activities. Although 'you hardly ever have a time when everybody is paying attention', she was concerned about the students who did not participate.

> The kids were interested, for the most part. But being the kind of person I am, I guess one thing that stands out in my mind is that there were some who were not ... it seemed to me that most of them were but there seemed to be probably, maybe six or eight that weren't really ... paying attention.

Jim's Classroom Teaching

Jim taught junior high school science for four years prior to our study. Although he is a biologist by training, we observed him teaching a unit on force and work in a semester-long Grade 8 physical sciences class. He had taught the course three times prior to our observations. One of Jim's strong pedagogical content beliefs is that science should be taught using a discovery method:

> My philosophy for science is let them explore it and come up with an hypothesis after they've seen it happen, rather than give them an hypothesis and say, 'This is what the law is', and then prove the law. I have them do it and then come up with the law. And then I say, 'Oh, guess what, you came up with the same thing as back in the 1800s' ... It's more meaningful that way.

According to Jim, the teacher's role is to provide students with opportunities to explore. Demonstrating his understanding of junior high students, he explained:

> With middle schoolers, it's got to be very activity oriented, very tactile ... I always have believed the only way you learn something is by playing with it, doing it, tearing it apart and putting it back together again. That's what I try to get them to do.

He tried to have many 'hands-on activities ... to bring the concepts to reality for the students'. Jim also stated that it is very important for students to see that life and science are 'interrelated'.

> I think, 'OK, what examples can they relate to in life?' And I try to bring those into the classroom.

Planning

Each semester Jim coordinated his teaching with the other instructor for the Grade 8 physical sciences course. They decided who would teach chemistry first and who would teach physics first, in order to avoid competing for equipment, films and other resources.

> That's as much long term planning as I do ... I make a decision: I'll teach chemistry first and she'll teach physics first. I gave up on long range plans ... [because] it used to be so frustrating. You would sit there and write out all those plans and they're invalid after a week.

Jim did make out a monthly calendar listing topics for each day and an occasional page number from the text, and he posted the calendar on a bulletin board in the classroom. All other planning that he did was in preparation for daily activities.

Jim was not as consistent or routinized in his daily planning as was Nina. He usually planned a day or so before each lesson, typically looking through several textbooks for ideas. Some of the ideas for activities 'get put into folders, if I know they are real successful'. More often he wrote them in the margins of the assigned text for the course 'because I know I look at the textbook first all of the time'. Jim's daily plans were fairly general and were never written down.

> I pretty much get the concept together and then let the lesson flow. I don't really plan what I'm going to say step by step. I just know that I'm going to do this activity and this activity and that makes up my lesson. And however it comes out, it comes out. There's not a lot of thought to every little word I'm going to say in that sense.

He typically planned several activities for each topic and made final decisions about which activities to use during the class session, guided by his sense of how quickly students seemed to understand the concept being taught.

Interactive teaching

Jim was much more likely than Nina to make decisions about activities during the class session.

> I typically let these types of things evolve. I know what I have to discuss basically, and the student questioning normally prompts me enough to remember, 'these are things I have to bring out' ... A lot of times an idea hits me that will bring a point home. I'll see their confusion and I'll realize I need another way to say the same thing, or make it visible to them, so they can see it happen. I'll probably have to pull out a fulcrum and a meter stick and a resistance, so they can at least see ... That's not written in my lesson plan, but I kind of have that in my mind. I know I can pull on that if they don't see it from diagramming it on the board.

One example of this spontaneity occurred during a discussion of the concept of work. The example also illustrates Jim's skill in drawing connections between scientific concepts and students' experiences. Jim asked the question, 'Which is more work, lifting a suitcase half a meter or pushing it half a meter, and why?' After he solved the problem using the formula $Work = Force \times Distance$, the class could not understand how lifting could be more work than pushing. Several called out that because of friction it should take more work to push it. Jim brought out a 200 gram mass saying 'All right, here's my suitcase', and demonstrated the problem using the 'suitcase', a spring scale, and a meter stick.

Reflections

Jim's reactions to lessons usually focused on student understanding. His comment, 'I think we got the point across ... I feel good that they understood forces', is typical of the reflections he shared with the researcher after observed lessons. Like Nina, his assessments of lessons often involved comparisons with expectations based on previous experiences teaching the same content.

> Some years a lot of the students don't question the fact that ... lifting a suitcase is more work than pushing a suitcase. And this year it happened that they didn't see that, and so therefore I needed to demonstrate it ... It took up some class time that I hadn't planned on. ...

Patterns across the Science Experts

As the illustrations from Nina's and Jim's teaching indicate, despite differences in instructional approaches, the expert teachers drew upon their pedagogical content knowledge, beliefs and experience in planning and teaching. All the teachers knew several ways to present lesson content. They had strategies for keeping track of these activities from year to year, including folders of activities, a notebook of factual materials, plan books from previous years and annotations in the margins of the textbook. They did little or no written planning other than to prepare monthly or weekly schedules of topics and assignments.

In keeping with their beliefs about science teaching, these teachers were skillful at drawing connections between classroom activities and students' lives. Also, they were able to skillfully combine demonstrations and explanations into presentations that seemed to guide students toward intended learning outcomes. They involved students in these presentations, controlling the direction of the discussion by acknowledging some student responses but not others and by elaborating on some of the responses they acknowledged. Also in keeping with the teachers' pedagogical content beliefs, laboratory exercises comprised a major component of their science teaching. Their introductions to these exercises emphasized areas in which previous classes had run into difficulties. During the exercises the teachers moved from group to group to monitor and assist. Many of their questions and comments were procedural in nature; however, they sometimes attempted to extend students' content knowledge and conceptual understandings in these one-to-one interactions. The teachers' post-lesson reflections focused on students. Again, their knowledge of junior high school students was revealed by comparisons they drew between the observed lessons and their previous experiences teaching the same content.

Patterns in the Novices' Science Teaching

A number of the patterns in the thinking and actions of the novice teachers contrasted with patterns in the experts' teaching. For example, in no case did a student teacher reveal clear, well-developed beliefs about teaching and learning during the course of the data collection. All the novices engaged in planning that was much more detailed and time-consuming than the experts' planning. None incorporated into lessons the variety of activity types utilized by the experts.

To a large extent, characteristics of pedagogical thinking and actions *differed* across the student teachers. Therefore, in contrast to our presentation of the experts' teaching, we do not attempt to illustrate patterns in the novices' teaching by presenting an abbreviated case description of each participant's planning, teaching and post-lesson reflections. Rather, we draw examples from two of the novices to highlight the ways in which 'noviceness' was revealed.

Shari's Classroom Teaching

Shari's demonstrations and her monitoring of laboratory exercises shared many characteristics with the actions of the experienced teachers, yet her teaching differed from theirs in several important ways. During the data collection interviews, Shari mentioned several weaknesses in her own teaching and attributed these to a lack of knowledge and experience.

> I'm very weak in knowing how much kids can handle, just because I don't have any experience with these kids. I mean ... as far as the amount of content ... how much detail to go into things, am I going way over their heads ... what can you expect of them?

She was also unable to anticipate how long activity segments would take.

> I have no idea, I've never done this at this age before ... How do I know how long this is going to take them to go through this unless I've done it before?

Despite her lack of experience and knowledge Shari was determined to conduct smoothly running class sessions. To do so, she planned extensively. For the frog dissection unit, the preparation of procedural guidelines, activity sheets, overhead transparencies and quizzes (one on lab safety and procedures, one on content) comprised a large portion of her planning time and effort. Shari also dissected a frog and then planned the demonstration for students based on the difficulties she had encountered.

> When I did it myself I figured out that, I mean what kinds of problems I had, you know, you had to pick up the skin and cut ... make sure they could see the tympanic membranes, behind the ears, and they lifted the skin and that kind of thing.

And she thought through details of procedures and classroom management strategies.

> For cleanup I'm going to discuss that at the beginning of the class ... We're going to stop earlier than I did yesterday, because I think that I was rushed at the end ... So I'm going to stop a little bit earlier, give more specific directions on cleanup. Like 'This side, one side of the room, all right, you guys can start with this table, working back toward the end, two at a time at the sink. When they

come back, you can go'. That kind of thing, much more clear directions on the cleanup and washing hands and that kind of thing.

Not surprisingly, Shari considered planning to be a 'monumental task', but her planning paid off. Her demonstrations included good procedural explanations with some content woven in. During laboratory activities, she walked around the room providing both procedural and conceptual assistance. For example, her demonstration-explanation of how to cut open the frog highlighted potentially difficult procedures.

When you pick up this layer here, that is the skin layer, and you're not going into the muscle. When you do this, it's all very lightly because if you jab in here you're going to cut the organs inside. So you have to be very light ... You want to pick up the skin, like this. [She punctures the skin with scissors and begins to cut.] You are not going to stop at the chest up here, but continue up [toward the head] ... you must be very careful because the heart is right underneath here. [She points with scissors to the region where the heart is located.] And if you go too far, you're going to cut the heart in half.

When walking around the room to monitor and assist during the dissection lab, Shari noticed that one group found flies in their frog's stomach. She used this situation to encourage the students to think about functions of the digestive system. She told the group members to describe the stage of digestion in the stomach represented by the flies. She then announced to the entire class:

When you are going through the digestive tract, if you find flies in the stomach, tell me what stage of digestion it is ... I want diagrams. I want an explanation of what's going on here. What do you see? Write as much down of what is going on.

Steve's Classroom Teaching

Steve had the strongest content background of all the student teachers, and possibly of all the study participants. He received a baccalaureate degree in chemistry in 1986 and returned to university two years later to earn a second baccalaureate in education and obtain teaching certification. He won the Outstanding Undergraduate Student Award in the year of the study, and his transcript showed 150 semester hours with a grade point average of 4.0 (on a 4-point scale). For this study, he was observed teaching the conclusion of a chemistry unit in Jim's Grade 8 physical sciences class.

Despite Steve's exemplary academic record, little about his teaching resembled the teaching of experts. His pedagogical knowledge and pedago-gical content knowledge seemed particularly limited, perhaps in part be-cause of his own experiences as a student:

> I don't think I'd use myself as a very good model for how to teach, because I think I'm a lot different than most people ... the teacher doesn't matter to me. I just read the book and study ... but probably most people can't do that.

Steve prepared detailed written plans for each lesson, usually on the night before the lesson. His plans followed a format provided in his teacher education program and included objectives, lesson outline with procedures, list of resources, assignment for students, reminders or special notes to the teacher, and sections for student evaluation and self-evaluation. Notes to himself included reminders about pedagogical strategies, diagrams to draw on the board, and subject matter content. Steve rarely used his plans during class sessions. He met with his cooperating teacher several times throughout the day, and these meetings frequently resulted in major changes in subse-quent class sessions.

Although Steve seemed to be aware that most students do not learn from books without the assistance of teachers, his teaching did not reflect that awareness. He relied heavily on the text during class sessions and did not seem to know how to explain concepts to others. In fact, fieldnotes for the entire observation cycle do not contain a single example of explanation of a concept, although there were several occasions on which such an explanation would have been appropriate. For example, on the first day he was observed, Steve planned to 'review one small section [of the text] that didn't get covered'. He called on one student to read aloud a paragraph from the book. He then announced to the class, 'OK, you can use that table [on the same page] today in the lab activity', and proceeded to the next activity.

Steve spent very little time interacting with the whole class. For more than 40 per cent of class time, students worked independently at their desks and Steve walked around the room, stopping to talk with individual stu-dents. Typically, many students were off task during these activities. When Steve did work with the class as a whole, he typically had students work problems independently and then asked one student to explain what he or she had done. Usually only the student explaining the problem and a very few others attended to the discussion. As the observer noted in her fieldnotes, 'For most of this time only six or seven students were following him at the board. Since he has a soft voice, it was almost like a private conversation between the student and the teacher'. On one occasion a student asked Steve to work a problem himself rather than having another student do it. Steve agreed to do so but then worked the problem by asking students questions to guide them step by step to the solution. During the process he provided only procedural comments and no conceptual explanation.

Steve: OK, number four. Aluminum and nitrate. [He writes 'Al'.]
        OK, what's the charge? What's the oxidation number?
When he hears the correct answer he writes: 'Al^{+3}' and continues:
OK, what's the formula for nitrate ion?
When students respond he writes 'NO_3' and then suggests that students 'look on page 145. What's its charge?'
There is no response, and after a few seconds he repeats: 'I'm still waiting, what's it's charge?' There is still no response.

Steve: Look at the table in the book entitled 'polyatomic ions', find nitrate, move over, negative one. It is very important to be able to look at the table and find what you're looking for. OK 3+ and 1−. What are we going to do to make it equal? So we use the crisscross method'.

He writes on the board: '$Al(NO_3)_3$'.

Steve: You put the parentheses outside the 3; since you have the three you put the parentheses outside to separate them. OK, if you have any questions, I'll be coming around to answer them.

Interpreting Expert-Novice Differences

Many of these characteristics of experts' and novices' teaching can be understood using the conceptual framework of teaching as a cognitive skill. That is, if novices' cognitive schemata are less elaborate, interconnected and accessible than experts', we can account for several of the differences in their planning, teaching and post-lesson reflections.

Experts' planning can be interpreted as a process of combining information from existing schemata to fit the particulars of a given lesson. Because experts have well-developed and easily accessible schemata for such aspects of teaching as content, students and instructional activities, they are able to plan quickly and efficiently. Further, once they select the desired activities, they need only pull the appropriate materials from their extensive activity files. The benefits of well-developed knowledge systems were evident in the expert teachers' introductions to laboratory activities as well. These teachers drew upon their pedagogical content knowledge, which includes knowledge of students and content, to anticipate difficulties the students were likely to encounter and to devise introductory explanations and demonstrations to minimize the difficulties.

The success of the experts' explanations and demonstrations seemed to depend upon their ability to assess student understanding and to provide quickly examples when students were uncertain or confused. In terms of cognitive structure, this ability to be responsive to students when providing explanations and demonstrations requires that the teacher have an extensive network of interconnected, easily accessible schemata and be able to select information from these schemata during actual teaching and learning interactions, based on specific classroom events. Jim's strategy of deciding which activities to use when explaining a concept is illustrative: 'I'll see their confusion and I'll realize I need another way to say the same thing, or make it visible to them, so they can see it happen'.

Novices, in contrast to experts, often have to develop or at least modify and elaborate their schemata as they plan. Their schemata for pedagogical content knowledge seem particularly limited. While experts' knowledge structures include stores of powerful explanations, demonstrations and examples for representing subject matter to students, novices must develop these representations as part of the planning process for each lesson. Because their pedagogical reasoning skills are less well-developed than those of experts, planning is often a very time-consuming activity. Then once they have planned the content of their lessons, novices must often prepare the materials needed to carry out the plan. It is not surprising that Shari viewed planning as a 'monumental task'.

Difficulties that novices encounter when they do not make or follow detailed lesson plans can be understood as the result of limitations in their knowledge systems. In comparison to experts, novices do not have as many potentially appropriate schemata for instructional strategies to draw upon in a given classroom situation. Nor do they have sufficiently well-developed schemata for pedagogical content knowledge to enable the construction of explanations or examples on the spot. Because their schemata for content knowledge are not easily accessible, they are sometimes unable to answer the questions that students ask.

A Comparison of Science and Mathematics Teachers

One of our intentions in conducting this study was to examine patterns of expert and novice teaching across the disciplines of science and mathematics by comparing our results with findings from the earlier study of mathematics instruction (Borko and Livingston, 1989). Some differences in teachers' thinking and action were apparent. Expert science teachers employed a *greater variety* of instructional strategies than their colleagues in mathematics, and there was *more diversity* in the student teaching performances of novice science teachers than in those of novice mathematics teachers. These differences must be interpreted with caution, given the small sample sizes, differences in grade levels (elementary and high school mathematics versus junior high science), and the fact that the student teachers, although from the same university, were enrolled in different teacher preparation programs.

Perhaps more interesting than the differences among the participants is our conclusion that patterns in the data provide no disconfirming evidence for the analysis of teaching as a complex cognitive skill. Although they differed in teaching style, the expert teachers in both studies were able to teach in a manner that was flexible and responsive to cues about student understanding. For the expert mathematics teachers, responsiveness often entailed developing an explanation of a mathematical concept or skill from a student question. Responsiveness in Jim's teaching was exemplified by his on-the-spot decisions to add unplanned demonstrations to his lessons. To be able to teach flexibly, he kept handy a variety of 'props' including a spring scale, fulcrum, meter sticks and weights. In all cases the flexibility and responsiveness of the experts' teaching seemed to depend upon quick access to an extensive, well-developed system of knowledge.

A cognitive analysis suggests that the different patterns of strengths and weaknesses shown by the novice teachers correspond to differences in their knowledge systems and pedagogical reasoning skills. Steve's content knowledge was strong but his pedagogical knowledge and pedagogical content knowledge were quite limited. Thus he was unable to work successfully with a large group and at times seemed unaware of the large number of students who were off task. In contrast, Shari (like the three novice mathematics teachers) was able to work successfully with the large group when her lessons were carefully planned and rehearsed in advance. The knowledge systems and pedagogical reasoning skills of most of the novice teachers were sufficiently well developed to enable them to plan successful classroom activities, although planning was a very time-consuming task.

While this investigation of expertise in science teaching provides further illustration of the potential of conceptualizing teaching as a complex cognitive skill, there is still much to learn about the nature of pedagogical expertise and about differences between expert and novice teachers. For example, most investigations of pedagogical expertise have compared experts and novices at a single point in time or over a period of weeks or months. The few longitudinal studies of learning to teach have examined only the initial stages of the process, through student teaching or the first year of teaching. The long process of becoming an expert teacher requires detailed study. Research comparing expert and novice teachers has focused primarily on the content areas of science and mathematics. Our comparison of this study with the similar investigation of mathematics instruction revealed differences in pedagogical thinking and action across these two disciplines, and Shulman (1988) and colleagues have also reported differences across subject matter areas in novices' use of content knowledge in classroom practice. Findings from these investigations suggest a need for studies of the development of pedagogical expertise across a wide range of subject areas.

Acknowledgments

An earlier version of this chapter was presented at the Annual Meeting of the American Educational Research Association, March, 1989. The research we report was partially supported by the Center for Educational Research and Development, College of Education, University of Maryland. We thank Dr. Julie Sanford for her role in the initial conceptualization and data collection for the project and Dr. Joseph Krajcik for his editorial comments. We also extend special thanks to the student teachers and teachers who participated in this investigation.

References

ANDERSON, R.C. (1984) 'Some reflections on the acquisition of knowledge', *Educational Researcher*, **13**, 10, pp. 5–10.

BERLINER, D.C. (1986) 'In pursuit of the expert pedagogue', *Educational Researcher*, **15**, 7, pp. 5–13.

BERLINER, D.C. (1987) 'Ways of thinking about students and classrooms by more and less experienced teachers', in CALDERHEAD, J. (Ed.) *Exploring Teachers' Thinking*, London, Cassell Educational, pp. 60–83.

BERLINER, D.C. (1988, February) *The Development of Expertise in Pedagogy*, Charles W. Hunt Memorial Lecture presented at the annual meeting of the American Association of Colleges for Teacher Education, New Orleans, LA.

BORKO, H. and LIVINGSTON, C. (1989) 'Expert and novice teachers' mathematics instruction: Planning, teaching, and post-lesson reflections', *American Educational Research Journal*, **26**, pp. 473–498.

BORKO, H. and SHAVELSON, R.J. (1990) 'Teachers' decision making', in JONES, B. and IDOLS, L. (Eds) *Dimensions of Thinking and Cognitive Instruction*, Hillsdale, NJ, Erlbaum, pp. 311–346.

CALDERHEAD, J. (1983, April) *Research into Teachers' and Student Teachers' Cognitions: Exploring the Nature of Classroom Practice*, paper presented at the annual meeting of the American Educational Research Association, Montreal, Canada.

CARTER, K., CUSHING, K., SABERS, D., STEIN, P. and BERLINER, D. (1988) 'Expert-novice differences in perceiving and processing visual classroom stimuli', *Journal of Teacher Education*, **39**, 3, pp. 25–31.

CARTER, K., SABERS, D., CUSHING, K., PINNEGAR, S. and BERLINER, D. (1987) 'Processing and using information about students: A study of expert, novice and postulant teachers', *Teaching and Teacher Education*, **3**, pp. 147–157.

CHI, M., FELTOVICH, P. and GLASER, R. (1981) 'Categorization and representation of physics problems by experts and novices', *Cognitive Science*, **5**, 2, pp. 121–152.

DEGROOT, A.D. (1965) *Thought and Choice in Chess*, The Hague, Mouton.

DREYFUS, H.L. and DREYFUS, S.E. (1986) *Mind over Machine*, New York, Free Press.

FEIMAN-NEMSER, S. and BUCHMANN, M. (1986) 'The first year of teacher preparation: Transition to pedagogical thinking?', *Journal of Curriculum Studies*, **18**, pp. 239–256.

FEIMAN-NEMSER, S. and BUCHMANN, M. (1987) 'When is student teaching teacher education?', *Teaching and Teacher Education*, **3**, pp. 255–273.

FREDERICKSEN, N. (1984) 'Implications of cognitive theory for instruction in problem solving', *Review of Educational Research*, **54**, pp. 363–408.

LEINHARDT, G. and GREENO, J.G. (1986) 'The cognitive skill of teaching', *Journal of Educational Psychology*, **78**, pp. 75–95.

LEINHARDT, G. and SMITH, D. (1985) 'Expertise in mathematics instruction: Subject matter knowledge', *Journal of Educational Psychology*, **77**, pp. 241–247.

PETERSON, P.L. and COMEAUX, M.A. (1987) 'Teachers' schemata for classroom events: The mental scaffolding of teachers' thinking during classroom instruction', *Teaching and Teacher Education*, **3**, pp. 319–331.

SABERS, D., CUSHING, K. and BERLINER, D.C. (1991) 'Differences among expert, novice and postulant teachers in a task characterized by simultaneity, multidimensionality and immediacy', *American Educational Research Journal*, **28**, pp. 63–88.

SHULMAN, L.S. (1987) 'Knowledge and teaching: Foundations of the new reform', *Harvard Educational Review*, **57**, 1, pp. 1–22.

SHULMAN, L.S. (1988) *Knowledge Growth in Teaching: A Final Report to the Spencer Foundation*, Palo Alto, CA, Stanford University.

SPRADLEY, J.P. (1979) *The Ethnographic Interview*, New York, Holt, Rinehart and Winston.

SPRADLEY, J.P. (1980) *Participant Observation*, New York, Holt, Rinehart and Winston.

WILSON, S.M., SHULMAN, L.S. and RICHERT, A.E. (1987) '"150 different ways" of knowing: Representations of knowledge in teaching', in CALDERHEAD, J. (Ed.) *Exploring Teachers' Thinking*, London, Cassell Educational, pp. 104–124.

5   Philosophical, Subject Matter and Classroom Understandings: A Case of History Teaching

Brent Kilbourn

In this chapter I argue that elegant practice in teaching requires the integration of philosophical, subject matter and classroom understandings. Teaching that is in a period of change can vividly show the integrated character of the three domains. Bill Lander, a grade 7 history teacher, acknowledged the difficulty in moving from a transmission style to a more interactive form of teaching. The first part of the chapter is a discussion of the kinds of understandings that, from my point of view, would be relevant to Bill's agenda for change. The second part of the chapter is an analysis of selected portions of one of Bill's lessons. I show how he acted on his agenda and I develop a plausible explanation for his actions.

I particularly want to explore how the pedagogical moves made in teacher-student interaction are influenced by an understanding of the subject matter; it will be apparent that my treatment of these issues is related to Shulman's (1987) construct of 'pedagogical content knowledge'. At places in the analysis alternative pedagogical moves are suggested as a way of exploring directions for future practice. Data from the transcript of Bill's history lesson are used, not to uncover some essential reality about a particular teaching episode, but rather, through the plausibility of the account, to contribute to conversation about the nature and improvement of teaching. A philosophical view of teaching is the first domain of understanding relevant to Bill Lander's situation.

Philosophical Views of Teaching

Every teacher has a philosophical view about teaching, a view that guides classroom practice. Such views may be implicit and unsystematic or, at the other end of the continuum, articulated and internally consistent. In the case of Bill Lander, the work of two writers are particularly important. Within the context of a graduate course on teaching, Bill had read writings of Thomas Green and Israel Scheffler and found them useful in guiding his attempt to become a more interactive teacher, engaging his students in the 'doing' of historical inquiry rather than passively remembering things.

Green develops the concept of a 'conversation of instruction' in his attempt to distinguish certain kinds of teaching from such things as conditioning, training, intimidation, physical threat, indoctrinating, propagandizing and lying. Although he agrees that the distinctions are blurred, nevertheless, 'the concept of teaching, as we normally use it, includes within its limits a whole family of activities, and we can recognize that some of these are more centrally related to teaching than others' (Green, 1968, p. 35).

Green reserves the term 'instructing' for teaching in which students and teachers engage in genuine conversation about issues concerning knowledge and belief (clearly areas of relevance to history as a discipline and as a school subject) rather than repeating standard patterns of accepted knowledge. Not any conversation will do; rather, it is to be conversation characterized by the giving of reasons, arguments, evidence and objections with the intent of arriving at the 'truth' of the matter at hand. But for a teacher like Bill Lander important pedagogical questions emerge: Whose reasons? How many reasons are to be given? What constitutes their character? How are good reasons and bad to be distinguished in the context of a grade 7 classroom? Where are the students to begin if they are naive learners, if they are used to a 'rhetoric of conclusions'? Where is the teacher to begin?

Scheffler's discussion of rule-model teaching contributes to Green's idea of a conversation of instruction by giving it more shape. The 'rules' of which Scheffler speaks are those of deliberation and judgment, and they apply to both cognition and conduct. 'The concepts of *principles*, *reasons*, and *consistency* thus go together and they apply both in the cognitive judgment of beliefs and the moral assessment of conduct' (Scheffler, 1965, p. 140). Scheffler implicitly suggests what such teaching might look like and highlights its opposition to transmission teaching and to mechanical application. The teacher still has the myriad of on-the-spot decisions that involve deliberative and intuitive choices, but they are made in conjunction with an understanding of the nature of subject-matter and inquiry.

> Teaching, [the rule model] suggests, should be geared not simply to the transfer of information nor even to the development of insight, but to the inculcation of principled judgment and conduct, the building of autonomous and rational character which underlies the enterprises of science, morality and culture. Such inculcation should not, of course, be construed mechanically. Rational character and critical judgment grow only through increased participation in adult experience and criticism, through treatment which respects the

dignity of learner as well as teacher. We have here, again, a radical gap which cannot be closed by the teacher's efforts alone. He must rely on the spirit of acknowledging that this implies the freedom to reject as well as to accept what is taught. (Scheffler, 1965, pp. 140–141)

Where do the rules, the principles, come from? Scheffler argues for the notion of 'tradition' within a discipline and gives an example from history.

> Scholarship in history is [analogous to science], for beyond the formal demands of reason, in the sense of consistency, there is a concrete tradition of technique and methodology defining the historian's procedure and his assessment of reasons for or against particular historical accounts. To teach rationality in history is, in effect, here also to introduce the student to a live tradition of historical scholarship. (Scheffler, 1965, p. 142)

One body of 'understanding' that serves as a backdrop to a teacher's practice, then, is the philosophical stance taken toward the aims of teaching. Bill's attempt at a more interactive classroom was shaped by his growing understanding of Green and Scheffler. It could be said that he was attempting to implement an image of rule model teaching and a conversation of instruction. (See Munby, 1969, for illustration of Scheffler's work to analysis of teaching in science.) The positions articulated by Green and Scheffler respect Bill's desire for increased interaction in his history class while preserving a sense of rigor in his lessons. As Scheffler points out, such philosophical positions 'orient' teaching.

Given Bill's customary transmission mode of teaching it might be expected that tensions would emerge as he tried to teach in a new way. The tensions could be seen in terms of his understanding of subject matter and classroom practice. His transmission mode of teaching consisted of a 'balance', acquired through the years, between information-to-be-transmitted (facts, dates, people, etc.) and his understanding of how, in a classroom, best to transmit the information. A dynamic balance would develop between content to be taught and the manner of teaching it. The balance would become disturbed when a 'new philosophy' is tried and that has consequences for what is done in teaching.

Subject Matter

Bill's traditional tack on subject matter is a common phenomenon and well understood: facts of history to transmit. However, he was frustrated with the 'dull-as-dust' chronicle approach to history teaching and wanted to move toward more active and rigorous inquiry in his classroom. What kinds of subject matter understandings would be relevant to his attempt to implement rule model teaching, teaching in which active historical inquiry was at the core of classroom practice? What kinds of understandings about historical inquiry are relevant to his work as a *teacher* of history? What understandings would be relevant to his ability to work with his 12-year-old students to develop the kind of discussion and principled inquiry he wants to foster?

Insofar as historical inquiry is integrally connected to the nature of historical argument, a start can be made by looking at some of the structural features of argument, in general; Toulmin (1958) provides an account that is useful in this context. According to Toulmin, arguments have certain structural similarities. In addition to the *claim* or conclusion being argued there are the *data* mustered in its support. *Warrants* are those kinds of statements that link, or show the relevance, of data to conclusions. Toulmin also notes that the conclusions that are reached in an argument are usually *qualified*, a point that seems particularly relevant to the nature of claims about the past (Toulmin, 1958, pp. 94–107).

Much could be said about each of these elements of argument, but several points about data are illustrative of principles of historical inquiry. One concerns the quality of data. So, for example, secondary accounts are generally less well regarded than primary accounts, but even primary sources such as letters or eye-witness interviews raise questions about vested interests and personal perspectives. Another point concerns data selection. An historian would seldom, if ever, have all the data that might be relevant to the explanation of an historical event, and even the data used to support a claim are selected from those available. Historical context is also important: data should be interpreted from the point of view of the period they represent. And it is commonplace that historians themselves cannot escape their own cultural heritage. Issues of personal biography, gender, ideology and politics all help shape the decisions about selection and interpretation that an historian must make. Historical inquiry is very much the product of human construction that serves as an overriding qualifier to every historical claim.

Understanding basic principles of historical inquiry affords a more textured account of the role of reasons in teaching. Sometimes when a teacher asks for or gives reasons, the 'reasons' refer to data. At other times, 'reasons' refer to warrants or to the backing for warrants. And in many classroom situations 'reasons' would be more generally understood to refer to all of these. But the important point is that, in any particular interaction with a child in which the teacher has the intention of inculcating the rules of historical inquiry, it will be useful for the teacher to understand when the problem of teaching-learning involves lack of data (the child cannot understand the reasoning because the relevant data are not apparent) and when the child is asking for or providing the connection (warrant) between data and conclusions. In other words, understanding the varied texture of reasons has the potential for contributing to a teacher's repertoire of pedagogical moves. (Russell's (1983) use of Toulmin's argument-pattern to examine aspects of science teaching is relevant to this discussion.)

Classroom Understanding

The kinds of understandings that would be helpful if 'rule-model teaching' and 'conversations of instruction' were to orient teaching represent two domains of teaching — philosophical and subject matter. The aim here is to articulate these domains of teaching so that Bill Lander's teaching can be understood and so that we can imagine, were we in his position, what might be done differently in the future. A third domain relates to a teacher's understanding of classrooms, the ability to function well as a teacher in a classroom setting where there are (typically) twenty-five, thirty or more students. One way of looking at classroom understandings of accomplished practitioners is to recognize that they have efficient, moral and integrative dimensions. The efficient dimension incorporates all manner of understandings and abilities related to the smooth conduct of classroom life. Motivation, classroom management, timing, humour, pace and momentum are but a few of the issues related to efficiency.

The ethical dimension concerns understandings about what is fitting and proper to do with students. On the one hand, there are norms relating to the role of the teacher as a member of society, with respect to the boundaries of interpersonal relations between teacher and student (in and out of the classroom setting), for instance. On the other hand, there are ethical considerations that relate more particularly to the character of classroom interaction, such as the teacher's sense of fairness (e.g., taking turns, giving each child a chance in discussion), equality and justice.

Finally, there are integrative understandings that concern the relationships among the three domains (philosophy of teaching, understandings about subject matter and understanding the efficient and ethical dimensions of classrooms). Integrative understandings enable the teacher to act appropriately and spontaneously in the heat of the moment. For instance, they enable a teacher to see the potential of the subject matter for teaching, which might include telling a relevant fact about the subject at an appropriate time or directing discussion in a way that capitalizes on the students' present understanding.

Teachers frequently talk about 'teachable moments' and in order to exploit a teachable moment the teacher must have insight as to *what* is teachable and how it 'fits' into the teaching situation at hand. As suggested, in some cases this requires simple knowledge of the 'stuff' of a discipline — facts, dates, key people and events, and so on. In other cases, it requires knowledge of the nature of the discipline, including its principles of inquiry. But, in any case, it requires integrating this knowledge with understandings about efficient and ethical classroom conduct. It is the integration of these 'understandings' that allows a teacher to know how to foster discussion not just for its own sake but for the sake of helping students learn. These three dimensions — efficient, ethical and integrative — mark out the kinds of classroom understandings that serve as a backdrop against which a teacher such as Bill Lander must bring to life the intent to have a conversation of instruction suffused with reasons, evidence, argument and objections.

A Grade 7 History Lesson

I am arguing that the backdrop to acts of teaching can be conceptualized as 'understandings' in three major domains — philosophy of teaching, understanding of subject matter from a pedagogical perspective and classroom understanding. I maintain that these understandings contribute both in obvious ways and in subtle ways to the particular pedagogical moves that a teacher makes in a given teaching situation. Teaching is informed by understandings in these three domains even in those circumstances where we would correctly say that a pedagogical move has been intuitive or spontaneous. In practice, of course, such understandings act in concert. They are integrated, and they tend to fade from a teacher's explicit awareness. But their integrated quality means that one set of understandings cannot be radically changed without affecting the others. Each domain, through a teacher's habits, can resist efforts to modify practice.

The transcript that follows shows that Bill was able to shift from a transmission mode to one in which his students began to engage in historical inquiry and where they began to have a conversation of instruction. But not surprisingly, his movement from transmission was uneven: two steps forward, one step back. Toward the end of the lesson, Bill was still able to stay away from a transmission mode of teaching, but his interaction seems to drift from what he apparently intended. My notes indicate that, although the students participated more than usual, less than a quarter were actually involved and Bill was disappointed about the extent and quality of their participation.

Bill found it hard to change and it is important here to try to understand why by developing a *reasonable explanation* for what happens in the lesson. The concrete data with which I am working are a transcription of the lesson and my notes indicating his overall intentions and his reactions to the transcript (which he outlined in his own analysis of his teaching). In the discussion that follows I make inferences, related to the three domains, about why Bill might have made the particular pedagogical moves he did. Obviously, I cannot read his mind, and reading Bill's mind is not necessary for a useful conversation about an instance of his teaching. As with most interpretive work, plausibility is the key. In the last analysis, I am more interested in generating useful conversation about teaching than in constructing a faithful description of 'reality'. The interpretations that follow are influenced by discussion of the transcript with more than 150 experienced teachers who have participated in one of my courses in the last twelve years.

It is possible to construct a plausible account of Bill's situation as he approached this lesson. Of the three domains of understanding, his philosophical view of teaching and his understanding of subject matter would be in disequilibrium. His classroom understandings, however, remain stable and implicit, reflecting his years as an accomplished practitioner. Thus all his habits and routines surrounding efficiency and morality (issues of pace, sense of fairness, how to get a task accomplished in a given time, and so on) would be implicit and stable *even though these would be affected in trying a new way of teaching*.

Bill had several goals for teaching and learning that he was working on with this group of students in the following lesson. He wanted them to become more actively involved; specifically, he wanted to talk less and have the students talk more. In keeping with Green's argument, he was aiming for more genuine conversation about substantive matters in history. In keeping with Scheffler's 'rule model', students' talk was to reflect, in some way, the rules or principles of historical inquiry. The intent was not to just talk about those rules, but to have students involved in their application.

At the time of the lesson that follows, Bill Lander was a department head in a large metropolitan junior high school (ages 12 to 15). He was participating in a graduate course in education that emphasized systematic reflection on one's own teaching as a vehicle for understanding its character and as a starting point for changing practice where personally desired. It is relevant to note that the lesson discussed here occurred two months into the school year, so the students were habituated to Bill's customary transmission style.

The immediate intent of the lesson was to have students make historical claims and support those claims with evidence. Students were to use their prior work (develop a historical theme and show present-day examples) to construct an evidential argument in which they would make historical claims and claims about the relationship of the past to the present, supporting these claims with evidence from their readings. The transcript shows Bill repeatedly asking for and helping students provide evidence for the claims they made.

The lesson started with Bill stating that he had had some difficulty in explaining the nature of the assignment. Several students articulated what they were to do and the interaction began with Bill asking Kent a question. Statements are numbered for later reference, with 'T' denoting Teacher and 'S' denoting a student not identified by name. Statements are in their original sequence but may not be consecutive.

1	T:	What do you sincerely believe to be the prevalent theme up until the year 1760, the past? Kent?
2	Kent:	(no response)
3	T:	How many people have a theme, have chosen their word? A word that explains generally what occurred — the idea is generally there. What is yours, Don?
4	Don:	(inaudible)
5	T:	Are there any others who have chosen this, or something close to this theme? Yes.
6	S:	Fighting.
7	T:	A different choice of words, though.
8	S:	(inaudible)
9	T:	No.
10	Ed:	Greed.
11	T:	No. This suggests violence, which is war ...

Perhaps these interchanges hint at some of what could have been troubling Bill. Responses do not seem to be tumbling forward as a teacher might hope, and when they do come they are relatively abbreviated and in some way 'off-the-mark' for Bill. At least two possibilities emerge. First, although the lesson started with reference to 'themes' (and this is continued throughout the lesson), early in the above interaction Bill used the term 'word' in place of 'themes' (3, 7). By focusing on a single 'word' (3, '... have chosen their word?'), Bill may have unwittingly and unduly restricted the initial responses to his question. It is not hard to imagine a grade 7 student thinking that a single word was what the teacher wanted and, not being prepared with a single word, being reluctant to respond.

Second, interchanges 5 to 11 show Bill asking for a response (sometimes implicitly) on three occasions; he denies two responses (9, 11) and asks for a modification in the third (7). Again, it can be hypothesized that this interaction might do little to promote participation. But this too is connected to the request for a single word, the substance of the questions, and Bill's desire for rigor. Bill (3) has asked students to contribute their theme (word), which Don does (unfortunately, what Don said was not audible). Question 5 is *not* a repeat of 3, although it would be plausible that some students might think so; rather its force is to ask for one word responses similar to Don's. Presumably, Bill does not want the range of themes students have developed, but only those similar to Don's. His own sense that students should respond accurately to the specific question (5) moves the interaction toward getting the 'correct word' rather than developing a conversation.

However, it is also evident that Bill encourages students to participate with more than a word. Although Kent originally had nothing to say (2), after the above series of interactions Bill returns to Kent, whose theme is 'disagreement'. The following excerpts illustrate Bill's press for evidential argument and how, at times, he encourages elaboration on a response.

12   T: All right, so we now have these people, at least, tuned in that this is the area that they must defend. Kent, defend yourself.

13 Kent: OK, uh, when Christopher Columbus was so mad at Italy for disagreeing ... [Kent's relatively lengthy response, culminates in a reference to an English attack on Port Royal in 1613 and Champlain's battle with the Huron Indians.]

Bill asks for elaboration, in keeping with Green's notion of a 'conversation of instruction':

14   T: What was the reason for the English attack on Port Royal?

15 Kent: It was disagreement. The English said that they owned Port Royal and the French said it was theirs, and they disagreed over who was going to get it and they were going to have a war.

In the next utterance Bill presses Kent for more substance; he wants Kent to articulate the *reason* for the disagreement.

16   T: OK, but before you go on, Kent, I'm going to suggest that you add one little extra thing on to your theory of 'disagreement'. Disagreement over the thing that is really important in this period.

Kent seems unsure of himself and does not give the response that Bill apparently had in mind and Bill turns to Stan:

17 Kent: (pause) Over people?

18   T: Uh, Stan?

19 Stan: Over land. Like, uh, they were disagreeing over land. We've got what? The French and the English? And some had better land than others.

20   T: All right ...

Here again, notice that in turning immediately to Stan and not pursuing the reasoning behind Kent's tentative response, Bill limits the potential for a richer conversation of instruction, at least with Kent in this instance. But, of course, there are pedagogical trade-offs, even in such a short episode

(16–19). Bill has not pursued Kent's reasoning but he *has* brought another student into the discussion and has done so in a way that moves the discussion in a direction that also meets his vision of the concrete historical information he wants them to acquire. It is not hard to infer that some of the 'reasoning' for Bill's pedagogical moves lies in his classroom understandings related to pace of the lesson and the value he places on giving people a turn.

While Bill has not pursued the 'reasoning' or the principles by which they reached their conclusions with either Kent (who had the 'wrong' answer) or Stan (who had the 'right' one), the avenues Bill could pursue with respect to a conversation of instruction and rules of historical inquiry are different in the two instances. Kent could be helped to articulate his reasoning ('Why do you say "people", Kent?', or 'What kinds of evidence are you using when you suggest the disagreement is over people, Kent?'), whereas Stan, in his own way, *has given a reason* for his claim that it was over land (19: 'And some had better land than others'). There are several options: A teacher could make a meta-comment on what Stan has just done as a way of helping students become aware of the fundamental rules of inquiry ('Notice, Stan has given a reason for thinking that . . .'), or a teacher might wish to go further in the articulation of rules of historical inquiry by continuing with a statement such as the following:

> And notice that Stan's reason for saying 'land' is a claim itself, a claim that some people's land was more valuable than others; so, Stan, what I'm wondering is, given our aim of understanding how historians work, what kind of evidence might be used to support the hypothesis that some pieces of land were more valuable than others?

These options illustrate the value of having different theoretical positions as a backdrop from which to make appropriate, intuitive pedagogical responses. Green's idea of *giving reasons*, within the context of a conversation of instruction, is sufficient to extend the conversation with Kent, but a more textured elaboration (as provided by Toulmin) helps provide a corridor for pedagogical action once those reasons have been given, as in the case of Stan. In other words, these more elaborate frameworks help suggest how Bill could pursue the conversation, once initial reasons had been given by a student.

As a reminder, this prescriptive analysis concerns what *could* have been done, given stated teaching intentions relating to the role of reasons and the nature of historical inquiry. It is not an argument for what *should* have been done, given the broader context of the entire situation. It could well be the case that the moves Bill made were entirely appropriate given the broader context, and those moves might be driven by his understanding of classrooms and these particular students. Perhaps Bill suspects that Kent's response is a wild guess; Kent doesn't have a reason and other students' interest is wavering; the pace is slowing to a critical point and now is not the time to pursue the issue with Kent; he is a strong student and is unlikely to be discouraged and, anyway, he is going to finish his theme of 'disagreement' in a few seconds, and so on. Hypothesizing about Bill's intuitive reasoning assumes that he is cognizant of the variety of options with regard to his intentions. On the other hand, he may not have been aware of the alternative moves he could make. One intent of this analysis, then, is to explore alternative pedagogical moves with a view to informed choice.

After responding to Stan, Bill turns back to Kent and again we see continued reference to reasons, evidence and argument:

21   T: Can I write down this word 'conflict' as your main theme? Prevalent conflict, disagreement and fighting. OK, keep on backing up your argument.

22 Kent: OK, it [the attack on Port Royal] caused the Kirk battle in 1628 and it caused the turning point in religion in New France ... It caused David Thompson to go out and get a chance to map most of Canada because he was so mad at the Hudson's Bay Company ... [Kent continues his theme]

23   T: Is there any more proof that, [do] other people feel that would prove that 'disagreement' and 'conflict' are themes of this period? Cliff, you had your hand up ...

24 Cliff: Mine is 'war' and I had ... [reads, finishing with:] The English then fought against the Americans who were fighting for freedom.

Part of the context of this lesson would be previous discussion of the central terms: 'evidence', 'data', 'claim', 'conclusion', 'hypothesis', 'theory', 'explanation', 'argument', 'reasons', 'backup', 'proof' and 'conjecture'. These terms are central because they are integrally related to the epistemology of historical inquiry and they are, in no small way, essential to the substance of this lesson. Unfortunately, we do not know how these terms have been used previously by Bill and his students and so we have only the most speculative grasp on what they might mean to these students. Nevertheless, it is important to note that he uses a variety of terms interchangeably. For example, at one point he asks, 'other examples of people in their search for freedom?' and, in that instance, 'evidence' could be used in place of 'example'. The lesson tends to be in 'layman's' language with respect to epistemological issues which would not usually be problematic, and it is difficult to see much difference in meaning between 'other *examples* ...' and 'other *evidence* ...'. However, it is worth hypothesizing that, for a grade 7 student unfamiliar with this kind of talk, too much variability in terminology could be confusing and, therefore, might curtail participation.

For instance, Bill's use of the term 'proof' may have unintended effects. Again, we do not know what meaning these students give to 'proof' and our hypotheses about the effect of using it must be tentative, but the use of 'proof' seems a bit strong in this context. Even a layman's sense of 'proof' might be equated with 'ironclad evidence', while its more technical meaning typically refers to the realm of mathematics: the familiar idea of *necessary* relationships in geometrical proofs, for example (which may or may not be familiar to a grade 7 student). More likely for a 12-year-old, there is the idea of proof associated with jurisprudence. Here, although the topic is clearly about contingent rather than necessary relationships, 'proof' is used to indicate certainty beyond reasonable doubt. In either case, the term 'proof' is a more stringent requirement for belief than many of the terms that might be used in its place.

In terms of a student's willingness to take a risk by offering a response in front of classmates, classroom interaction will vary according to whether a teacher says 'What proof do you have?' or 'What evidence do you have?' or 'Why do you say that?' or 'Interesting point, what were you thinking there?' It is important to remember that these are peer-sensitive 12-year-olds whose past experience in this class has been oriented toward providing right answers. Consequently, it is reasonable to imagine that they will need encouragement to take the more active role that Bill wants. It is not unreasonable to imagine that at this stage Bill's agenda for an interactive discussion is fairly fragile. The possibility that a term such as 'proof' may inhibit (or fail to promote) a conversation of instruction is an important point for consideration.

In addition to this analysis of classroom interaction, a further comment should be made about the relationship between interaction and the nature of the subject matter. Interaction and substance are often integrated and certainly do not exist as separate categories in the phenomenology of the classroom. The use of the term 'proof' (23) is a good example of the integration of interaction and substance. Bill has asked a question that can be seen, in general terms, as promoting interaction. But the terms that he uses also convey something about the nature of history, correctly or incorrectly. Here it could be argued that 'proof' is inconsistent with the spirit of the nature of historical inquiry and, consequently, with one of the primary intentions for the lesson, which was to 'inculcate' the principles or rules that represent that spirit. (I use the term 'spirit' deliberately because it seems to capture the force of Scheffler's articulation of 'rule model' and Green's 'conversation of instruction'. I am not arguing that there are no contexts in which historians would be found using the term 'proof', but in those cases its meaning would incorporate a commonly agreed understanding about the epistemological character of historical inquiry. Yet that is precisely what these students are attempting to learn. Other meanings of 'proof', more colloquial and more suggestive of certainty that might be expected in historical claims, could inhibit the students' ability to understand the spirit of historical inquiry.)

In some teaching situations part of the skill is to honour the demands of one agenda without sacrificing the integrity of another. How can interaction be promoted while maintaining a degree of rigor with regard to the subject, and how can the nature of the subject be respected while encouraging a more active role for students, a role that undoubtedly means they will take risks and make mistakes? Inevitably there will be trade-offs, but as familiarity and skill increase, a teacher becomes more adept at finessing such competing demands. Bill turns to Jill:

25	T:	Any other proofs? Can you back up this theme further?
26	Jill:	Would 'revolution' be one?
27	T:	Well, why don't we listen to what you have to say about 'revolution' and let the class decide?
28	Jill:	OK, uh, Cartier came ... [Jill provides a lengthy response, ending with:] ... and the British people in North America were disgusted and started a revolution against England ...

It is not entirely clear what the class will be deciding in question 27; Bill has asked for evidence (25), but Jill's response is not as much evidence as it is another theme. However, within that theme she cites historical happenings. What is confusing is whether the class is to decide if her theme (revolution) is similar to the previously discussed theme (war) or whether her instances count as evidence for her claim that revolution is a theme in this period of history. Bill uses the technique of polling the students as a way of drawing them into the interaction, a pattern that occurs seven times in the lesson. Toward the end, for example, Bill says:

> T: How many people found disagreement, conflict and fighting to be the major themes during this period? Showing of hands. Two, four, six, eight, nine. Nine or ten out of a class of thirty. One in three found that. How about 'freedom' or 'search of freedom'? How many found that? Less. All right, what else?

But it is important to realize that historical claims are not supported by recourse to a vote. Thus there is an inconsistency between a pedagogical device for encouraging interaction and the (unintended) substantive message about historical inquiry that that device might, in some circumstances, convey.

After Jill's offering (28), Bill asks what a revolt is and continues to encourage students to participate by supporting the claims they make.

29	T:	What is a revolt? What is a revolt or revolution? What does it suggest? Ian?
30	Ian:	People or countries, like, when they disagree they fight against each other.
31	T:	Yes.
32	S:	(inaudible)
33	T:	Yes, it is that as well. There are missed proofs. Do they back up this basic theme? What do you think? What do you think, having said them now?
34	S:	Yes. They back them up.
35	T:	Do you agree with this? Anybody disagree? Does anybody disagree that 'Conflict' and 'Disagreement' and 'Fighting' and 'Revolution' are possible themes that are prevalent during this period? Is there anyone who disagrees with this? All right then, another one, Ian.

As at the beginning of the lesson, Ian responds with a single word, but this time Bill sticks with him. Bill engages Ian in a conversation, brings another student into the interaction, and then returns to Ian (43).

36	Ian:	Freedom.
37	T:	What do you mean?
38	Ian:	Well, like, uh (pause)
39	T:	Yes, go ahead.
40	Ian:	Well, the French and the English, they, uh, were all loyal to their country.
41	T:	But loyalty and freedom are two different things. Now, let's work off what Cliff said about 'freedom'. I'd like to get an explanation of what Ian means. Yes?
42	Cliff:	Freedom of worship, in religion.
43	T:	Could we say the 'search for freedom' and Cliff starts us off when he says, 'religion' — people searching for freedom of religion. Now, Ian, it's back to you.

In the next interchange it is important to notice another dimension of Bill's sense of rigor. Of the many things he must 'juggle' in this lesson, one concerns whether or not the conversation is based on information commonly regarded as 'true'. My inference that he is, understandably, concerned with correct information emerges in 49–53.

44	Ian:	OK. The Jesuit missionaries, the (inaudible), and the Quakers came to Canada and America to freedom.
45	T:	Does anyone disagree with any of his information so far? Yes?

46	Pete:	(inaudible)
47	T:	I beg your pardon.
48	Pete:	The Jesuits didn't come to Canada.
49	T:	There's more misinformation.
50	Ian:	But I said, 'America'.
51	T:	Yes?
52	Bev:	The Jesuits didn't come to get away from England. They came to Christianize the Indians, not to search for freedom.
53	T:	OK, keep on going, Ian, as long as we don't set off on the wrong track.

This account of parts of Bill Lander's Grade 7 history lesson is an effort to show the complex relationship between the pedagogical moves that a teacher makes and substantive issues regarding the subject matter, rather than an attempt to provide, in any sense, a 'complete' account. It can be seen that Bill must travel a difficult road in unfamiliar territory, given his customary 'transmission' mode of teaching. He is trying to promote a more active role on the part of the students while also trying to honour both the process and the products of historical inquiry, all within a vision of 'rule model' teaching and a 'conversation of instruction'. The task Bill has set for himself is a demanding one and neither he nor we should be surprised if he occasionally stumbles.

But if we look closely, his occasional stumble can teach us something about the process of changing practice and can point the way toward future practice. With that in mind, then, I turn to an episode near the end of the lesson that is a particularly complex and vivid example of the issues I have been discussing. A number of interchanges have occurred since the interaction with Ian.

54	T:	Are there any other examples of freedom during this period? Yes?
55	Lyn:	Freedom of lifestyle [pause] because, like, the habitants, like they weren't having their rights and so they were very unhappy.
56	T:	When?
57	Lyn:	Uhm, at the Seven Years' War. No, wait (inaudible) like, uh, their reputation and everything.
58	T:	What proof do you have that the habitants were very unhappy and were involved in a search for freedom?
59	Lyn:	It says, uh, that they had poor families, and they couldn't go any higher because, like [T interrupts]
60	T:	My question was, 'What proof do you have that they were unhappy?'

61 Lyn: I don't know, [pause] you see [pause] ...

62 T: But the instructions were, last class, that you must find specific proof and be able to back it up; and your idea is conjecture as to whether they were unhappy or not. We know that the English did do things, if you remember back, the English did do things to try to win the French Canadians back. Do you remember what they were? Yes?

This is a complex bit of interaction. Bill is pushing Lyn to provide evidence for what she says, and this is consistent with his approach to the whole lesson and with his intent to have students become more actively involved, at their level, by engaging in historical inquiry. It seems clear that Bill wants students to understand that there is a difference between unfounded opinion and evidential argument. Several interchanges after 62, he says:

63 T: So clearly we have an example that the English did things for the French. Maybe the French were still unhappy. The only proof we do have is that the English did go out of their way in passing these laws to make things easy on the French.

While it can be argued that Bill's reiteration of the task (62) is pedagogically appropriate, there is something perplexing about this interaction (54–62) that is worth exploring. My concern is less with the general form in which Bill has proceeded with Lyn than it is with the manner in which the interaction has been played out. Consistent with his intent to have students become more actively involved, at their level, by engaging in historical inquiry, Bill is pushing Lyn to provide evidence for what she says. In the context, it is plausible to imagine that he wants students to understand the difference between unfounded opinion and evidential argument. While the pedagogical moves (54–62) are in the spirit of distinguishing opinion from argument, nevertheless, the tone of the interaction is 'challenging' rather than 'assisting' and seems unlikely to contribute to the kind of participation Bill wants to foster. It might be hypothesized that, in this brief episode, his drive for rigor has put aside another goal related to participation.

Of the many possible explanations for the character of the interaction with Lyn (gender bias, for example), I suggest that such interaction demonstrates an underlying tension between Bill's developing sense of the subject matter as interpreted through a 'rule model' teaching philosophy and his familiar classroom understandings. On this interpretation it is not coincidental that the critical episode (54–62) occurs near the end of the lesson. Assuming Bill to be like many teachers, it would be toward the end of the lesson that he would quicken the pace in an effort to conclude. His (efficient) pedagogical moves toward an appropriate conclusion to the lesson, coming out of his classroom understandings, would tend to take precedence over the slower pace and longer amount of time it would take to work with Lyn.

But let us assume that, in another 'take' of this interaction, Bill did have the time to work with Lyn. Here it should be pointed out that rigor need not be sacrificed for participation, nor for a more 'assisting' role for Bill. He could have responded (58) with something like, 'What kinds of evidence might support the idea that . . .', thus taking some of the harshness out of his question while still pedagogically 'inculcating' (Scheffler's term) the principles of historical inquiry. Lyn's contributions (55: her major claim that the habitants were unhappy; 59: reasons they were unhappy) suggest that she does not articulate her thoughts smoothly or that her thoughts are not well developed. Yet clearly she has the structure of an argument: she has *reasons* why she thinks the habitants were unhappy. One reason concerns a commonplace observation that poverty and misery are highly associated phenomena of the human condition. The other reason involves an argument from analogy with present-day experiences, that frustrated upward mobility often leads to unhappiness. Such an analogy may or may not pertain to the habitants but it is a point for exploration in classroom interaction, exploration that might entail explicitly noting the kind of historical argument being made.

It would appear, then, that Lyn (59) is trying to fulfil one of the stated parts of the assignment, which was to develop a theme from the past and compare it with the present. Her reasons, sketchy though they may be, provide a good base for pedagogically making points about historical inquiry by engaging in it and reflecting on that engagement. So, for instance, Bill could have responded (60) with something like, 'Nice point, Lyn; now, given what we said yesterday about how historians work, what kinds of evidence would suggest that the habitants were poor?' and then engaged Lyn and her classmates in a conversation about how letters, diaries and other documents are data to a historian and can be used to make inferences about the past.

The concepts of dilemma and tension are useful here. The complexities of classroom life frequently present competing demands for action. Deeply held views about efficiency (timing, pace, etc.), ethics (participation, equality, fairness), subject matter (principles of inquiry, knowledge), philosophy of teaching (in this case, 'rule model'), and rigor (conversation that stays on track) cannot all be satisfied within a given interaction. In the interchange with Lyn, for example, it might be hypothesized that a richer fulfilment of the teaching demands of rigor, fairness and inquiry will require an adjustment of 'classroom understandings', to a diminished role for fast pace, to less emphasis on acquired knowledge and to a different kind to conclusion to the lesson.

Conclusion

Exploring alternative pedagogical moves by treating a transcript like a playscript in which things may be changed within a 'corridor' of teaching intent and style is one way to come to a deeper understanding of the teaching act. Two outcomes emerge from this glimpse at Bill Lander's lesson: One involves seeing what it means for a teacher to try something different, something as fundamental as trying to change a teaching style. With Bill Lander we see this not just in general terms but as it relates to the particulars of what he says and does with his students. Learning something new and complex often involves instances of success as well as stumbles. Examining the character of the successes and stumbles is one way of charting a course for future action. Bill Lander is an 'old pro' within his familiar transmission style but when he tries a more interactive style he becomes 'deskilled'. We see striking successes, as when he repeatedly asks students to support the claims they are making. We also see stumbles, instances where, for example, the push for evidence seems to become overly aggressive.

A second outcome reveals something about the relationship between pedagogy and subject matter, as well as pointing the direction for future development. Bill Lander wanted to move his teaching style from transmission to a more interactive mode, and I have couched the discussion in terms of the kinds of understandings a teacher might benefit from in order to move on that agenda. Elegant teaching requires *integration* of understandings about philosophy of teaching, subject matter and pedagogy. It is in this area that we gain insight into the nature of the transitional stumbles in Bill's lesson, revealing a need for greater integration of pedagogical moves (poll-taking, questioning, redirecting, etc.) with the nuances of the subject matter of history, all within a point of view about teaching represented in this case by the work of Scheffler and Green.

It is not surprising that Bill occasionally 'stumbles' since his customary transmission style would not have required that kind of integration. It is evident that he has the skill to pursue a conversation with students. And, clearly, he knows how to get students to support claims as an historian might. What could be cultivated is a more finely-grained integration of these skills, an integration that would be sensitive to the nuances of subject *and* interaction at the same time: sensitivity to the possibility that interchangeable use of central epistemological terms might be confusing to students and, consequently, might inhibit their willingness to participate, or sensitivity to the possibility that some poll-taking could be misinterpreted by students as conveying a message about the nature of historical inquiry.

One way of moving toward such integration would be for a teacher to talk more explicitly about the substantive-pedagogical issue at stake; that is, a teacher might be forthcoming about what teacher and students are *doing* in the teaching-learning situation. At times it is appropriate that a teacher talk *explicitly* about pedagogical reasons so as to help students become clear about the activities of which they are a part. So, for example, on the issue of poll-taking, a teacher might say, 'OK, it looks like we're all agreed on that interpretation, but is our agreement grounds for believing it to be true?' On the issue of 'correct' and 'incorrect' information, a teacher might say, 'Nice point, Steve, and well argued. It so happens, that, based on other bits of evidence it is now conventionally understood that ...'. On the dilemma of student involvement, the teacher might say, 'That is a great line of reasoning, Kent, but I'm going to stop you there so that some others can get a chance to develop their ideas. Lyn, you wanted to say some more about the habitants?' Notice that although these kinds of moves are basically pedagogical, their shape and tone is heavily influenced by philosophical understandings about teaching *and* by the nature of the subject matter.

In the interest of integrating subject matter and classroom understandings, the 'conversation of instruction' can begin to include the reasons why certain pedagogical moves are made. There is strong evidence in the transcript that these are skills that Bill Lander is developing and it is exciting to see him work on his teaching. Our fortunate opportunity to see him in transition, to catch a glimpse of his growth, allows us to gain further insight into the relationship between the substance and manner of teaching.

Acknowledgement

Earlier versions of this chapter were presented at the annual meetings of the American Educational Research Association (Boston, April 1990) and the Canadian Society for the Study of Education (Victoria, BC, June, 1990).

References

GREEN, T. (1968) 'A topology of the teaching concept', in MACMILLAN, C.J.B. and NELSON, T.W. (Eds) *Concepts of Teaching: Philosophical Essays*, Chicago, Rand-McNally, pp. 28–62.

MUNBY, H. (1969) *Analyzing Science Teaching: A Case Study Based on Three Philosophical Models of Teaching*, unpublished MA thesis, University of Toronto.

RUSSELL, T.L. (1983) 'Analyzing arguments in science classroom discourse: Can teachers' questions distort scientific authority?', *Journal of Research in Science Teaching*, **20**, pp. 27–45.

SCHEFFLER, I. (1965) 'Philosophical models of teaching', *Harvard Educational Review*, **35**, pp. 131–143.

SHULMAN, L.S. (1987) 'Knowledge and teaching: Foundations of the new reform', *Harvard Educational Review*, **57**, 1, pp. 1–22.

TOULMIN, S. (1958) *The Uses of Argument*, Cambridge, Cambridge University Press.

6 Transforming Chemistry Research into Chemistry Teaching: The Complexities of Adopting New Frames for Experience

Hugh Munby and Tom Russell

Introduction

This is a case study of a science teacher ('Debra') learning to teach, with special attention to her learning from experience. The case is unusual because Debra worked for eleven years as a research technician in chemistry before she shifted to teaching chemistry in a secondary school. Much attention is being given to 'pedagogical content knowledge' and to 'reflection' in discussions about how individuals learn to teach, and we believe this case makes an important contribution to how those terms are understood and used in working with student and first-year teachers. We find this case particularly interesting for its suggestions about possible ways in which professional knowledge is acquired. One unique feature of this case is Debra's knowledge of chemistry not just from a student's perspective but from extensive laboratory experience. A second unique feature is the role of the observer who was asked to offer assistance as he also gathered observational and interview data for understanding Debra's teaching.

We have long known that the earliest years of teaching transform one's understanding of the subject one is teaching. Organizing a subject for presentation to others and responding to students' questions and difficulties stimulates a beginning teacher to see his or her subject in new ways, to make new connections and to better appreciate how theory and data interact in a disciplined way. Shulman (1987, p. 15) has proposed a 'model of pedagogical reasoning and action' that includes Comprehension, Transformation, Instruction, Evaluation, Reflection and New Comprehensions. Like Shulman, we have developed case studies of beginning and experienced teachers, but we have focused attention on metaphor and reflection (Schön, 1983). We believe that the case of Debra suggests important insights into the nature and complexity of 'reflection' as part of the process of learning from experience.

With respect to learning from experience, it is evident that some teachers are more predisposed than others to reframing the puzzles of practice. This finding has prompted a series of case studies designed to look closely at possible relationships between the knowledge teachers bring to the classroom and the events of teaching (Russell and Munby, 1989, 1991). Specifically, we are investigating teachers' constructions of their subject matter (or discipline) with particular interest in changes in the earliest years of teaching.

Special attention is given here to two aspects of Debra's development as a beginning teacher. Her subject matter knowledge appears to be *context-dependent* in ways that can be related to her prior experiences as a research technician, and her manner of interpreting her teaching experiences also seems influenced by her prior work in a research laboratory. The chapter has three parts. The case data are presented as descriptively as possible, in sections on background, Debra's teaching, the observer's interventions and Debra's interview responses. Analysis of the case follows, with more interpretive moves in the argument. The chapter concludes with discussion in which we return to the issue of reframing in reflection that leads to developing pedagogical content knowledge from experience.

Background to the Case

Debra graduated with a B.Sc. (Hons.) degree in Biochemistry in 1978. She worked as a laboratory technician full-time until the summer of 1980 when she enrolled part-time in an M.Sc. program, completing the thesis in 1985. From that point until she began teaching in September 1989, she worked part-time as a research technician in a hospital. She completed a Bachelor of Education degree on a part-time basis in the 1987–89 academic years and began teaching in 1989–90.

The course that we observed Debra teaching during the semester in which she participated in the research is the Grade 12 (Ontario) Chemistry Course. The first unit is essentially a review of chemistry topics in Grade 9 and 10 General Science: measurement, physical and chemical change, states, and elements, compounds and mixtures. This is followed by units on periodicity, structure, compounds and formulae, reactions and equations, stoichiometry (molar problems), acids and bases and gas laws.

Debra joined the study in late October, seven weeks after the beginning of her first semester of teaching. She was known to us by her presence in one of our courses (taught by Russell) during her B.Ed. program; her considerable experience as a technician suggested an interesting perspective on her subject, and her securing a position locally made her classroom conveniently accessible. She readily agreed to participate when an inquiry was made.

Debra's class (lasting seventy-five minutes) was observed six times over two months, and each observation was followed by an interview. Data collection ended with a seventh interview conducted during the examination period at the end of the semester. Each classroom observation yielded two types of data: an audiotape of the lesson and observer's notes. After the observation, the observer-interviewer (Munby) composed an account of the lesson from the notes and the tape. The interviews were transcribed and then checked for accuracy. Copies of the lesson accounts and interviews were given to Debra as soon as they became available. Early in the period of her participation, she was lent tapes and observer notes, but she found she did not have the time to attend to these, so the practice was discontinued. Data were given to Debra as a deliberate part of the research strategy, included in the written agreement that also allowed her to withdraw at any time without further inquiry. There was an additional reason in Debra's case: she had asked the observer/interviewer to 'watch for and talk about classroom management' (Interview 1 41D1; this code identifies the location of the data in our files, with 41D1 designating speech 41 in Debra's first interview). As shown below, steps were taken to draw attention to patterns in Debra's teaching that might be non-productive and to advance suggestions that she could attempt during the semester. Debra did not contribute written data in response to the observation and interview data returned to her.

The data and their initial analyses were read by the three members of the research team (Munby, Russell and Johnston), whose subsequent discussion identified principal patterns in the teaching and in the interviews. This analysis is reported following sections describing the patterns in the teaching, in the interviewer's interventions and in Debra's interview responses.

Debra's Teaching

Debra's teaching can be described in terms of the patterns that were identified by the observer/interviewer and confirmed by discussion with the other two members of the research team. These patterns are the most obvious regularities in Debra's teaching, when examined with awareness of her special concern for classroom management. The patterns are described under the following headings: Beginning, End and Transitions; Connections and Clarity; Interactions; Guided but not Independent Practice; and Laboratory Work.

Beginning, End and Transitions

Debra's class enters the room with a considerable amount of noise for its complement of twelve students. Invariably, the students take time to settle down and are generally unresponsive to Debra's various calls that they pay attention. Getting their attention is achieved somewhat informally by calling the roll. Thereafter, Debra begins to teach, but with no explicit signal that the lesson has begun. A lack of explicit signals is also evident in transitions to a new model of instruction, such as taking up homework. Equally, Debra gives no clear signal at the end of the period that she has finished and that the students may leave. Such messages are conveyed implicitly by the assignment of homework and by the school bell. Sometimes students are leaving the room as the last details of homework are being given.

For instance, Lesson 4 opens with four students at the board balancing equations from the homework assignment. There is noise as the roll is called. Students talk about doing the homework, one announcing loudly that he has not done it. Debra does not respond to this but repeats the page number of the text to which they are meant to turn. The noise continues with only two of those not at the board appearing to attend to the lesson. Later, when the discussion of homework is finished, Debra moves toward classifying chemical reactions. But the transition is given as 'What do chemical equations tell us ...? Why do you write chemical equations? What does the chemical equation tell us?' This leads to a response about products. Only after this do the students get a signal about what is coming: 'Now chemists like to categorize things because it is much easier to handle information that is categorized'.

Another example occurs at the end of Lesson 3 with Debra saying 'Homework' and setting a reading assignment to the accompaniment of considerable noise. One student asks if they are just to read it and Debra responds with a question about a sheet distributed the previous day, but not all are attending. Debra announces, 'You have until next Wednesday to choose a topic [for a project]'. There is more noise, and some students leave before the end of the lesson has been signalled explicitly.

Connections and Clarity

Debra's chemistry instruction is consistently clear and precise, and the content is always scientifically accurate. Her manner toward the students is friendly and smiling, and there is a business-like air to the teaching, but the students appear not to respond to this. Instead they display reluctance to work seriously in class and take advantage of opportunities to distract one another. Debra provides very few signals about the ways in which each part of her instruction is related to the unit under consideration. This is especially noticeable at the beginning of each class and at transitions. There is nothing here that shows the students how the forthcoming material is conceptually or otherwise related to the material just treated. Lesson 2, for example, opens with Debra writing on the board, in chart form: acids, radicals, prefixes, suffixes. She says to the class, 'OK, do you want to get out your books? Open to page 15'. She then begins explaining what is on the board before the students have settled and before there is an introduction about what is going to be done and why. 'Who can tell me what the parent oxyacids [of the compounds listed in the book] are?'

Interactions

Debra encourages considerable student participation with her questioning. Generally, a question is asked, a student (often called upon) answers, and Debra repeats or corrects the response. There are few instances in which a response is given to the class for judgment or continuing discussion.

Guided but not Independent Practice

The concepts 'guided practice' and 'independent practice' used in the problem-solving literature of instructional psychology (Rosenshine and Stevens, 1986) are helpful here. When Debra introduces a new type of problem, such as working out chemical formulae using oxidation numbers, she carefully guides the students through the steps, asking questions as she goes. This guided practice is effective, but the ability to solve such problems depends on knowing the series of steps to be followed. Invariably, Debra omits the independent practice that is effective for accomplishing this learning, and she provides the students with the next step, cueing them toward solution.

In Lesson 1, formulas for simple compounds are derived from knowledge of electronic structure and bonding capacity. Questioning proceeds as follows:

> What about phosphorus and potassium? Potassium belongs to what group? (One) How many electrons in the outer shell? (One) Phosphorus fits under what group? (Five) So the bonding capacity of potassium is? (One) And the bonding capacity of phosphorus is? (Three) And the compound will be?

Lesson 5 has Debra guiding the class through 'mole' problems:

> You have to know how to name them, how to write the equation ... then you have to know how to balance the equation. We have nitrogen reacting with hydrogen to produce ammonia. Now the question is what? (A student reads the question). How many moles of hydrogen are required to produce five moles of ammonia? OK. So what is our unknown? (A student responds) The amount of hydrogen. They are telling us ... If you start with the balanced

equation (writing it on the board), we know that three moles of hydrogen are required to produce two moles of ammonia ... I've got to rewrite the statement, OK? Where are we going to put our unknown? (Student: On the right side) On the right side ...

In the lessons observed, Debra provides little or no opportunities in class for students to independently pursue the steps to solving problems.

Laboratory Work

Debra's management of laboratory activities and students' laboratory performance contrasts sharply with the other patterns. Her procedural instructions are clear and explicit, and the students work with scrupulous attention to safety and with the same business-like air that characterizes their teacher's teaching. They do not seem to attempt to distract one another, nor to talk about anything save the work. For instance, the 'Procedure' section of the written instructions for laboratory work on 'The Behaviour of Solid Cu in an Aqueous Solution of Silver Nitrate' begins with:

1. Obtain a 4–5 cm strip of Cu wire. Coil the wire by wrapping it around a pencil.
2. As precisely as possible, determine the mass of the wire. Record this in an observation table.
3. Using masking tape, label a test tube with your name. Determine and record the mass of this test tube.

Observer's Interventions

The observer's undertaking to examine the teaching for anything that was of concern to Debra gave an interesting quality to this case study. Debra's invitation to the observer generated an opportunity to be an active participant in her professional learning process. Thus some interventions took the form of the observer drawing explicit attention to patterns in the teaching. In Interview 2, for example, the pattern of not giving independent practice in problem solving was discussed:

[They] had no trouble when you said, 'OK, this is the step you do next. What is such-and-such?' And they give you the answer. But they seem not to know what was the next step ... I was struck by the way in which they can answer the individual questions with which you move them along the path to the solution, but you were giving them the path, and I wondered what would happen if you stripped the path-giving away. (following 6D2)

We returned to this issue in later interviews, just as we returned to the idea of providing the class with an agenda each day, together with connections to previous and future work, an issue raised by the observer in Interview 4:

> I've noticed that the lesson has implicit beginning, transition and end, by which I mean they're not explicit. I'm interested in how the students are to know how each piece fits, how they're meant to take the responsibility for their learning. (following 18D4)

The pattern in which Debra interacts with one student at a time ('Interactions', above) was also discussed in Interview 4.

> I found an interesting way in which conversations were going on in the last lesson I listened to. Group discussions tended to be of this sort: You'd ask a question and someone would answer, and then it would be your move to someone else, and back to you. So the pattern was from you to someone and back, and from you to someone and back, and so forth. (following 14D4)

The observer's deliberate strategy, illustrated in the data cited, was to describe patterns that seemed related to Debra's concerns about management. The intention was to suggest alternative ways of looking at the situation without insisting on their use.

Patterns in Debra's Interview Responses

Subject-Matter Orientation

The extent of Debra's preparation and experience in science is evident in the biographical sketch, above. None of that, however, shows the degree of her ease within the discipline. Some of this is apparent in the interview data. For instance, in Interview 3 she compares her own calculation of solution strengths as a technician with teaching students to do it:

> For me, it's easy to calculate solutions ... I guess it's so sort of second nature for *me*. It's difficult to sort of start to tell them exactly how to do it and be consistent, because I never approach it in the same way. (8D3)

The same message reappears in Interview 7:

> In chemistry, I use all kinds of shortcuts, and my work too, I do the same kind of thing, and I've never really suffered — short forms and not using the correct nomenclature, and things like that. And

you still get away with it, and there's no problem ... Maybe I shouldn't expect that of the kids if I don't do it all the time. How can I expect the students to follow rules to the letter if I don't do it all the time? (16D7)

Debra's strong application-based orientation to science stands in contrast to her concern for her knowledge of more rudimentary science, and with what she finds that the students have not remembered from earlier grades. In Interview 6 she describes her dilemma in the following terms:

I'm not worried about the material itself, but I'm more worried about getting the material across to the kids. I think my initial worry was that I wouldn't be able to know the stuff well enough to teach it, whereas now I'm worried that I can't make it easy enough or clear enough for the kids to understand. And that's what my worry is now, because now I realize how easy it is for *me*. But for them ... the first part of the semester I was always baffled by what they *didn't* know ... because I taught the chemistry unit in Grade 9 and a lot of it is repeated in Grade 11 at the beginning of the year. (1D6)

Content: What Students Need to Know

Mention of 'material' and 'stuff' in the above extract is just part of the evidence that *covering the content* is a preoccupation for Debra. In Interview 5, she describes her planning:

I have the [Ministry of Education] guidelines with how many hours, and this is the stuff I have to cover, essentially; so it's just a general outline in the guidelines. And I sit down and say, 'Well, I need sixteen hours, let's say, for gases', and I'll try to fit in topics. (9D5)

Debra admits (29D2) that she was not sure where she was heading at the beginning of the course and that she relied upon another teacher for guidance about the pace of the course. This type of deference to other and more senior teachers appears elsewhere, as in Interview 7 (7-8D7). Later in the same interview Debra says, 'You know, I felt like I was tied to the guidelines. I think if the kids don't learn the material, there's no point covering all the material' (25D7), and she admits to feeling that she had to keep up with the other teachers for examination purposes. 'That was what essentially ruled what I was doing' (27D7). The theme of 'what they have to know' is central to a segment of Interview 6 in which Debra describes a portion of the course that she has yet to teach: 'So I'm just going to go through the guidelines and tell them what they have to know' (18D9).

Battle of Rules

Debra's concern for controlling this class is voiced frequently throughout the series of interviews. In Interview 1, for example, she reports that 'This is the most difficult class I have to keep settled' (22D1) and that she feels that she is 'sort of on the edge between control and not having control' (38D1). In an early segment of Interview 2, Debra expresses concern that they were chatting constantly. Interview 2 also contains a description of an incident in which Debra finds herself having to confront a student about taking a test outside class hours according to the rules she has established for missing class tests: 'It was the sort of behaviour that I found unacceptable'. Similar concern for class behavior appears in Interview 3, in which the class is described as too 'busy'. Here (24D3) a good class is defined as one in which students are not disruptive. Debra remains concerned in Interview 5: 'Well, I had — I still have the catcalls from — well, not catcalls, but the comments from [student's name] and it was going on anyways, and things like that, from a few of the kids' (3D5).

Debra's Responses to Suggestions

There is evidence that the observer's interventions caused Debra to begin to look at her teaching differently, finding new frames for some of her concerns. It is clear in Interview 2 that she sees that she is not allowing the students to learn how to solve problems independently of the steps that she provides. In Interview 5 she connects the 'Guided Practice' pattern to student outcomes: 'They're not learning as much because I'm doing it all for them — I think it's probably your tip — to get them to give me the steps' (14D5). And in Interview 3 it is evident that she picked up on the observation that explicit agendas were not being provided for each class and for problem solving; she generated a flow chart for naming, 'because of what you said. That's why I did it. I did what you said' (11D3). Debra appears to use the same sort of chart or model to help the students identify the types of mole problems they are to solve (9D4). In contrast, although she recognizes the pattern of interaction in which all discussion passes through her, she does not seem to attempt to change it: 'Am I doing what I think I'm doing . . . Maybe I'm not exactly clear on what it is that I'm not doing' (9D6).

Getting students to do homework remains a frustration for Debra. In Interview 6, the observer suggests a procedure of randomly selecting someone to solve a homework problem on the board and then having other randomly selected students comment on each step of the solution. Debra refers to this in Interview 7: 'They should be involved anyway if I say "It's *your* problem. You tell me if it's right". Then they can . . . it'll be worthwhile if they can correct the board' (14D7).

Frequently, Debra expresses gratitude to the observer: 'I know I find the hints helpful, like letting them know where they are going' (24D4), and 'Your comments are too kind' (28D4). Sometimes the expressions were uncomfortable for the interviewer because they seemed to convey a sense of guilt: 'I find this so helpful because I don't realize what I'm doing wrong, really' (5D5).

The Guilt-Trip

Discussion of management and other problems is frequently accompanied by language suggesting that Debra is assuming something akin to guilt for what happens in the lessons. The first sign of this comes early in Interview 1 when she discusses failures on a test in terms of not providing students with enough time to study the material: 'The kids who did do the work managed to do fairly well on the test. So in a sense I'm at fault, and in a sense they're not doing their full participation ... I'm guilty and they're guilty too' (21D1). In the same interview, we hear Debra discussing the rule she has established about handing in assignments: 'I think I'm too much of a pushover when it comes to handing in assignments ... it's still one mark per day, it's too much of a problem for me to calculate ... But I'm still not tough enough on the day they hand it in' (51D1).

This sort of talk appears in Interview 2, when Debra blames herself for seeing students breaking rules, and in the way Debra begins Interviews 3 and 4: 'Horrible lesson'. Her view of the third lesson, the topic for Interview 3, is that she 'made it more complicated than it had to be' (1D3) and that she 'didn't represent [molar mass] properly' (2D3). Later in the same interview Debra speaks about what she noticed from listening to the tape of the second lesson: 'I repeat things all the time. I keep coming back with the same thing' (5D3). When asked if this is a concern, she responds, 'I haven't decided if it is a concern or not'. Then, referring to the pattern concerning steps (called 'Guided Practice', above), Debra offers:

> I sort of help them along too much and I end up repeating it again
> rather than getting it from them maybe? ... So what worries me
> then ... Is it because of the way that *I'm* teaching it to them? Is it
> what *I'm* doing that they can't fill in the blanks? ... Am I allowing
> them to be too dependent? (5D3)

In the same interview she refers to her problems of control by saying 'I find this group an abusive group' and by speculating, 'Maybe I'm just avoiding confrontations most of the time' (31D3).

The general theme of guilt extends into the final interview. She believes, for instance, that she didn't and still doesn't set reasonable expectations. And she seems to excuse management problems with 'as long as they're *doing* the work, as long as they're *learning* the work, I shouldn't really care. That's why I broke down, I think' (17D7). On four occasions in this final interview, Debra explains how she felt about her hesitance in enforcing her own rules:

> The minute you let it go once or twice, you're finished. (17D7)
> I didn't really follow through with everything. (18D7)
> You can't sort of change your ways halfway through. It's much easier to start off one way and then live with your mistakes. (21D7)
> Those kids that I have this year are suffering through *my* first year, and it's sort of unfortunate. It's their luck of the draw that they didn't get someone else who's experienced. (36D7)

Despite this, Debra did change some of her rules during the semester. Between Interviews 3 and 4 she rearranged the seating so that there were no pairs. This was to reduce the 'chatter' and she appeared pleased with the result.

Learning How to Teach

As noted in the discussions of responses to suggestions and of 'guilt', Debra has learned from the experiences of her first semester of teaching. In Interview 3 she shows that she spotted the way in which she repeated herself and provided the steps for the students when they were engaged in learning to solve problems: 'When I ask a question, I'm not giving them the chance to let me know they actually have that point. I sort of help them along too much, and I end up repeating it again rather than getting it from them, maybe? I'm not waiting long enough for an answer?' (5D3) Additionally, the final interview (Interview 7) contains many instances of what she views as 'mistakes' from which she is clearly developing ideas about teaching: 'I won't be nice at the beginning of the semester' (9D7), and 'They have to do it my way' (11D7) suggest that she hopes to enforce her rules more than she admits to doing this semester.

For us, Debra's view of learning from experience is particularly interesting: 'I think you can only learn this by doing it. I mean, you think one thing but it doesn't always work that way ... you don't really learn to do it until you've done it ... It's the same in the lab. You can read over procedure, and until you actually do the actual setting up to do it, you don't realize what you have missed' (47D7). We return to this statement in the analysis.

Analysis of the Case

Our interest in Debra's case and in others like it relates to the goal of understanding possible ways in which professional knowledge is acquired.

Interpretation of Debra's case is made more intriguing by two factors: Debra's extensive knowledge of and laboratory experience with science, and the observer's dual role of offering assistance while gathering data about Debra's teaching and understanding of her own teaching. As in our previous research, we look at Debra's case from the perspective of Schön's (1983) theoretical framework to understand the part experience plays in the development of professional knowledge.

For Schön, experience plays two significant roles. In the first, it is the data that are used when we reflect logically and systematically on past events, and Schön calls this attending to the feedback of experience 'reflection-on-action'. Feedback, though, is a limited concept simply because it is based on rather elementary predictions: such and such will work, or it won't. In this way feedback is almost reduced to being binary: this or that, yes or no. The binary property of feedback is not a function of the experience itself, but rather of what we expect the experience to be. Experience yields feedback, then, only when the feedback is recognized as such. This does not diminish the place of feedback in learning from experience; it simply puts it in its place as limited.

The concept of feedback would not be limited were experience simple and predictable, but usually it is anything but simple and predictable. Rather, experience has the potential for complexity and uncertainty, and this certainly seems true of classroom teaching experience. Schön refers to the unpredictable offerings of experience as 'backtalk', a term that recalls the idea of unanticipated talking back. 'Backtalk' suggests the second role experience can play in the development of professional knowledge: For Schön, attempts to make backtalk sensible require us to develop a framework for it that, almost by definition, must be different from the framework that was used in forming expectations and assessing feedback. Schön terms the process 'reframing', and marks off its non-logical nature by referring to the reflection involved as 'reflection-in-action'. We rarely have deliberate control of coming to see actions in new frames, and we only fully understand the new frames when we take them back into the action context by modifying our practices.

These concepts enable to us to ask particular questions about Debra's teaching and about her professional knowledge and its development:

> Does she reframe and come to see things differently, and possibly more productively?
> Can we detect anything in the data that either encourages or discourages her reframing?

The laboratory orientation that Debra brings to her teaching appears to provide her with a productive frame for interpreting some of what transpires in her teaching, but it seems not to be brought into play for interpreting all of her experiences. The productive, quiet and orderly work of the students in the laboratory activities of the course stands in marked contrast to the disorderly beginnings and endings of lessons. The evidence is that Debra has spent time making laboratory safety procedures clear and significant. Additionally, each laboratory activity is carefully introduced, talked through, and accompanied by a sheet of ordered instructions.

It seems appropriate to assume that the many years Debra has spent as a laboratory technician have generated very detailed practical knowledge of how to arrange people, materials and equipment so that useful results are achieved safely. Debra's point, cited above, that laboratory work is learned from having to walk through it is apt here.

Importantly, this careful approach to management seems not to extend into the non-laboratory portions of the teaching — the 'beginning, end, and transitions' pattern is evidence, as is the continual 'battle of the rules'. Neither do the carefully ordered presentations of laboratory activities have their parallel in the presentation of content: 'connections and clarity' are rarely evident, and the problem of 'guided and independent practice' seems related. The latter is particularly interesting because Debra seems not to see the importance of providing clear plans for problem-solving nor of rehearsing whole solutions; instead, as we have seen, she offers the steps herself.

Much of this can be explained in terms of Debra's own understanding of chemistry from a laboratory technician's point of view. As she says, 'For me, it's easy to calculate solutions ... I guess it's so sort of second nature that for me it's difficult to sort of start to tell them exactly how to do it and be consistent, because I never approached it the same way'. And, in a later interview, she talks of the short cuts she took as a technician. Debra appears to have acquired a view of chemistry, especially of stoichiometry, that is neither linear nor hierarchical, but integrated. Everything is connected, theoretically and practically, with everything else. And the challenge facing Debra is to construct a linear approach to the discipline so that it can be learned. In this light, it is hardly surprising that the task is not yet complete, and that problem solving is not presented to students serially or as a decision tree.

At a common-sense level, it seems straightforward that those who have studied a particular subject (such as chemistry) at university would view the courses recorded on transcripts as the major source of their knowledge of the subject. By virtue of the shift from student to teacher, the initial years of teaching a subject are years of deepening one's understanding of the subject as one plans lessons and responds to students' questions and misunderstandings. A teacher's interaction with the subject during teaching is quite different from the university's lecture-and-lab setting with an examination at the end. We are only beginning to understand how teachers' knowledge of content becomes linked to the pedagogical context of the classroom, but it is clear that such links do form.

It seems crucial to attend to Debra's *laboratory content knowledge* as knowledge and understanding grounded in her research experience. Thus her learning to teach may be more complex and demanding than that of the new teacher straight from university courses. Debra must come to understand how the laboratory context of knowledge differs from the classroom context, so that she can appropriately reinterpret ('reframe') the subject she is teaching.

Quite clearly, Debra has met a large measure of the initial challenge. The course she teaches is sequenced, although the overall sequence and the sequence of each lesson may not be explicated for the students. So the frame of seeing chemistry differently than through the laboratory technician's eyes is not uniformly applied: It is far easier for her to frame the laboratory work than to frame the lessons, where events more readily remind her of the pressures of teaching a new course combined with the need to keep abreast of colleagues teaching the same course. The pressure to 'cover the curriculum' as well as to learn it may consume all planning time, leaving little time to consider what has occurred during lessons. This explanation is limited, however. It does not seem to explain the 'battle of the rules', a pattern in the interviews in which Debra returns to the theme of the struggle she perceives in maintaining order and in getting the students to adhere to rules that she wants her class to follow. Alternative ways of dealing with such situations are available, of course, but these seem to have been put aside for this semester. Instead, Debra invokes what might be called a 'guilt-trip', apparent in the pattern of blaming herself for the errant behavior of her class. A far more productive pattern would involve seeing that the problem areas are just those that the laboratory-technician frame is least likely to accommodate.

Framing part of her teaching in terms of guilt permits Debra to identify the problem in a way that allows her to postpone treating the problem until she begins work with another class in the semester that follows. Indeed, in the final interview in the case, Debra talks about the many things that she will do differently, such as 'I won't be nice at the beginning of the semester' (9D7), and she gives details of how she will enforce the rules she plans to impose.

From the perspective of learning from experience, the guilt frame is limiting in two fundamental ways. First, it discourages Debra from seeing that she need not wait until the next semester to correct what she views as her mistakes. Second, the guilt she experiences and the discomforts that come with being on the receiving end of resistance, gratuitous comments and other mild abuses become 'punishment' for her mistakes within the guilt perspective.

The management and behavior problems can be viewed differently, however. But for this to happen, Debra needs to reframe her view of *how she learns from her experiences* of teaching. In brief, she needs to move away from feeling guilty about 'mistakes' and toward seeing experiences of this sort as inevitable and as the essential stimuli for her own professional learning. The evidence that she does not presently do this resides in Debra's characteristic description of the researcher's suggestions as 'tips'. Although they may be seen in this frame, the intent of the suggestions was twofold: to draw attention to using the evidence of patterns in teaching to promote productive thinking about teaching, and to suggest ways of looking at connections between teacher behavior and student behavior.

The final and summarizing issue in this analysis concerns the stark difference between Debra's view of how she learned as a laboratory technician and the mistake-making frame she imposes on her initial teaching experiences. The laboratory-technician frame evidently works well for her when she instructs her students in laboratory activities. But this view of instruction is not extended, in interview or in action, to the other forms in which she gives instruction. Perhaps Debra has accepted the familiar idea that her teacher education program constitutes a complete preparation for professional life. This view is consistent with the idea that unanticipated outbursts constitute 'mistakes' on the teacher's part. Indeed, this view may be powerful enough to submerge the view that the evidence of teaching can be treated systematically like any other evidence, leaving Debra with the view that her instruction in laboratory activity works well simply because she has enjoyed good laboratory experience herself.

This extended sequence of observations and interviews from one of Debra's first groups of students reveals a split between laboratory work and classroom instruction. The frames from years of laboratory experiences in research appear to serve her well in the laboratory component of science teaching, but she seems unable to extend them to her classroom activities. The new frames implied by the observer's comments in reply to her management concerns seem to be taken as 'tips' rather than internalized as significant new perspectives suggesting alternative patterns of action. Minor changes are made, and some have good effect, but experience has not yet become a stimulus to what Schön refers to as 'reflection-*in*-action'. Here it is fascinating to see the context-dependency of Debra's subject-matter knowledge. She almost seemed to predict the problem in a passage she wrote at the conclusion of her BEd program:

> My greatest reservations about teaching stem from the fact that I feel very comfortable in my present job. It is something I have been working at for the better part of the last eleven years. The level of comfort has accrued over the last six or seven years and I would agree that it is due to the reasonable assimilation of theory and a good mix of practice. When a problem comes up in the laboratory, or when I set out to design an experiment, I can draw on past experience to give me an overview of the problem and confidence in my approach. With teaching, it is like starting all over again. I have learned — or tried to — some tricks and some do's and don'ts, am reasonably familiar with the curriculum guidelines and duties of a

teacher, but I have not actually lived the life of a teacher without an easy escape route. I am semi-dreading the first year or so; it is impossible to set a time frame. I am very sure the first year will be most trying but also the most important step into this new career. I won't be able to judge what works best for me until I have tried it.

Debra's anticipation of the complexity of learning to teach suggests that she may recall elements of the complexity of learning to do research. It is useful to return to her comment about the necessity of learning by doing. What is fascinating is that her words make so much sense, yet at the level of action and practice, *she applies this view neither to her own learning to teach nor to her students' learning of chemistry*. What she says is very insightful, but nothing in her professional education has prepared her for the complex process of acting on these words.

> And I think you can only learn this by doing it. I mean, you think one thing but it doesn't always work that way, or — and you don't really *learn* to do it until you've done it. You don't actually know how to do it until you've done it at least once. It's the same in the lab. You can read over procedure, and until you actually do the actual setting-up to do it, you don't realize what you've missed. You think, 'Oh, I'll do this concentration and this and this', and you realize when you set it up that it wasn't molar concentration percent by mass, it was something else that you need a bit more work for calculating. And until you've actually tried to do it, or done it, you don't realize that. You just sort of skim-over.

There is more here than the words themselves indicate. It is not uncommon to find that we do not connect one set of experiences with another set in a different context. The essence of reframing is seeing new connections, and the process is not automatic. Even more, Debra seems unprepared for the reality that her new perspectives *on* practice must be played out *in* practice. This is a major flaw in the linear view, implicit in everyday language, in which reflection *follows* action. Even the explicit realization that 'you can only learn by doing' has no useful meaning unless it is deliberately taken back *into* the practice context. Left on its own as a generalization, it naturally fades away under the pressure to transmit the content of the curriculum and is of little help when specific puzzles arise in that transmission process. For Debra's particular situation, this may hold the key to her *reinterpreting* her subject matter knowledge from the laboratory context to the classroom context. The complexity of the frames and their interaction in Debra's case testify to the position that the way in which experience is framed (or had) is central to any account of the development of professional knowledge.

Discussion

Earlier, we introduced Schön's distinction between feedback and backtalk as one way to describe the importance to 'seeing' of the framework with which one interprets classroom events. While Schön suggests that new frames are an essential aspect of learning from experience, frames simply do not feature in Shulman's account. Instead, knowledge and experience are separated as though there is nothing in knowledge that influences *having* experience. Shulman's (1987, p. 19) brief account of 'reflection' includes these statements:

> [Reflection] is what a teacher does when he or she looks back at the teaching and learning that has occurred, and reconstructs, reenacts, and/or recaptures the events, the emotions, and the accomplishments. It is that set of processes through which a professional learns from experience. It can be done alone or in concert, with the help of recording devices or solely through memory ... Central to this process will be a review of the teaching in comparison to the ends that were sought.

We find this account much too general, even vague, to be helpful in working with a student or first-year teacher, and Debra's case is helpful in explaining why. Debra did have someone with whom to work, and their discussions were assisted by tape-recordings, although these guided only the observer as Debra tended to rely on memory. The observer was guided by the importance of frames and the importance of reframing in developing new approaches to pedagogical problems. Seven interviews is a rare opportunity in current support for most beginning teachers, yet these were not enough to enable Debra to make significant shifts in practice. The guilt pattern led her to blame herself rather than to objectify her own actions, and she was thus led to postponing significant reframing.

Few beginning teachers have Debra's elaborate laboratory-technician frame, which proved to be an asset in the school laboratory but a liability in the classroom. Yet all beginning teachers do have 'student' frames that accompany their knowledge of the subject they intend to teach. While the laboratory-technician frame is specialized and can be interpreted from a common sense perspective, the student frame is so universal that its features are difficult to see. We believe that this is one of the reasons why reframing as a central feature of learning from experience to develop pedagogical content knowledge is easily overlooked — by those learning to teach, by teacher educators, and by those who carry out research on learning to teach. A further reason relates to the everyday use (by teachers and others) of 'reflection' in ways that do not imply the development of new frames for events.

Adopting new frames for her teaching was *not* an easy or straightforward matter for Debra. Extensive reflection-on-action, over a period of weeks, with documentation of her teaching and discussion with an interested observer did not lead quickly to changes that would resolve her concerns about managing classroom interaction. If Debra had been having problems with laboratory activities, perhaps her years of laboratory experience would have been helpful in the reframing process. But her concerns were about classroom discussion, and transforming her knowledge of chemistry for laboratory research purposes into knowledge of chemistry for pedagogical purposes was not a simple matter.

Most teachers develop pedagogical content knowledge by building on their undergraduate study of the subject at university; working with the subject for purposes of teaching prompts them to recognize and fill in the interconnections and incomplete understandings that remained after university study. For those who go on to graduate study of the subject, similar 'filling in' can be assumed to occur during those further studies. In Debra's case, it appears that extending her undergraduate study of chemistry by using it in a research laboratory and by studying for a graduate degree produced an understanding of her subject so integrated that it became a potential barrier to reworking the subject for teaching purposes. The teacher question-student answer-teacher elaboration pattern so familiar to all teachers from personal classroom experiences as students led Debra to provide heavily guided practice without the independent practice that could have led to greater understanding of chemistry by her students. Our overriding impression from the work with Debra is of a knowledge of chemistry so complete that she found it difficult to provide classroom experiences that would leave her students with a sense of accumulating understanding of the subject. This is not to suggest that *all* who shift from laboratory research to teaching will have difficulties similar to those experienced by Debra. The data provided by Debra do demonstrate that significant experiences using a subject outside of teaching can complicate the process of learning to teach.

Acknowledgments

An earlier version of this chapter was presented at the annual conference of the Canadian Society for the Study of Education, Victoria, June 1990, and discussed at an invitational conference of the University of Toronto/OISE Joint Centre for Teacher Development, Stoney Lake, Ontario, May 1990. The paper is part of the authors' study of 'The Development of Teachers' Professional Knowledge', funded by the Social Sciences and Humanities Research Council of Canada; Phyllis Johnston is the study's research officer. Chris Kyriacou of the University of York provided valuable comments on the chapter.

Hugh Munby and Tom Russell

References

ROSENSHINE, B. and STEVENS, R. (1986) 'Teaching functions', in WITTROCK, M. (Ed.) *Third Handbook of Research on Teaching*, 3rd ed., New York, Macmillan, pp. 376–391.

RUSSELL, T. and MUNBY, H. (1989) 'Science as a discipline, science as seen by students, and teachers' professional knowledge', in MILLAR, R. (Ed.) *Doing Science: Images of Science in Science Education*, London, Falmer Press, pp. 107–125.

RUSSELL, T. and MUNBY, H. (1991) 'Reframing: The role of experience in developing teachers' professional knowledge', in SCHÖN, D.A. (Ed.) *The Reflective Turn: Case Studies In and On Educational Practice*, New York, Teachers College Press, pp. 164–187.

SCHÖN, D.A. (1983) *The Reflective Practitioner: How Professionals Think in Action*, New York, Basic Books.

SHULMAN, L.S. (1987) 'Knowledge and teaching: Foundations of the new reform', *Harvard Educational Review*, **57**, 1, pp. 1–22.

7 Creating Cases for the Development of Teacher Knowledge

Kathy Carter

When a new teacher is learning to teach, what is she or he learning? When an experienced teacher 'knows' how to teach, what is that teacher smart about? Despite a growing literature on teacher education, the first of these questions, which centers on the 'learning' in the learning to teach process, has often been evaded. Studies of learning to teach have focused on the socialization of teachers (for example, Zeichner, 1987; Zeichner and Tabachnick, 1985), the impact of particular programs (Feiman-Nemser, 1983), the effect of cooperating teacher and university supervisors (Richardson-Koehler, 1988; Zimpher, 1987), and similar topics, but few studies have directly addressed what is learned. And despite a substantial data base on teacher effectiveness, knowledge about what teachers know has been elusive.

The argument is developed in three stages. I first describe recent work that has begun to address the critical questions of what new teachers learn and what experienced teachers know. I then connect this work to some of the underlying reasons for the recent emergence of the case method in teacher education. Finally, I explore in some detail the implications of these analyses for the writing of cases about teachers and teaching and the use of cases in teacher education.

Conceptions of Teachers' Knowledge and Learning to Teach

There are many reasons, historically, why the questions of learning and knowledge in teaching have not been addressed adequately (for more comprehensive discussions, see Carter, 1990a; Doyle, 1990; Richardson, 1990). Chief among these may be the long-held conceptions of teaching that ignore cognition and the mental work required of teachers. Notions of teaching underlying early research implied that a 'smart' teacher had a well-refined set of skills, an image derived from studies that focused on correlating teacher behavior with student outcomes or on controlling aspects of teacher behavior to gain experimental 'proof' for prescriptions for practice (Peck and Tucker, 1973; Waxman and Walberg, 1986).

The focus for teacher education paralleled the views of teaching and learning to teach represented in the research. The spotlight of professional preparation was on teaching performance, or more precisely on controlling or changing teacher performance so that it became technically true to skills-based models extracted from teacher-effects research. Under these behaviorist notions of change, a teacher became 'knowledgeable' about teaching by 'exposure' to studies of teacher effectiveness (e.g., Stallings, 1987) and by behavioral 'training'.

> Behavior analysis and behavioral training may have particular value in changing teacher behaviors that for some reason are difficult to establish, to modify, or to extinguish. (Gliessman, 1984, p. 102)

Many teacher educators and researchers are now reformulating their conceptions of what it means to be knowledgeable about teaching and to learn to teach. Foolproof techniques have fallen into disfavor along the road to practice, as both new and practising teachers become increasingly vocal about the flaws in simplistic views of teaching and how teaching practices change.

Emerging Conceptions of Teachers' Knowledge

Recent developments in research on teacher education are suggesting a radically different sense of teachers' knowledge and how it is acquired. Here I summarize some of the major lines of thinking that are emerging from this work (for elaboration see Carter, 1990a).

Teachers' knowledge is practical and 'contextualized' in the sense that it is knowledge of common dilemmas teachers face in classroom life
With this conception of teachers' knowledge, what one knows is derived in part from having to act and react to the dilemmas that present themselves daily in classroom contexts. Teaching dilemmas, by their very nature, do not lend themselves to direct and decisive courses of action. Instead, they are paradoxes for teachers in that a chosen course of action may simultaneously correct one problem and prompt others. By facing these complexities and 'coping' (Lampert, 1985) with the cognitive demands of teaching, teachers develop 'practical arguments' (Fenstermacher, 1986) that are closely connected to their classroom decisions and actions. These practical arguments are a form of knowledge about teaching, though they may not represent traditional notions of what that knowledge is or should be.

Teachers' knowledge is personal, in the sense that teachers formulate and draw upon their personal understandings of the practical circumstances in which they work

Lampert (1985) has suggested that knowing about teaching involves continuously carrying out a very personal argument with oneself about how to go about teaching. For it is the person, the person working as teacher, who holds beliefs about what teaching is and should be (Connelly and Clandinin, 1985; Clandinin and Connelly, 1986; Elbaz, 1983, 1987; Munby, 1986; Russell and Johnston, 1988; Russell, 1989). Armed with the best practices that science has to offer, it is the person who makes inferences about when particular practices are appropriate for use. Moreover, what those skills 'look like' when they are implemented is the product of the personal voice of the teacher. The work of Amarel and Feiman-Nemser (1988), Grossman (1987) and Richert (1987) has illustrated clearly how the personal biographies and individual orientations of teachers are played out in their understandings of their work and ultimately in their actions in classrooms.

Teachers' disciplinary knowledge affects how teachers organize instruction and represent the curriculum to students

Research by Gudmundsdottir (in press) has suggested that teachers have acquired, as a result of their own education, a mental map for their subject-area specialization. These mental frameworks for a disciplinary field define areas of focus for the teacher, suggest how the teacher sees the relationships among these areas of focus, and hint at the scope and depth of one's view of the subject matter. Gudmundsdottir argues that uncovering these mental representations is a fruitful way to understand the representations of the content (Doyle, 1983; in press) that teachers provide when they translate that content, through their instructional choices and means, into academic work for their students. Importantly, this aspect of teacher knowledge also does not lend itself to skills-based approaches, for as Ball (1988) notes, what one knows and perhaps can know about teaching is tied to how and how well one understands the content one teaches.

Teachers' knowledge is task-specific and event-structured

At the core, teachers' knowledge is connected to the tasks in which they engage and to the events in which they and their students commonly participate in classrooms. Doyle (1986) argues that teachers must accomplish two major tasks in teaching: achieving order, and representing and enacting the curriculum in classrooms. This is to say that teachers must fill the role of both manager and instructor. They must do so by using their knowledge to develop solution strategies to help them deal with the dilemmas they encounter in classroom events. While events that take place in classrooms are jointly constructed and enacted, it is the teacher who must draw on her memory of how previous and similar events were enacted in order to guide them in ways that help students accomplish academic work. This event-structured knowledge is akin to the 'know-how' (which is much richer than simply knowing how to do things) that successful practitioners gain from recurring experiences with similar events. Just as a good basketball player can read a defense and use her knowledge of previous events to make the play, a teacher can interpret what certain behaviors and interactions within events mean for her tasks of management and instruction, and can use this event-structured knowledge to sustain cooperation and structure school work for students.

Teachers' knowledge is constructed and invented from repeated experience in accomplishing tasks or close approximations of tasks in a domain
While teachers' knowledge includes stored knowledge of events in classrooms, such knowledge is not static. Although teachers draw upon their event-structured knowledge to make predictions about trajectories for students' behavior, they also invent knowledge by mentally acting on new information as they experience unexpected events. Thus teachers' knowledge is constructed in a social setting with students (Carter and Doyle, 1987), and teachers are frequently forced to formulate fresh interpretations of students' actions and reactions when the original sense made of events no longer seems sensible.

These emerging conceptions of teachers' knowledge owe a considerable debt to case study approaches to research on teaching and learning to teach, and they emphasize the value of examining the work of individual teachers in detail. Quite naturally, then, teacher educators are becoming increasingly interested in the potential contribution of case studies to the experience of learning to teach.

Conceptions of Teachers' Knowledge and the Case for the Case Method

The case method is being put forward as one possible means by which the content and processes of both preservice and inservice teacher education might be redesigned (Carter and Richardson, 1989; Carter and Unklesbay, 1989; Shulman and Nelson, in press; Shulman, 1986). Many of these proposals rest on the premise that the case method can convey the complexity of teachers' cognitive work. Indeed, Richert (1990) suggests that cases are potentially powerful pedagogical tools for helping people develop teaching knowledge, for unlike a number of traditional methods employed by teacher education, cases present teaching 'as it is — infinitely complex, changing, and uncertain'.

> The teaching moment or moments 'frozen' in the case description allow the teacher to think about what has occurred in the particular

situation described. Teachers can ask themselves, or ask one another, what the case is about, what the actors are doing or saying, what circumstances seem to determine what people do and say in the situation described, and what they might do in similar situations. (Richert, 1990, p. 11)

Proponents of the case method suggest that cases are a logical basis for the kind of reflective inquiry that engages teachers as they attempt to learn from their experiences (Carter, 1990b; Noordhoff and Kleinfeld, 1990). Finally, Kleinfeld (1988) argues that carefully-constructed cases may heighten our consciousness and cause us to consider more carefully the contextual and multicultural issues that are intrinsic to functional understandings about teaching.

Thus it appears that for many, cases are a cause for celebration in this time of reform in teacher education. But for these hopes to be realized, it would seem of considerable importance to develop and use cases in ways that reflect current conceptions of teacher knowledge. If cases are ill-connected to teachers' everyday cognitions and modes of knowing about teaching, they will likely add little to the educative process in which many beginning and experienced teachers wish to engage.

Conceptions of Teachers' Knowledge and Case Construction

Unlike those professions that have a long history of case literatures, for which the writing is 'regulated' by rich traditions, teacher education lacks a shared sense of what constitutes a written case. Given the recent ground-swell of support for case methods in the literature of teacher education, it seems somewhat surprising, perhaps even unsettling, that written debate about the fundamentals of form and substance of cases in teacher education has not ensued with equal enthusiasm. Basic questions about the size, substance and shape of cases, while debated in conferences concerned with the case method (Harrington, 1991), have taken a back seat to the business of promoting the possibilities of case use. While there is widespread senti-ment that cases may serve as a means to prepare new teachers or to assist experienced teachers as they evolve in their own work, it is difficult to locate a literature that provides guidelines to teachers who wish to use or write their own cases or to teacher educators who hope to generate and teach with cases. Shulman and Nelson's (in press) *The Teacher Educator's Casebook* is a notable exception, but even here the debate on what constitutes a case is secondary to displaying various types of cases developed recently by teachers and teacher educators. Perhaps the emerging conceptions of teacher knowledge can serve as a starting place to begin this necessary debate and to direct, though certainly not dictate, case construction efforts. I turn now to the question 'What do current conceptions of teachers' knowledge suggest about basic issues in case construction?' by considering the issues of the size, substance and shape of cases of teachers' knowledge.

Size

When we begin to write we often ask, as our students ask, 'How long does it need to be?' As I think now about case writing, I realize that I appreciate more fully how maddening my typical response ('long enough to cover the subject') must have been to my own students. Indeed, the issue of the size of a case seems central to the question of what constitutes a well-written case of teaching. Yet general guidelines are often left unspecified and, perhaps more importantly, undebated in the emerging literature on case methods for teacher education. Current conceptions of teacher knowledge complicate rather than resolve the problem, but the complications are instructive.

One useful way to think about the length of a case is to ask if the case relates a 'story' of teaching in a unit that is meaningful to experienced teachers. Teachers' knowledge appears to be shaped by repeated experiences of similar or associated events. In other words, a teacher makes sense — forms her knowledge of separate events — by making connections among similar events and by reframing the meaning of those events for her teaching. If teaching knowledge is event-structured, then it seems to follow that a case should describe well a series of classroom events that teachers typically encounter. Thus one must ask if the case is 'long enough' to allow the reader to detect patterns in the teacher's reactions to the events.

Unconnected events as vignettes

There is some evidence that unconnected but well-remembered events in teaching (Carter and Gonzales, 1990) vary widely in duration. A description of one event, whatever its size, may be powerful in eliciting a teacher's immediate reactions and may elicit her thinking about a particular scene or scenario. This event, translated into writing, might be called a 'vignette' or 'critical incident' in teaching. Here one would expect the narrative summary to be short. These vignettes, while useful for some pedagogical purposes, probably do not constitute cases of teacher knowledge. They are, instead, 'free floating' instances of teaching until they are carefully connected to one another and, importantly, to a description of the meaning that the teacher in the case has made of them. A detailed description of events is not a case; rather, it is the material from which cases are constructed.

Making a case

To be a case of teachers' knowledge, events must be connected to form a 'story' that tells the reader important information about the teacher (usually the main character), the students and other salient characters, and about their actions and reactions over time in relation to one another. To be a case of teacher knowledge, the text must allow the reader to interpret, as the story is told, what sense the teacher seemed to make of similar events. Importantly, a teacher's actions and reactions to events will reveal much about the extent to which classroom problems are seen and solved. This information gives the reader some sense of what the teacher knows and understands about classroom events (Carter, 1990a).

The issue of appropriate size, then, cannot be separated from the issue of how to represent teachers' knowledge in appropriate ways. If the written case is so short that it trivializes teaching decisions into critical incidents in which right or wrong choices are made, then the description is too short to be a case. If, however, the case is stretched beyond a description that can be made sensible by teachers, it is probably too long to be called a case of teaching.

Guidelines from research on teacher knowledge are imprecise with respect to the length of a case. This much, however, can be said: It is likely that all cases of teachers' knowledge are characterized by some of the structures of story, including exposition, narration and timing. Constructing a case to reveal teacher knowledge, then, is writing a story that reveals a teacher's knowledge without telling it directly. While much might vary in the way the story unfolds in the written case, it would seem that there are some fundamental characteristics of a written case of teacher knowledge. (McNair, 1971, and Merliss, 1986, provide related discussion regarding the elements of case construction for business schools.) First, the case should be expository. This means that the case writer will elucidate critical contextual information. Second, the case should take the form of narrative, to allow the reader to perceive relationships and interactions among classroom incidents and events. Third, the case should answer questions about time structure so that the reader knows when events occurred and how long they lasted. For example, does the case take place during the latter part of the spring semester or in a particular grading period? Do the events transpire in one lesson or over several lessons, in one day or over several days?

Substance

Next is the matter of the substance of a case. Few would disagree that the 'stuff' of cases must be something of substance to teachers' thinking. Yet I suspect there is wide difference of opinion about what might be called the central foci of cases of teacher knowledge. I argue here that cases of teacher knowledge, if they represent current conceptions of how teachers' knowledge is organized, will have the tasks of teaching as the undergirding substance of case stories. Carter and Doyle (1987) have argued that classroom tasks provide a window into the cognitive world of teaching. The concept of 'task' calls attention to three basic dimensions of action-situation relationships: a goal state or end product to be achieved, a problem space or set of conditions and resources available to reach the goal state, and the operations involved in assembling and using available resources.

Broadly speaking, teachers face two interrelated tasks in classrooms: establishing and maintaining social order, and representing and enacting the curriculum. Teachers must, in other words, organize groups of students, establish rules and procedures, elicit students' cooperation in classroom activities, and sustain order for designated blocks of time across several months. At the same time, teachers must create work for students that conveys the curriculum, explain the intellectual processes involved in doing the work, and provide assistance and feedback as students carry out and complete assignments. The tasks of social order and curriculum enactment are constituted by teachers *and* students (Erickson and Shultz, 1981). This interactive property of task accomplishment, combined with the inherent complexity of the classroom environment (Doyle, 1986), makes teaching in classrooms an extraordinarily difficult enterprise.

Teachers carry out these tasks by navigating the course of events in classrooms (Doyle, in press). Through a detailed description of these events, a reader of a case should be able to gain a sense of how a teacher attempts to solve the problem of order and enact the curriculum with students. Familiar issues such as motivation, planning, discipline and methods of teaching will be addressed in cases of teachers' knowledge, but these are the lenses through which we view 'lived out' events in classrooms.

By constructing cases broadly organized around teachers' tasks, tasks that are carried out in the course of classroom events, readers are better able to suspend their disbelief about the story told through the case (McNair, 1971) and to enter into the 'problem space' of a particular task of teaching. They will, in other words, be asked to 'think' like a teacher because they will be asked to organize their cognitions around the major tasks of teaching. This knowledge will, like that of practising teachers, be constructed and reconstructed from their developing personal understandings of the practical dilemmas described in case materials.

Shape

Recent conceptions of teacher knowledge also suggest questions about the structure or 'shape' of a case.

Is the case 'contextualized' and 'situated'?
It has been suggested earlier that teacher knowledge about and comprehension of their tasks is tied to particular classrooms and situations. What actions a teacher takes to accomplish the tasks of teaching may depend on the distinct features of a given class. It is quite important then for the case to begin with a detailed description of the class so that the case can have the

particulars it needs to be perceived as believable. 'Armchair' cases often lack the contextual details that allow readers to learn from the case. For this reason, I have argued that cases should be grounded in descriptions of naturally-occurring classroom life (Carter, 1990b). To clarify the context for a case, the case writer will need, for example, to portray carefully the physical environment of the classroom. (Perhaps a sketch or photograph of the classroom might be included in the case). Moreover, students (age, socioeconomic status, numbers, culture, characteristics) will need to be detailed. Also, salient information about the teacher (age, years of teaching experience, statements about teaching, intentions for lessons, etc.) will need to be provided for the reader. It is the work of the case writer to ensure that the cases are both 'peopled' and 'placed'. If such conditions prevail, the reader of the case will be able to 'observe' the teacher, 'watch' visible students interacting with the teacher, 'hear' their verbal responses, 'see' their non-verbal behavior, 'witness' the action that takes place in a particular context, and 'feel' the emotional arena in which all of this takes place.

Are the teacher's solutions revealed in the case description?

Access to teachers' knowledge is seldom direct (Ericcson and Simon, 1980). It is unlikely that anyone can readily provide an analytical description of personal knowledge and how it is used to comprehend and carry out events. Yet it may be possible to construct a case in ways that indirectly reveal a teacher's knowledge structures and comprehension processes. To do this, a case writer must shape the case so that a teacher's solutions to dilemmas are implied through a teacher's patterns of acting and reacting to problems that present themselves in classroom events. A case of teacher knowledge, then, will describe in detail *how a teacher accomplished a major task of teaching*, including such matters as what the teacher attended to, talked about and did in the task environment. With this design for case construction, information about the task itself and how it was accomplished will be obtained by the case writer from extended classroom observations, often conducted on a daily basis over several weeks. The case write-up will not be a record of the teacher's conscious thoughts but rather a written analysis of a teacher's solutions to the tasks of order and instruction. A teacher's solution strategies appear to be central to understanding what that teacher knows. With this strategy, the student of the case will be asked to make inferences about a teacher's thinking from a studied analysis of a teacher's preoccupations and actions in accomplishing classroom tasks. As suggested, if the solution is summarized directly for the reader, the writer may fail to transfer ownership of thought to the student of the case. This would seem to violate one of the intended purposes of case method.

One alternative to including information indirectly about a teacher's solutions to her teaching tasks is to omit the teacher's solutions from the description entirely and to ask the reader to formulate personal responses to the classroom problems posed in the case. This option has been debated in other fields (Merliss, 1986) and has sometimes proven troublesome because case readers are inclined to develop a 'right answer' rather than reason carefully about the case.

Should questions be included at the end of a case?

The issue of questions for the reader is widely debated in other fields in which case pedagogy has a long history, and the issue seems to be the object of much discussion in current conversations about cases in teacher education. This much seems certain: Attaching questions to the case must be done carefully to preserve the complexity of teaching. If case writers choose to include questions at the end of a case, the following guidelines seem warranted in light of what is known about teachers' professional knowledge:

Case writers should design questions in such a way that the reader's development of an analysis is pushed forward, not backward through the text of the case. Questions should not ask the case reader simply to 'search and match' information or recall parts of the text. Teaching involves much more than retrieval of information for transmission to students. The development of teachers' professional knowledge involves reframing and reflecting on events of one's practice (Munby, 1989; Russell, 1989).

Questions should not elicit 'Yes or No' responses. Doyle (1990) has argued that the core problem in learning to teach is learning how to enact curriculum with students in complex instructional settings. On the surface this problem may seem a simple one, but teaching is an intricate social event shaped powerfully by the understandings, dispositions, resources and goals of the teacher and students. Judgments about the appropriateness of teaching decisions are rarely so straightforward that they can be summed up in one-word responses to case-based questions.

Questions should be broad enough to lead to analysis rather than answers. Questions should be designed to 'throw open' alternate pathways of thought rather than to steer readers down well-worn roads to 'right' answers.

What principles might guide the construction of commentary at the end of a case?

In fields with established case traditions, case commentaries are designed to allow readers to view a case from different vantage points or alternate perspectives. Given the complexity of the cognitive work required of teaching, commentary would seem to be a useful way to explore different ways of thinking about classroom events. If commentary is included as the answer in disguise, however, it will cut off deliberations about the case.

Should teaching notes be included with a case?

In other fields in which case methods are used, teaching notes may be written by the case writer or by others who have used the case in their teaching. Similarly, teaching notes might be useful to teacher educators to predict or track such features as the issues that seem pertinent to the case, students' reactions to cases, activities useful in teaching the case, and materials and resources that might supplement the case discussion. Given how little is known about how cases function in teacher education, however, teaching notes are probably best considered as 'optional' in the case construction effort. If teaching notes are to be included, they should be written in ways that reflect the complexity of the issues raised in the case. Specifically, this means that they should not be prescriptive nor should they represent a singular view of teaching.

Thoughts on Case Pedagogy

Conceptions of teacher knowledge not only suggest considerations in case construction but also have implications for thinking about how cases might actually be used. What do conceptions of teacher knowledge suggest about learning to teach? Concomitantly, what do these views of learning to teach suggest for case pedagogy?

First, learning to teach involves the acquisition of practical wisdom about the circumstances in which teachers work. To be knowledgeable about teaching, teachers must become thoughtful about how to carry out the tasks of teaching in classrooms characterized by unpredictability, simultaneity and complexity (Doyle, 1986). To do this, they must develop 'case knowledge' of classroom events. Teachers must gain a rich store of situated knowledge of content, classroom social processes, academic tasks and students' understanding and intentions. They must create meaning from related events in classrooms and they must continually question and draw upon their understandings to think about navigating new events. (For further discussion of teacher comprehension see Carter, 1990a.)

I have recently argued that teachers can achieve these ends by participating in the development of cases, by engaging in the long-term study of cases of teacher knowledge and by carefully constructing conversations around cases of teaching (Carter, 1990b). These conversations, however, are likely to look radically different from typical and traditional conversations in formal teacher education classes. If case pedagogy is consistent with conceptions of teacher knowledge, reasoning and reflection will replace talk of right answers, complex choices will challenge catalogued lists of best practices, and the development of practical arguments (Richardson, Anders, Tidwell and Loyd, in press) will preempt teaching prescriptions.

Second, learning to teach is both biographical and developmental. It is a person with a unique biography who comes to the task of learning to teach (Feiman-Nemser, 1990; Grossman, 1990). This suggests that individuals' responses will vary to the stories they read of different teachers' strategies for accomplishing the tasks of teaching. Thus students of a case may differ in what they regard as salient information because of their own individual histories. On the other hand, case methods can provide unique opportunities for those who study teaching to unpack their personal understandings and to reflect on their preconceptions and evolving understandings of teaching and learning.

Third, learning to teach demands reconstructing one's content knowledge as curricular events for students in classrooms (Doyle, in press). Teachers must learn, in other words, to translate their knowledge of a subject area into subject matter for pupils in classrooms. This is often a difficult learning experience for new teachers, for it means that one's mental frames for a content area become cluttered with classroom contingencies such as time, space, resources and pupils' willingness and interest to strive to learn the subject.

Case methods may hold promise for revealing the contingencies and constraints on teachers as they work to engage students in the content they intend to explore with them. What will be required of case teachers is tough and time-consuming work in helping prospective and practising teachers confront these contingencies and constraints in ways that do not lead them to retreat to individualistic defenses about their disciplinary knowledge and to set them up for feelings of helplessness. The problematics revealed in cases will need to be presented, then, as lifetime, preoccupying puzzles. A new teacher may discover, through study by the case method, that learning to teach the curriculum is much more difficult than expected because it is such difficult work to transform disciplinary knowledge into classroom content. It is, they may find, as much a matter of labor *with* the subject as it is a matter of love *for* one's subject.

Finally, learning to teach is both intervention and invention. Organized, formal, educative experiences wherein a professional literature is examined, analyzed and applied to teaching is an important but insufficient means by which teaching knowledge is acquired. To learn to teach one must not only gain access to practices developed through research on teaching but must also practise inventing knowledge through 'experiencing' teaching. This does not necessarily mean that to experience teaching one must assume responsibility for large groups of students over time. As suggested here, intentional cognitive experiences may be designed through the development and use of case methods to allow teachers to begin to develop the event-structured, experiential knowledge necessary to teach.

The Case for Cases in Teacher Education

Until recently, much of the research on learning to teach has focused on either the acquisition of specific teaching skills or teachers' socialization into the norms and dispositions of the occupation. It is increasingly recognized that teachers' learning also involves knowledge about subject matter, pedagogy, learning and motivation, and the personally and culturally embedded nature of students' conceptions and aspirations. Indeed, teaching is increasingly seen as an intellectual activity in the sense that successful practice rests fundamentally on interpretation, problem-solving and reflection rather than simply on mastery of an assortment of teaching skills. The major theme that surfaces clearly in the current literature on teacher knowledge is a theme of *complexity*. It would seem, then, that teacher education will be successful only to the extent that this complexity is recognized. In the midst of cries for reform, the case method presents itself as a possible means by which to conduct the professional preparation of teachers in ways that reflect the complexity of teachers' thought about their work. Yet a long history with the swinging pendulums of reforms in education (Cuban, 1990) suggests that there is no magic in any method. Unless we examine and act on the connections between current conceptions of teaching and the case method, and unless we are quite careful to reflect what we know of teacher knowledge in the construction and use of cases in teacher education, we run the risk 'of recruiting reformers for the ride on one more teacher education bandwagon, and we will find, as we so often have in the past, that the bandwagon will break down ... once again' (an anonymous teacher education colleague).

References

AMAREL, M. and FEIMAN-NEMSER, S. (1988) *Prospective Teachers' Views of Learning to Teach*, paper presented at the annual meeting of the American Educational Research Association, New Orleans.

BALL, D. (1988) *Prospective Teachers' Understandings of Mathematics*, paper presented at the annual meeting of the American Educational Research Association, New Orleans.

CARTER, K. (1990a) 'Teachers' knowledge and learning to teach', in HOUSTON, R. (Ed.) *Handbook of Research on Teacher Education*, New York, Macmillan, pp. 291–310.

CARTER, K. (1990b) 'Meaning and metaphor: Case knowledge in teaching', *Theory into Practice*, **29**, pp. 109–115.

CARTER, K. and DOYLE, W. (1987) 'Teachers' knowledge structures and comprehension processes', in CALDERHEAD, J. (Ed.) *Exploring Teachers' Thinking*, London, Cassell, pp. 147–160.

CARTER, K. and GONZALEZ, L. (1990) *Teachers' Knowledge of Classrooms and Classroom Events*, paper presented at the annual meeting of the American Educational Research Association, Boston.

CARTER, K. and RICHARDSON, V. (1989) 'Toward a curriculum for initial year of teaching programs', *Elementary School Journal*, **89**, pp. 405–420.

CARTER, K. and UNKLESBAY, R. (1989) 'Cases in teaching and law', *Journal of Curriculum Studies*, **21**, pp. 527–536.

CLANDININ, D.J. and CONNELLY, F.M. (1986) 'Rhythms in teaching: The narrative study of teachers' personal practical knowledge of classrooms', *Teaching and Teacher Education*, **2**, pp. 377–387.

CONNELLY, F.M. and CLANDININ, D.J. (1985) 'Personal practical knowledge and the modes of knowing: Relevance for teaching and learning', in EISNER, E. (Ed.)

Learning and Teaching the Ways of Knowing, Eighty-fourth Yearbook of the National Society for the Study of Education, Chicago, University of Chicago Press, pp. 174–198.

CUBAN, L. (1990) 'Reforming again, again, and again', *Educational Researcher*, **19**, 1, pp. 3–13.

DOYLE, W. (1983) 'Academic work', *Review of Educational Research*, **53**, pp. 159–199.

DOYLE, W. (1986) 'Classroom organization and management', in WITTROCK, M.C. (Ed.) *Handbook of Research on Teaching*, 3rd ed., New York, Macmillan, pp. 392–431.

DOYLE, W. (1990) 'Themes in teacher education research', in HOUSTON, R. (Ed.) *Handbook of Research on Teacher Education*, New York, Macmillan, pp. 3–24.

DOYLE, W. (in press) 'Curriculum and pedagogy', in JACKSON, P. (Ed.) *Handbook of Research on Curriculum*, New York, Macmillan.

ELBAZ, F. (1983) *Teacher Thinking: A Study of Practical Knowledge*, New York, Nichols.

ELBAZ, F. (1987) 'Teachers knowledge of teaching: Strategies for reflection', in SMYTH, J. (Ed.) *Educating Teachers: Changing the Nature of Pedagogical Knowledge*, London, Falmer Press, pp. 45–53.

ERICCSON, K. and SIMON, H. (1980) 'Verbal reports as data', *Psychological Review*, **87**, pp. 215–251.

ERICKSON, F. and SHULTZ, J. (1981) 'When is a context? Some issues and methods in the analysis of social competence', in GREEN, J. and WALLAT, C. (Eds) *Ethnography and Language in Educational Settings*, Norwood, NJ, Ablex, pp. 147–160.

FEIMAN-NEMSER, S. (1983) 'Learning to teach', in SHULMAN, L. and SYKES, G. (Eds) *Handbook of Teaching and Policy*, New York, Longman, pp. 150–170.

FEIMAN-NEMSER, S. (1990) 'Teacher preparation: Structural and conceptual alternatives', in HOUSTON, R. (Ed.) *Handbook of Research on Teacher Education*, New York, Macmillan, pp. 212–233.

FENSTERMACHER, G. (1986) 'Philosophy of research on teaching: Three aspects', in WITTROCK, M.C. (Ed.) *Handbook of Research on Teaching*, 3rd ed., New York, Macmillan, pp. 37–49.

GLIESSMAN, D.H. (1984) 'Changing teacher performance', in KATZ, L.G. and RATHS, J.D. (Eds) *Advances in Teacher Education, Vol. 1*, Norwood, NJ, Ablex, pp. 95–111.

GROSSMAN, P. (1987) *A Tale of Two Teachers: The Role of Subject Matter Orientation in Teaching*, paper presented at the annual meeting of the American Educational Research Association, Washington, DC.

GROSSMAN, P. (1990) *Knowing, Believing, and Valuing: The Role of Subject Matter*, paper presented at the annual meeting of the American Educational Research Association, Boston.

GUDMUNDSDOTTIR, S. (in press) 'Pedagogical models of subject matter', in BROPHY, J. (Ed.) *Advances in Research on Teaching*, Greenwich, CT, JAI Press Inc.

HARRINGTON, H. (1991) *The Case Method in Teacher Education: Issues and Considerations*, paper presented at the annual meeting of the American Educational Research Association, Chicago.

KLEINFELD, J. (1988) *Learning to Think Like a Teacher*, unpublished manuscript, Fairbanks, Center for Cross-Cultural Studies, Rural College, University of Alaska.

LAMPERT, M. (1985) 'How do teachers manage to teach? Perspectives on problems in practice', *Harvard Educational Review*, **55**, pp. 178–184.

McNAIR, M. (1971) 'McNair on cases', *Harvard Business School Bulletin* Reprint No. 9-372-303, Cambridge, Harvard University Graduate School of Business.

MERLISS, P. (1986) *Case Preparation: A Guide for Research Assistants at the Harvard Business School*, Cambridge, MA, Harvard Business School.

MUNBY, H. (1986) 'Metaphor in the thinking of teachers: An exploratory study', *Journal of Curriculum Studies*, **18**, pp. 197–209.

MUNBY, H. (1989) *Reflection in Action and Reflection on Action*, paper presented at the meeting of the American Educational Research Association, San Francisco.

NOORDHOFF, K. and KLEINFELD, J. (1990) 'Shaping the rhetoric of reflection for multicultural settings', in CLIFT, R., HOUSTON, W. and PUGACH, M. (Eds) *Encouraging Reflective Practice in Education*, New York, Teachers College Press, pp. 163–185.

PECK, R. and TUCKER, J. (1973) 'Research on teacher education', in TRAVERS, R.M. (Ed.) *Second Handbook of Research on Teaching*, Chicago, Rand McNally, pp. 940–978.

RICHARDSON, V. (1990) 'Significant and worthwhile changes in teaching practice', *Educational Researcher*, **19**, 7, pp. 10–18.

RICHARDSON, V., ANDERS, P., TIDWELL, D. and LOYD, C. (in press) 'The relationship between teachers' beliefs and practices in reading comprehension instruction', *American Educational Research Journal*.

RICHARDSON-KOEHLER, V. (1988) 'Barriers to the effective supervision of student teachers', *Journal of Teacher Education*, **39**, pp. 28–34.

RICHERT, A. (1987) *The Voices Within: Knowledge and Experience in Teacher Education*, paper presented at the annual meeting of the American Educational Research Association Special Interest Group for Women and Education, Portland, OR.

RICHERT, A. (1990) 'Using teacher cases for reflection and enhanced understanding', in LIEBERMAN, A. and MILLER, L. (Eds) *Teachers: their World and their Work*, 2nd ed., New York, Teachers College Press.

RUSSELL, T. (1989) *The Role of Research Knowledge and Knowing-in-Action in Teachers' Development of Professional Knowledge*, paper presented at the annual meeting of the American Educational Research Association, San Francisco.

RUSSELL, T. and JOHNSTON, P. (1988) *Teachers' Learning from Experiences of Teaching: Analyses Based on Metaphor and Reflection*, paper presented at the annual meeting of the American Educational Research Association, New Orleans.

SHULMAN, J. and NELSON, L. (Eds) (in press) *Case Methods in Teacher Education*, New York, Teachers College Press.

SHULMAN, L. (1986) 'Those who understand: Knowledge growth in teaching', *Educational Researcher*, **15**, 2, pp. 4–14.

STALLINGS, J. (1987) 'Implications from the research on teaching for teacher preparation', in HABERMAN, M. and BACKUS, J. (Eds) *Advances in Teacher Education, Vol. 3*, Norwood, NJ, Ablex, pp. 57–74.

WAXMAN, H.C. and WALBERG, H.J. (1986) 'Effects of early field experiences', in RATHS, J.D. and KATZ, L.G. (Eds) *Advances in Teacher Education, Vol. 2*, Norwood, N.J, Ablex, pp. 165–184.

ZEICHNER, K. (1987) 'The ecology of field experience: Toward an understanding of the role of field experiences in teacher development', in HABERMAN, M. and BACKUS, J. (Eds) *Advances in Teacher Education, Vol. 3*, Norwood, NJ, Ablex, pp. 94–117.

ZEICHNER, K. and TABACHNICK, B. (1985) 'The development of teacher perspectives: Social strategies and institutional control in the socialization of beginning teachers', *Journal of Education for Teachers*, **11**, pp. 1–25.

ZIMPHER, N. (1987) 'Current trends in research on university supervision of student teaching', in HABERMAN, M. and BACKUS, J. (Eds) *Advances in Teacher Education, Vol. 3*, Norwood, NJ, Ablex, pp. 118–150.

8 Narrative and Story in Teacher Education

D. Jean Clandinin

Introduction

> Current research on women often focuses on a single aspect or stage of life. Dissection is an essential part of scientific method and it is particularly tempting to disassemble a life composed of odds and ends, to describe the pieces separately. (Bateson, 1989, p. 10)

In *Composing a Life*, Bateson draws our attention to the importance of looking more holistically at our lives. She emphasizes the temptation of trying to make sense of pieces of our lives without understanding the narrative wholes in which the pieces are embedded. While Bateson is looking at women's lives, her words have particular significance for teacher education. Too often we look at teacher education as separate from the ongoing lives of teachers and student teachers. We pull out the years of teacher education to examine them. In so doing, we separate teacher education experiences from the pasts and futures of our student teachers' lives. We do not create spaces to acknowledge either the ways they have already written their lives prior to teacher education or to the ways they continue to live their stories in the context of teacher education. Bateson's words taken into the teacher education context highlight the importance of making sense of teachers' and student teachers' lives as narratives of experience, a living-out of the stories we tell ourselves in order to make meaning of our experience.

In our work with teachers (Connelly and Clandinin, 1988) we came to understand our own lives as teachers and researchers as well as the lives of teachers, student teachers and children narratively. Our work on narratives of experience draws attention to the broad sweep of our lives, to the ways our pasts are connected to our presents and futures as we live out and tell our stories. Looking at life as narrative or storied allows us to see the unities, continuities and discontinuities, images and rhythms in our lives. We take the view that one of the basic human forms of experience of the world is as story and that the storied quality of experience is both unconsciously restoried in life and consciously restoried, retold and relived through processes of reflection (Connelly and Clandinin, 1990).

> Narrative, for us, is the study of how humans make meaning of experience by endlessly telling and retelling stories about themselves that both refigure the past and create purpose in the future. Deliberately storying and restorying one's life or a group or cultural story is, therefore, a fundamental method of personal and social growth: it is a fundamental quality of education. (Connelly and Clandinin, 1990, p. 24)

Our use of the terms 'narrative' and 'story' draws on distinctions that other researchers have developed. In social science research the two terms are often collapsed with no great loss of precision. Polkinghorne (1988, p. 13), for example, reviews possible uses of both terms and concludes by treating them as equivalent — a position close to that adopted by Carr (1986). We have an in-between usage. When referring to participant situations (such as classroom field records and interview data) we tend to use 'story' to talk about particular situations and 'narrative' to refer to longer term life events. Everyday speech patterns modify this loose distinction and we would more often say 'deliberately storying and restorying one's life ...' rather than 'deliberately narrating and renarrating one's life...'. We would, however, follow Carr and Polkinghorne here and treat the two expressions as equivalent. When we refer to research, research method and researchers we use the term 'narrative' exclusively. For example, we would say 'narrative researchers, as Mishler (1986) shows, are engaged in the collection of stories when conducting interviews'. Our ideas on narrative method are elaborated in Connelly and Clandinin (1990).

Personal Practical Knowledge as Narratively Constructed Knowledge

To speak of teachers' knowledge of schools and classrooms as personal practical knowledge (Clandinin, 1986; Connelly and Clandinin, 1988) is to capture the idea of experience in a way that allows us to talk about teachers as knowledgeable and knowing persons. We see personal practical knowledge as in the person's past experience, in the person's present mind and body and in the person's future plans and actions. It is knowledge that reflects the individual's prior knowledge and acknowledges the contextual nature of that teacher's knowledge. It is a kind of knowledge carved out of, and shaped by, situations; knowledge that is constructed and reconstructed as we live out our stories and retell and relive them through processes of reflection.

Our work to this point has explored experienced and novice teachers' personal practical knowledge. We do this experientially and biographically by understanding teachers' knowledge as constructions and reconstructions of their life narratives. We see this storying and restorying of each of our lives as going on in our work as teachers and researchers.

Narrative inquiry as research method builds on this process of growth, that is, on these constructions and reconstructions of personal practical knowledge as we story and restory our lives. Narrative inquiry is the storying and restorying of our narratives of educational experience. The narrative account of an educational event that we wrote as researchers constituted a restorying of that event. We saw those accounts, at least to the extent that they were a restorying of the event, as on a continuum with the processes of reflective restorying that goes on in each of our educational lives. We came to see narrative inquiry as going on, therefore, both in researchers' work as well as in each of our educational lives. It is, therefore, less a matter of the application of a scholarly technique to understanding phenomena than it is a matter of 'entering into' the phenomena and partaking of them. For us, we saw narrative as part of the phenomena of educational experience.

In this chapter, I briefly outline the process of narrative inquiry in order to set a context for viewing teacher education as a kind of narrative inquiry for all of the involved participants, university teachers, cooperating teachers and student teachers. In this work, I offer a view of teacher education as a way of composing our lives as teachers, a way to not disassemble but to bring back a more holistic way of seeing experience and teacher education. Seeing teacher education as narrative inquiry is, for me, a way to connect our pasts as children and students in school to our present experiences as student teachers, cooperating teachers and university teachers with our imagined future experiences.

This chapter offers an account of a particular narrative inquiry into teacher education. In the 1989–1990 academic year, a group of university teachers, cooperating teachers and student teachers worked together in order to explore an alternative approach to teacher education as narrative inquiry. This chapter describes how we conceived of teacher education as narrative inquiry and illustrates these ideas through a telling of one student's story in the program. The story of Julie illustrates the storying and restorying between one university teacher and one student teacher as we worked together in the inquiry. I attempt to highlight the growth and change as we both came to new ways of living our stories. The story also highlights the tensions as individuals live out their stories embedded within social, cultural and institutional narratives.

The Process of Narrative Inquiry

Prior to giving an account of teacher education as narrative inquiry, I briefly outline the process of narrative inquiry as we have engaged with it in our research. (More detailed accounts are presented in Connelly and Clandinin,

1990, and Clandinin and Connelly, 1991). Briefly stated, we have noted that narrative is both phenomenon and method. Narrative names the structured quality of experience to be studied and it names the patterns of inquiry for its study. In narrative inquiry, we say that people lead storied lives and tell stories of those lives and narrative researchers describe such lives, collect and tell stories of them and write narratives of experience.

We see our work as narrative inquirers as staying open to continually assessing the multiple levels (temporally continuous and socially interactive) at which the inquiry proceeds. The complexity of staying open to the multiple levels becomes apparent when we realize that people are both living their stories in an ongoing experiential text and telling their stories in words as they reflect upon life and explain themselves to others. For the researcher, this is the smallest portion of the complexity, since a life is also a matter of growth toward an imagined future and, therefore, involves re-storying and attempts at reliving. A person is, at once, then, engaged in living, telling, retelling and reliving stories. We have begun to work with teachers and other practitioners to give accounts of the storying and restorying that goes on in each of our lives. For example, in work with Stephanie, a primary teacher, I construct stories that illustrate how her image of the classroom as home is central to her storying and restorying of her classroom practices (Clandinin, 1986). Similarly, in our work with Phil, a school administrator, we illustrate the narrative unity of community that is a unifying thread through his storying and restorying (Clandinin and Connelly, 1991).

The possible entanglements of seeing and describing story in the everyday actions of teachers and children is particularly acute in the tellings and retellings for it is here that temporal and social-cultural horizons are set and reset. As narrative researchers we add to the complexity of the process for, as researchers, we become part of the process. Researchers' narratives are lived, told and retold in the research process. Thus the narratives of participants and researchers become, in part, shared narrative constructions and reconstructions through the inquiry.

Narrative method involves participant observation, shared work in a practical setting. The process is a joint living out of two persons' narratives, researcher and practitioner, so that both participants are continuing to tell their own stories but the stories are now being lived out in a collaborative setting. We see the initial process of beginning to work together as an ethical matter, a negotiation of a shared narrative unity.

We have shown how successful negotiation and the application of principles do not guarantee a fruitful study. The reason, of course, is that collaborative research constitutes a friendship. In everyday life, the idea of friendship implies a sharing, an interpenetration of two or more persons' spheres of experience. Mere contact is acquaintanceship, not friendship. The same may be said for collab-

orative research which requires a close relationship akin to friendship. Relationships are joined, as MacIntyre (1981) implies, by the
narrative unities of our lives. (Clandinin and Connelly, 1988, p. 281)

When we conceive of negotiation of entry in this way, we highlight the way
narrative inquiry occurs within collaborative relationships among researchers and practitioners (Connelly and Clandinin, 1990). Here I want
to emphasize that in the process of beginning to live the shared story
of narrative inquiry, the researcher needs to be aware of constructing a
relationship in which both voices are heard.

In narrative work on teachers' personal practical knowledge, data ori-
ginated in researcher observation, participant observation of practice and
observations by other participants, as well as through personally reflective
methods such as journal keeping, story telling, letter writing and autobio-
graphical work such as those involved in the writing of personal annals and
chronicles. In the research process, the researcher adds his or her own
reflective voice. For example, the researcher responded to teachers' stories
with questions about why the story was told in the way it was. By answering
the researcher's question, the participants were able to penetrate more
deeply to other experiences to trace the emotionality attached to their
particular way of storying events and this, from the point of view of research, also constituted data.

Movement from experience to researcher and practitioner field notes,
transcripts, documents and descriptive storying of the experienced narrative,
to a mutual reconstruction of a narrative account, characterizes the process
of narrative inquiry. Both researchers and practitioners are participants in
the research and, as such, engage in the collaborative process. Both work
through a mutual reconstruction of the telling of the story in practice that
has been captured in field notes, transcripts and documents. The narrative
inquiry process is a process of data collection, mutual narrative interpretation by practitioners and researchers, more data collection and further
narrative reconstruction. The narrative inquiry process itself is a narrative
one of storying, restorying and restorying again.

In narrative inquiry we offer ways of telling individuals' stories —
researcher's *and* participant's — as embedded within particular cultures and
histories. Accounts of how the individual is shaped by the larger professional knowledge context and also the ways in which the professional knowledge
context has been reshaped in the unique situation in which the individual
lives and works are constructed. Therefore, in narrative inquiry we both
understand and try to give an account of the ways in which the individual is
shaped by the situation and shapes the situation in the living out of the story
and in the storying of the experience.

There are many risks, dangers and abuses of narrative (Connelly and
Clandinin, 1990), including difficulties that arise such as 'narrative smoothing' (Spence, 1986). However, another risk that becomes particularly appar-

ent as we lived out our narrative inquiry in teacher education was the construction of a story by the university teacher-researcher that could be given as a kind of script to student teachers. In situations where some participants have been traditionally silenced, as student teachers have been, this risk becomes particularly acute.

One purpose of narrative inquiry is to foster reflection and restorying on the part of all participants in the inquiry. The first, and central, contribution lies in the interactive relations between practitioner and researcher that lead to a mutual, collaborative telling and retelling of the stories of the participants — both practitioner and researcher. This leads to a consideration of the way in which participation in a narrative inquiry opens participants to understanding change in their practices (Clandinin, 1989; Connelly and Clandinin, 1988). This change and growth occurs for all participants for no-one emerges unchanged from this process. We had begun to explore the ways in which change in practice occurs for teachers and researchers within the collaborative relationships of narrative inquiry as a process of 'giving back a story' (Connelly and Clandinin, 1985).

Teacher Education as Narrative Inquiry

Our insights into understanding narrative inquiry as an educative process that facilitates change and growth through reflective storying and restorying lead us to conceptualize teacher education as narrative inquiry. Some colleagues, both practising teachers and university teachers, worked together to explore the possibility of making sense of teacher education as narrative inquiry. In our inquiry we wanted to explore ways of constructing teacher education that would allow each of us, student teachers, cooperating teachers and university teachers, to tell our stories and, through the collaborative inquiry, to envisage new ways to tell and live our stories in teaching practice. We saw ourselves as engaged in a process of becoming attuned to hearing our own stories as they were lived out in our practice; to hearing others' stories as they were lived out in their practice; and, in hearing our stories as they were given back by other participants in the program, to see possibility for new stories of classroom practice and teacher education. We also wanted to stay attentive to the ways in which the cultural, historical and institutional narratives shaped the telling and living out of our new stories of teacher education.

Making sense of teacher education in this way allowed us to explore the personal knowledge of student teachers and to work with them in collaborative, supportive working relationships as their personal knowledge was made practical in classroom and school situations. As student teachers constructed and reconstructed their knowing, we, as university teachers and cooperating teachers, also engaged in a reflective restorying. We saw ourselves as engaged in learning to hear and tell our own stories as we worked with students in our classrooms and classes. Our work with them both helped us to see the stories we were living and telling even as their participation with us shaped the new stories we were learning to tell.

Our ideas of teacher education as narrative inquiry were shaped by what we understood it meant to engage both in a collaborative relationship and, within that relationship, to respond to another's story. The idea from our work as researchers seemed to fit with the kinds of teaching-learning relationships we were attempting to establish in our exploration of teacher education as narrative inquiry. We wanted to pay close attention to relationships between student teachers, university teachers and cooperating teachers that were akin to friendships, relationships that would be joined by the narrative unities constructed through our shared work.

Giving Back Stories: A Narrative Response

Notions about our collaborative relationships led us to explore the ideas of response. We had written about entering into another's story by becoming a participant in the shared story lived out in practice. We had only begun to explore the question of response. What did it mean to offer a response to another's story? What constituted a response that allowed space for all participants' stories? What kind of response allowed for a mutual reconstruction of all participants' stories? We were informed by the work of Belenky and her colleagues, who wrote about what they called a connected teacher:

> As a teacher, she believed she had to trust each student's experience, although as a person or a critic she might not agree with it. To trust means not just to tolerate a variety of viewpoints, acting as an impartial referee, assuring equal air time to all. It means to try to connect, to enter into each student's perspective. (Belenky *et al.*, 1986, p. 227)

Belenky draws attention to the importance of trying to respond from the perspective of the other, suggesting an attempt to understand the other's way of knowing. While we recognized the importance as educators of hearing the students' voices, we wanted the relationship between university teacher, student teacher and cooperating teacher to be educative for all participants, that is, to include space for all participants' stories. Bateson allowed us a way to make sense of what we wanted to do. She wrote that:

> Today, more than twenty years later, I see the next step in the concept of response. It is interesting that, in spite of the different emphasis, the word 'response' provides the etymology of 'respon-

sibility', whose central place in women's ethical sensitivities Carol Gilligan has so eloquently investigated. (Bateson, 1989, p. 234)

Bateson drew our attention to the ethical side of response and what it means to respond. It became important for us to consider how our response, that is, our way of connecting both the story given and the story given back, was a question of moral responsibility. Gilligan's work with young girls helped us think about our responses as moral.

> Yet to open oneself to another person creates great vulnerability, and thus the strength of girls' desire for relationship also engenders the need for protection from fraudulent relationships and psychic wounding. (Gilligan, Lyons and Hanmer, 1990, p. 21)

As we worked together, we came to understand the way shared stories were given and given back in the context of relationships. It was important to understand our responses as moral.

We also realized that the stories given back, the responses, were not only personal in the sense of coming from our own narratives of experiences, but were also embedded in particular social, cultural and institutional narratives. Not only our stories but our responses to others' stories were set within all of the contexts in which our stories were lived and told.

Reading and hearing others' stories became ways to help us hear our own stories and to understand the ways our stories are embedded in social and cultural stories. Bateson illustrated how reading others' stories help us become aware of our own when she wrote:

> Women today read and write biographies to gain perspective on their own lives. Each reading provokes a dialogue of comparison and recognition, a process of memory and articulation that makes one's own experience available as a lens of empathy. We gain even more from comparing notes and trying to understand the choices of our friends. (Bateson, 1989, p. 4)

Bateson's words also helped us see other possible ways of considering response. We came to see that it is from hearing the questions of our friends and teachers, that is, from within our trusted relationships that we learn to see new possibilities in living our stories. Her words drew our attention again to thinking about new possibilities for all participants, not only for students.

Initially we thought of our work as teacher educators, both university teachers and cooperating teachers, as giving back student teachers' stories. However, our work became a three-way dialogue between student teacher, cooperating teacher and university teacher in which stories were given and given back between all participants. These three-way dialogues were similar to the kinds of response we had given and received in discussion and narrative accounts written to and with, participants in our research projects. These given back stories picked up on ongoing narrative threads in a person's life and offered back other possible interpretations of these stories.

In our study of teacher education as narrative inquiry we struggled with the complexity of response for not only did university teachers, cooperating teachers and student teachers give back each other's stories but so did children, other colleagues, other staff members, parents and so on. These connected responses, these given-back stories, allowed us to see new narrative threads and tensions in all of our stories. Each of us began to see our work as teachers working with children in uncertain contexts as always living and telling, reliving and retelling our stories. We felt, as Bateson noted, that we needed 'to reinvent' ourselves 'again and again in response to a changing environment' (Bateson, 1989, p. 17).

As we worked together in the inquiry, we saw that each of our lives was being restoried through having our stories given back by others in our classroom and university contexts. Distinctions of role between student teacher, cooperating teacher and university teacher faded as we learned to hear the response of the other, to make sense of the new insights we had into our own storied lives. There were many tensions as we struggled to do this for we were living out our new stories within institutional narratives where teacher-student relationships are not founded on assumptions of equality and mutuality and where the constraints of time, position, power and evaluation shaped our collaboration. We struggled to establish relationships that would provide all of us with 'experiences of mutuality, equality and reciprocity' (Belenky *et al.*, 1986, p. 38). For student teachers and cooperating teachers who have often seen themselves as less important and less valued than university teachers, it was a difficult ongoing struggle to live new but connected stories within traditional institutional narratives.

Paley's (1990) description of Jason, a little boy in kindergarten, captures something of the feeling we all experienced at some time over the year.

> Jason, finally, has figured out his own way to use his most precious possession and private fantasy to enable him to play with others. He has, in a real sense, come home. Which is to say, school is starting to feel like home. He can breathe deeply and open the doors of his helicopter house to others. (Paley, 1990, p. 146)

Paley, in her description of Jason, gave us a way to express our struggle to learn to work together. We too found ways to open our 'doors' to each other, to share our stories and to hear them given back so we could begin to live them with new possibilities.

Giving Back Julie's Story

The following fragment of a story illustrates one instance of giving back a story in the context of teacher education as narrative inquiry. We have called it Julie's story. Julie was a student teacher in our program who worked in a Grade 3–4 classroom. One of the assignments in our program was to follow one child's development in mathematics for a short period of time. In her work on this assignment, Julie chose to follow a small group of boys who were working on a task that her cooperating teacher called the house project, a project in which the boys were to figure out how to design and cost out a house given a certain set of constraints. This was an enrichment task in the classroom. Julie advised me she was going to work with this group of boys as they worked on the house project. We talked very little about the project in our seminar although, as students worked on their assignments, many did discuss them with me or other instructors. In the first months of the project, Julie and I attempted to establish what I thought was a collaborative relationship. We engaged in an ongoing journal dialogue and met on a weekly basis in a seminar group. However, evaluation, an important thread in the institutional narrative of teacher education, had not become an apparent tension in what I thought was a relationship of mutuality, equality and reciprocity.

In November, Julie gave me her first paper, one she had written on her work with the boys. The paper was a mixture of transcribed notes from the boys' conversations interspersed with various quotations from learning theory texts and quotations from theoretical resources on mathematics learning. I was surprised for I had expected something much different from Julie. My surprise caused me to reflect on what I had expected. I had expected a paper that talked about the particular boys, the particular task and what she had learned from the experience. I gave back in my response to her paper a story of distance from the children, of lack of connection with the subject matter and a lack of her voice as she hid behind the various theoretical formulations displaying a kind of what Belenky *et al.* (1986) would call 'received knowing'. Julie was angry with me and with herself but she was able to begin to make sense of the given-back story. I began to be aware of the institutional narratives and the ways evaluation shaped and constrained the collaborative relationship that Julie and I were attempting to construct. Julie had, in the face of a university assignment, completed a paper that drew on quotations from experts and that silenced her own voice, accounts of her own narrative knowing.

We talked and wrote and responded to each other in her journal over the next months. Julie's story of mathematics began to emerge. Several months later, in April, she gave me a second paper that offered another account of her story with the young boys. It was a story that began with Julie's story of mathematics, a story of lack of connection, of fear, of humiliation in which she endured teachers who held up her papers as inadequate and of summer holidays spent practising mathematics 'facts'. It was also a story in which she learned to depend on friends to explain to her what mathematics was all about, to help her make the connections to a subject matter story that seemed distant from her. As she retold her own story of learning mathematics, she saw how she had relived that story in her relations with the boys and mathematics. In rewriting the paper she now began to see her choice of working with the house project in new ways as she wrote about wanting to see what would happen when children were allowed to work with their peers on mathematics projects and when mathematics seemed more relevant to real life.

As Julie retold her story of mathematics as a learner and her story of working with the young boys, she made more sense of the way her old story had been relived in the work with the house project. She had not been able to find a connection to either the boys who were doing the project nor to mathematics as a subject matter. She was reliving her story of lack of connection, of silence.

Julie came to understand her story of learning to be a teacher this year as one in which she needed to learn to live a new story of mathematics in order to teach it. She began to involve herself in educational situations, courses in which she could explore a new story of herself as a learner of mathematics. But she also became interested in exploring her experience of mathematics within the context of the larger story of girls and mathematics and science learning. She began to research the topic in the literature and to talk to her female colleagues about their experiences. She began to explore, with her cooperating teacher, her feelings of the need for her voice to be heard in the classroom and the ways in which the young girls in the classroom needed to have space for their voices to be heard as they tried to make connections to the subject matter of mathematics.

As I reflected on Julie's story then and now as I write this chapter, the ideas of giving back stories took on new meaning for me. In my work as a teacher educator, I understand the importance of staying open to other possible readings of story even as I recognize the difficulty of staying open to possibilities. It is a felt tension in how I construct the horizons of my knowing. The institutional narratives in which I am embedded become apparent as I try to live a new story of teacher education. Collaboration becomes particularly important in order that we might have a wide range of stories given back from many participants. The collaborative relationships help us become attuned to the tensions such as those evoked as the evaluation process became part of the stories that Julie and I were living out.

It was important for me to have my story of surprise at Julie's paper given back to me by other participants in our program. Their response caused me to wonder about young women who enter teacher education as received knowers and the challenge of having them become constructed knowers. But their responses also caused one to ask questions about my own lived story as a received knower. I also sensed the importance of telling stories such as my story with Julie so other readers might raise questions about their practices in teacher education. Other students and teachers might see reflections of their stories in the ways we have chosen to tell Julie's story. For us as we think about teacher education as narrative inquiry, we see again the ways in which narrative inquiry leads to growth and change, to educative possibilities.

Educative Possibilities in Narrative Inquiry

Practitioner-participant and researcher-participant goals in narrative inquiry (Clandinin and Connelly, 1991) are meaningful only within a larger social narrative shared by both. Practitioner and researcher continue to work, and so the restorying is expressed in reshaped relations with children, school, community, teachers and so on. A second goal for the researcher involves the more formal aspects of the story — a story in which the researcher has confidence may be read with meaning by others. We have written that the question of audience is what primarily separates the interests of researcher and practitioner-participant in narrative inquiry. The practitioner-participant, in the end, is storying his or her experience and so must live out the experience. The researcher, while also restorying his or her own experience wants others, an audience of other practitioners and researchers, to read narratively the one narrative presented in the research account. A third researcher goal is to develop theoretical constructs, which offer a language for thinking and talking about experience, practice and teacher knowledge.

As we reflect on teacher education as narrative inquiry we see the goals in educative terms. We want student teachers to learn to live their stories in practical situations and to see new possibilities for living out different stories than those they experienced as students. We also want cooperating teachers to live new stories in their practices with the children that allow for change and growth for them and the children. As cooperating teachers and university teachers we also want to live new ways of storying teacher education in our schools and universities.

There is, however, also a need to write narratives of our work in teacher education for a larger audience. We need to pay particular attention to how to write our accounts of teacher education as narrative inquiry and the ways in which such accounts should be read. Something of the spirit of action of the participants, students, teachers and university teachers needs to find a place in these stories. As in the accounts of research, issues of representation and audience are central concerns.

One purpose of narrative research is to have other readers raise questions about their practices, their ways of knowing. Narrative inquiries are shared in ways that help readers question their own stories, raise their own questions about practices and see in the narrative accounts stories of their own stories. The intent is to foster reflection, storying and restorying for readers. Rose (1983, p. 17) remarks that 'the work as a whole will suggest new truths especially the extent to which all living is a creative act of greater or less authenticity, hindered or helped by the fictions to which we submit ourselves'.

To be a reader of a narrative is to be drawn into a story, to find a place or way of seeing through participating in the story. Crites (1975, p. 26) reminds us that the completeness of a story consists:

> in the immediacy with which narrative is able to render the concrete particularities of experience. Its characteristic language is not conceptual but consists typically in the sort of verbal imagery we employ in referring to things as they appear to our senses or figure in our practical activities. Still more important the narrative form aesthetically reproduces the temporal tensions of experience, a moving present tensed between and every moment embracing a memory of what has gone before and an activity projected, underway.

Here Crites gives a sense of what narrative researchers try to capture in their narrative writing. They attempt to have readers understand enough of the participants' experiences so that they can share something of what the experience might have been for the participants. In order to do this a reader must make a genuine effort to share in the experience of the participants. It is something akin to what Elbow calls the 'believing game', 'an act of self-insertion' (1973, p. 149). At its best it is a dialogue that allows a reader to share some qualities of the participants' experience. Narrative researchers need to consider the ways in which readers are drawn into the narrative and see possibility for alternative possible stories.

These issues seem particularly important as we begin to tell stories of teacher education as narrative inquiry. We do not propose to offer solutions or models for teacher educators or student teachers. Rather, we want to tell the stories in ways that highlight the tensions between personal and institutional narratives, between university and cooperating teachers' stories and student teachers' stories, and through these stories to foster reflection on the ways individuals and institutions construct teacher education.

Acknowledgment

This work was supported in part by a grant from the Social Sciences and Humanities Research Council of Canada.

References

BATESON, M.C. (1989) *Composing a Life*, New York, The Atlantic Monthly Press.

BELENKY, M., CLINCHY, B., GOLDBERGER, N. and TARULE, J. (1986) *Women's Ways of Knowing*, New York, Basic Books.

CARR, D. (1986) *Time, Narrative and History*, Bloomington, Indiana University Press.

CLANDININ, D.J. (1986) *Classroom Practice: Teacher Images in Action*, London, Falmer Press.

CLANDININ, D.J. (1989) 'Developing rhythm in teaching: The narrative study of a beginning teacher's personal practical knowledge of classrooms', *Curriculum Inquiry*, **19**, 2, pp. 121–141.

CLANDININ, D.J. and CONNELLY, F.M. (1988) 'Studying teachers' knowledge of classrooms: Collaborative research, ethics and the negotiation of narrative', *Journal of Educational Thought*, **22**, 2A, pp. 269–282.

CLANDININ, D.J. and CONNELLY, F.M. (1991) 'Narrative and story in practice and research', in SCHÖN, D.A. (Ed.) *The Reflective Turn: Case Studies In and On Educational Practice*, New York, Teachers College Press, pp. 258–281.

CONNELLY, F.M. and CLANDININ, D.J. (1985) 'Personal practical knowledge and the modes of knowing: Relevance for teaching and learning', in EISNER, E. (Ed.) *Learning and Teaching the Ways of Knowing*, Eighty-fourth Yearbook of the National Society for the Study of Education, part 2, Chicago, University of Chicago Press, pp. 174–198.

CONNELLY, F.M. and CLANDININ, D.J. (1988) *Teachers as Curriculum Planners: Narratives of Experience*, New York, Teachers College Press.

CONNELLY, F.M. and CLANDININ, D.J. (1990) 'Stories of experience and narrative inquiry', *Educational Researcher*, **19**, 5, pp. 2–14.

CRITES, S. (1975) 'Angels we have heard', in WIGGINS, J.B. (Ed.) *Religion as Story*, Lanham, MD, University Press of America, pp. 26–63.

ELBOW, P. (1973) *Writing Without Teachers*, London, Oxford University Press.

GILLIGAN, C., LYONS, N. and HANMER, T. (Eds) (1990) *Making Connections: The Relational Worlds of Adolescent Girls at Emma Willard School*, Cambridge, MA, Harvard University Press.

MACINTYRE, A.C. (1981) *After Virtue: A Study in Moral Theory*, London, Duckworth.

MISHLER, E.G. (1986) *Research Interviewing: Context and Narrative*, Cambridge, MA, Harvard University Press.

PALEY, V. (1990) *The Boy Who Would Be A Helicopter*, Cambridge, MA, Harvard University Press.

POLKINGHORNE, D.E. (1988) *Narrative Knowing and the Human Sciences*, New York, State University of New York Press.

ROSE, P. (1983) *Parallel Lives*, New York, Vintage Books.

SPENCE, D.P. (1986) 'Narrative smoothing and clinical wisdom', in SARBIN, T.R. (Ed.) *Narrative Psychology: The Storied Nature of Human Conduct*, New York, Praeger, pp. 211–32.

9   Teaching for Reflection: Being Reflective

Antoinette A. Oberg and Sibylle Artz

Introduction

In any piece of writing in which a lot of oneself has been invested, there is
a story between the lines, and this chapter is no exception. Because it is
relevant to our topic and the topic of this book, we believe it is important to
tell how we came to write what we have in the way that we have, before we
share our experiences of teaching for reflection.

When Tom Russell and Hugh Munby first invited a chapter for this
book, I (Antoinette) was in the midst of reading the reflective journals
of the graduate students in my Curriculum Foundations class and was so
impressed with the questions they were asking themselves as teachers, that I
thought that I would write about their experiences as chronicled in their
writing. However, as I wrote to Tom and Hugh at the time, I was somewhat
dissatisfied at the prospect of saying, 'Look what happened here'. Even
comparing the paths of various students and the nature and quality of their
reflections seemed to miss an important dimension. I finally recognized what
that dimension was: the context in which all this was occurring, not the
context as given but the context as made. It was the context of the relationships between students and teacher, of the conceptualizations and con-
struals of what is and what might be, of the persons the students and teacher
were. And it was usually (though not always) the teacher who made the first
move to define that context by setting the tone, imagining the goals, orienting to the task in a certain way.

So I knew this chapter had to be about teaching rather than the results
of teaching. It had to tackle the questions, 'What is it to teach reflectively?'
and 'What is it to be a reflective teacher?' Of course, the setting would be
one in which the students were adults rather than children, and I (Antoinette) would be the teacher in question. The substance of this writing would
be my own experience of teaching for reflection. The aim would be to draw
out and to render into themes what is entailed in the sort of teaching that
makes intensive reflection possible.

The exercise is not a descriptive one, but a critical one. It requires intensive reflection on self as teacher — precisely the sort of reflection I request of my students. I must ask myself who I am, what I do, how I do it and with what implications when I invite students to become reflective about their practice. To work through such questions, I require a co-respondent, an other who understands but is not part of my quest (just as students require a respondent to their reflections). My hope is always that I may understand myself and my teaching more clearly as I see these reflected in the understanding of the other.

For me, this other has been Sibylle. She is also a teacher of adults (though not of teachers, but of battered women establishing their independence by returning to the workforce) and she also aims to deepen her students' awareness of that which grounds their words and actions, of what is implicit in the way they live their lives. Through other projects we have done together, we have come to realize that we share common interests, that is, that we stand on similar ground ('interest' coming from *inter esse*: to be or to stand in the midst of something). We are both interested in what it is to place oneself as a teacher in front of students and to invite them to become reflective. We are both interested in questions of meaning rather than questions of procedure and in understanding our own subjectivity in the context of our practice as reflective educators.

We agreed to work together at the task of understanding ourselves as educators. Having located reflective teaching in the complex mix of relationships and structures that are present in any given educational setting, we could do no more (and no less) than talk about what went on in our settings, what we pondered, what we struggled with and how we attempted to come to terms with our experiences and reflections. And so, in this chapter, we present our conversations about our experiences of teaching for reflection.

These conversations are to be understood as discourse and as action. They both express and show our understanding of what it means to be reflective in and about practice. In the process, we implicate ourselves as subjects who are creating ourselves in particular ways in particular times and places. Thus the form in which we present ourselves in this paper is as significant as what we say. We have presented conversations rather than arguments because our intent is to avoid abstracting, analyzing and concluding (in the same way we believe these must be avoided with our students if reflection is not to be foreclosed). We are not delivering already-formed understandings but inviting readers to enter our conversations wherever our reflections touch upon theirs.

Readers accustomed to analytic essays may experience a certain amount of frustration with our chapter, which may appear loosely structured, open-ended and inconclusive. The meanings may not be obvious, and our leaving openings for readers to participate in making sense of what we share may seem more like an abdication than an invitation. We have attempted to take these possibilities into account. With the help of Hugh Munby, who played devil's advocate for us, we have written into our conversations the anti-cipated concerns of such readers and our responses to them. Readers interested in other accounts of Oberg's work are referred to Oberg (1989, 1990), Oberg and Blades (1990) and Oberg and Underwood (in press).

About the Conversations

Sibylle and I met every week for three months to talk about our teaching. We had no preset agenda but we moved naturally from talking about how we would actually produce this chapter to sharing with each other stories and insights, questions and misgivings about our teaching, stimulated by our most recent class sessions.

I met with my classes in a typical sterile university classroom; Sibylle met with hers in downtown Victoria, British Columbia, in a complex of old brick buildings transformed into a shopping and office square. From the beginning, we knew our collaboration would work because neither of us understood reflection as acquired behaviours or skills; rather, we saw it as an attitude, an approach that permeates everything, something one becomes. It was not that either one of us had set out to learn how to 'teach reflectively'. Each of us was in the habit of standing in the midst of our practice with questions rather than certainties, looking back on what had transpired to deepen our understanding.

As we talked, we tape recorded and then transcribed by hand. Our conversations wandered, pulled this way and that by the enthusiasm of the moment — not off-topic, but not in a straight line towards a comforting conclusion. When we began to read the transcripts, we wondered how to give some shape to what we had accumulated. Eventually, the pages and pages of dialogue began to cohere around three themes of pedagogic significance: the place of the teacher, the difficulty of evaluating another's reflection, and what it means to be oriented or to have an orientation.

We rearranged our conversations to appear in three parts according to the three pedagogical themes we had identified. We refined the language only minimally and replaced words we misspoke with ones closer to the meanings we were trying to develop. These changes we could not avoid making as we reflected on the transcripts, and we felt free to make them because our words were not 'data' but illustrations of ourselves and our understandings, which are always and forever evolving.

You are invited to enter the vortex of our thought wherever you can. Do not expect a smooth ride or a predictable ending. You will have to work to keep your balance, to see through what appears superficial to what is going on underneath the surface. We ask that you suspend disbelief and judge this work on its own terms. For our part, we will try to be clear about what we are doing.

The Place of the Teacher

SA: Where shall we begin?

AO: I think we should begin with subjectivity. It's our subjectivity that comes to the fore during reflection. Who do we make ourselves out to be as human beings? Since the Cartesian move has separated us from the world and elevated objectivity to the status of a god, we need to reconnect ourselves to the world, literally, starting from the hermeneutic stance that the world is already intricate, whole, given before we do anything to it. What we are seeking is our connection with the world and with each other. When I'm trying to understand myself, I'm doing that *in relation* with you, another subject, not an object. I accord you the same status as I accord myself, as someone who has the capacity to know and is to a large extent unknown and becomes known in relationship. It's subject and subject, not subject and object.

SA: Yes, I think that this is key. Not only do we work with each other in this way, but we work in exactly the same way with our students.

AO: How do you work with your students?

SA: I introduce a series of topics which are mostly about concrete communication skills. The topics become lenses through which we look at our experiences together. So, for instance, if we talk about learning styles, we try to come to an understanding of each other through the structures offered in the literature on learning styles. The topic is no longer learning styles, but how I can understand myself and you better, now that I know how we each approach learning.

AO: So are your classes mostly activities and discussions?

SA: Yes and no. The discussion is dependent on a shared understanding of the material which I bring to the classes, so it's very important when I introduce a topic that I do it in a way that invites and welcomes discussion. I don't want to act in ways which imply that I am handing out expert knowledge which students are expected to hand back to me. So, for example, if we're dealing with handling conflict, we may do an activity together that centers us in the material and then we talk extensively about the meanings and implications of the experience and the material for each of us.

AO: My classes are a bit different. Most of the reflective work doesn't take place in the class as it does for you; it happens in the students' journal writing. In the journals students begin with descriptions from their everyday practice which then become the focus of their reflection. They are encouraged to seek out who they are as educators and what their educational practice is grounded in. The class discussions and the readings are all intended to further this questioning. So, in my classes as in yours, the topic of the day becomes a 'view-finder' through which people focus on their own experiences.

SA: Talking about teaching in this way brings up the issue of psychotherapy as a label that could be used as a way of understanding what it is that we do.

AO: Although my style of teaching has often been seen as analogous to therapy, it is not really my intention to interpret my teaching or yours in psychological terms.

SA: That's not an interpretation I want to use here either. All too often, psychotherapy or therapeutic teaching is a name given to an approach that conceives of teaching as an intervention with students in order to correct a deficit. Are we there to 'operate' on students in order to 'improve' the condition they are in, are we there because we 'know better' and must seek to change our students, or are we there for some very different reasons?

AO: I see myself leaving space so that people can get in touch with what they are doing and how that is shaped by their context, become aware of what kinds of people they are making themselves and their students into, and come to an understanding of how that is part of a whole life. Is that therapy? Is that something one can even give a name to?

SA: I don't know if I can name what I do exactly. The course I teach is called Life Skills, but what I'm actually working on with my students is the development of a voice, and how to speak in their own voices, all the way from being able to understand their own orientation to learning through to being able to handle confrontation and conflict. The most important thing is that we work together so that each individual can learn to speak in her own voice.

AO: That's quite similar to what I'm doing even if the way in which I do it is different. You work at finding a voice through engaging your students verbally and on a personal level in the classroom. I engage my students in written dialogue. The 'topic' if you will, is no longer the course content, but rather how we, teacher and student together, engage each other in order to discover ourselves in relation to each other and to the materials we bring to the course. That may be described by some as therapy.

SA: What does the word 'therapy' really mean?

AO: The dictionary (Webster's *New Collegiate Dictionary*, 1965, p. 1210) defines therapy as a remedial treatment, an approach designed to bring about social adjustment. That's quite instrumental. But it also says that the word originates from the Greek 'therapeuein', which means 'to attend', 'to treat'. That's better. It can be read as meaning 'to attend'.

SA: Well, I'm quite uncomfortable with the idea of myself as someone who adjusts others socially or applies treatment, but I like the notion of attending. It's a bit like standing by.

AO: Yes, that's interesting, 'to attend'. That's like Heidegger's 'attunement', and that's what Max van Manen's (in press) work on 'thoughtfulness' is derived from.

SA: Yes, I'm more at home with notions of attending, of attunement and of thoughtfulness. I don't want to engage in a technological, instrumental interaction with my students or anyone else.

AO: I think that in the instrumentally conceived teaching situation we are trying to deal primarily with external, received knowledge, a canonized body of knowledge that has been construed as somehow objectively true and universally relevant, while in our type of teaching situation we're dealing primarily with the display and interplay of multiple subjectivities.

SA: Yes, I think that might be the difference. I see that in a teaching situation like ours the relationship between teacher and student becomes part of what is taught, and in that case who and what we are becomes a major question.

AO: But remember, when I was talking to Hugh Munby, he warned us that speaking about teaching in this way might be considered by some as simple-minded, not clear enough, perhaps requiring more explication and examination in a scholarly fashion than we could do justice to in a conversation such as this one.

SA: Yes, I remember his questioning that. What did you say to him about that?

AO: Well, I said that this piece is never going to have the texture of an analytic essay because what we are showing here arises quite differently from the way an analytic essay arises. Our teaching has come to be what it is not by reflecting upon what others have said about teaching and joining it in some way with what each of us has experienced. We don't proceed that way at all, neither in our teaching, nor in our relationship to each other. The main reason we're proceeding conversationally is that we're not starting with external texts. We're starting and staying very close, quite intentionally, to our own experiences. The reason we think that is important is because precisely the quality of knowledge, the kind of knowledge and the source of knowledge that we're aiming for is to be found in reflection on our own discourse and actions. We're talking about knowledge that is retrieved from a critical look at experience, and that sort of knowledge doesn't take shape the way an analytical essay does. It looks simple-minded when you hold it up against a very well-worked out, well-grounded explanation of the issues, but its significance is quite different. Its significance is its location in relation to the personal. It isn't a question of analytical prowess; it's a question of who I am as teacher that makes the reflection possible. What I think I show is that I am not the person with the answers, nor even the one who sets the questions, but rather the one who prepares the ground for students to ask their own questions.

SA: In response to what you've just said, I feel a need to make it clear that I'm not aiming to push my students to 'spill their guts', to put it graphically.

AO: No, nor am I. I am not interested in pointed or public questioning of my students. I haven't done that in my teaching. My tendency has been to allow my students to choose what they write about and with whom they share their writing.

SA: Yes, I also prefer a more gentle invitation to share and reflect rather than challenging or confronting. It's important to me that my relationships, yours and mine for example, and mine with my students, be helpful, not harmful. My classes are about sharing all sorts of ways of knowing and coming to terms with oneself and the world. If people wish to share personal examples, fine, but I never demand it, nor do I make it a condition of participation or success. What's interesting is the amount of trust and involvement that builds up over time.

AO: Yes, I've found that too. And what seems to make it possible for me to ask the kinds of questions that precipitate deep reflection is that I have listened carefully and really heard what someone is trying to say.

SA: Yes. That kind of approach seems to be more like caring for people than being in charge or in control of them. I have the notion that teachers are really more trained to take charge than to take care.

AO: Absolutely, in much of teacher training the emphasis is on being in control. Sometimes that is the sole basis for evaluating success.

SA: Are you concerned with control at all in your class?

AO: No. I've written in my journal about the fact that I think of my classes as non-events. The emphasis is not on me and what I do at all, it's on my students.

SA: I have the impression that you create a very private and meaningful relationship with each of your students, and that as a teacher you are more a mentor.

AO: It's interesting that you should mention that word, especially in this context. The word 'mentor' actually has a history that goes back to the story of Mentor, a friend of Odysseus who was entrusted with the education of his son, Telemachus.

SA: So a mentor is someone you would trust to be an educator, someone who is capable of entering into an educational relationship.

AO: Yes. In my case, I offer myself as a mentor, but the choice lies with the student. It has to be the student's choice to take up what is offered. So the question is: 'What is the nature of the invitation, and what is the nature of the relationship that inspires the confidence to respond?'

SA: I think it's as we have already described it, an invitation to reflect, and an invitation to engage. I aspire to create that kind of experience in my class rather than to work at control.

AO: Yes, that's one of the big breakthroughs I made in the past year — to relinquish in one huge movement a great deal of the control I formerly retained, and give it over to my students.

SA: In responding to my students rather than controlling them, I've had to learn to listen to my inner voice, to attend to my own inner dialogue as I am teaching and allow myself to be guided by that. I've had to develop an ability not to overrule my inner voice when it gives me direction, but to attend to it carefully because it is often more able to see into the heart of things.

AO: Now that's exactly what I have to listen to when I respond to the journals that my students write. That is when my own experience comes into play because I see things in the journals that are significant to me, things that prompt me to ask questions. I used to hold back and I always wondered whether or not I should ask, should suggest that the writer might want to pursue this or that direction. But this year, I just asked my questions right out, and I think it was crucial. I think it resulted in a phenomenal move forward for many people.

SA: It seems to me you offered yourself just as you are and said to each student: 'In relation to you, this is who I am'.

AO: So what is it the instructor represents?

SA: Do you mean what does the instructor stand for?

AO: Yes. For me this is an important question, especially with the fragmentation of a field like Curriculum Studies and the dissolution of external authority in this field. What is it the instructor is presenting? The field itself is not simply an accumulation of uniform knowledge that the instructor-as-gatekeeper imparts to a passive audience whose duty it is to feed it back to her. The field has become a dynamic conversation among thinkers with very different orientations, emphasizing a variety of priorities. Is it possible for us to transcend this fragmentation?

SA: What do you mean 'transcend'?

AO: I mean, is there something that can lead to a convergence, a coming together with something beyond, something bigger than those who are converging; that can move us past our historicity, our limited viewpoint, into a larger truth?

SA: But is there this kind of truth, and where does this truth reside?

AO: Traditionally, it has been seen to reside in a spiritual or in a secular external authority. Truth has always resided outside the individual.

SA: So in the past we've always trusted in something outside ourselves which we've invested, often through belief or faith, with a greater power. We've had either religious or secular gods to turn to as our sources for truth. In order not to continue to substitute one external authority for another, one god for another, where can we go?

AO: It seems to me, we begin by holding in abeyance notions of external Truth with a capital T and try to work out our own understanding, and for that we go in precisely the opposite direction.

SA: To the self?

AO: Yes. But because we've always thought of authority as an external universal, we've therefore thought of self, by definition and in contrast with that, as shallow, unreliable, idiosyncratic, ephemeral, relative, subjective. It seems to me that that's because we haven't gone far enough. Stopping with self dissolves into solipsism. We have to keep on going past that, and when we do, it seems to me that we come to the other. So what we have is self and other, each providing the possibility for the other's self-understanding.

SA: So in turning away from the successive toppling of external gods, from the fallibilities found in received or canonized knowledge, we also turn away from being seduced by internal authority and unconnected subjective knowledge.

AO: Yes, the aim is not to allow transcendence to be replaced by immanence. I'd like to get beyond the either/or of choosing between the external and the internal, the self and the other, by continually remaining open and connected to both self and other.

SA: Yes, intuitively that has a lot of appeal for me, but I want to question that a bit more. The difficulty for me as a teacher is that it leaves unanswered the question of where to turn in order to judge what is right and true. I suppose I'm really concerned here with my personal use of authority and power. Am I to take my experience of connecting with a student as evidence that we have arrived at something that I am to invest with rightness? Am I to take the achievement of such resonance as meaningful, as signifying that we've reached beyond our limited viewpoints into a larger truth?

AO: What do you mean by that experience of resonance between student and teacher? Because if resonance is truly the experience of two people, each with their own understanding, finding that they share a kind of common ground, but each preserving independent status, isn't the risk considerably decreased that one will buy into the authority of the other? That is the really tough thing, isn't it, especially in an institutional context where the teacher is one of the people and the student is the other, because the relationship can so easily deteriorate into one in which the teacher has power over the student.

SA: Yes. And I question this whole thing also because I believe that it's possible to think I've connected with another when I may have just had my point of view validated, that is, found someone who agrees with me. I take seriously the problem of the power dynamic in the teacher-student relationship. I want to work with my students so that they have the power to understand, critically evaluate meaning, discern, and to decide for themselves what is to be done. I don't want to act in ways that compel agreement from them because they see me as the one who legitimates them by virtue of my position.

AO: I experience this kind of questioning daily. When I am using my judgment as I am reading my students' work trying to determine what it represents, and whether it's an example of the kind of probing that I'm asking for, I have to give a place to the knowledge that defines the field, and give students credit for mastering that generalized knowledge. It seems to me to be a continual movement between the particular and the general, the internal and the external. How do I decide what is the appropriate balance?

SA: So much seems to depend on where we start. I've noticed that with my students the particular can't seem to take shape until the general has been outlined. What I mean is that it's hard for my students to articulate their experiences until we have worked our way through some theoretical models of how people learn and experience the world.

AO: That's ironic, because I'm asking my students, who are more comfortable and proficient with general theories, to move away from the general and into the particular, to begin with their own experiences and not with theory, and that's what they find difficult.

SA: What is it we both hope to accomplish?

AO: I claim that my aim is that students should become reflective. I judge not what is revealed, but reflectiveness. I'm asking my students to throw their assumptions into question and to abandon the stance of theoretical knowing as the only valid kind of knowing, meaning that I want them to be concerned with their own reflections and responses rather than with giving me back in modified form the material I have shared with them.

SA: My aim is to stimulate an interest in awareness of the self. I think our intentions are not really very different.

AO: Talking about the role of the teacher in this way reminds me of another question Hugh asked. He wanted to know if the particular conversation we're having here is analogous to our own teaching, because we are, after all, two colleagues talking, and colleagues and students generally have very different power structures and very different understandings from teachers and students.

SA: That's an interesting question, especially because we are both colleagues and student and teacher at once since you are also my thesis supervisor. What did you say?

AO: Well, I said that it's analogous not so much in its structure, but in the kind of discourse it is. In fact, now that you remind me that we are teacher and student, I realize it is analogous in both structure and linguistic form. It's conversation and not didactic; it's not explanation. In that way this conversation is an analogy for the kind of interaction that is predominant in our classrooms. And that is part of what we're trying to say here. The reason that the role of teacher is an issue is precisely because we step aside from the notion of the teacher as the person who has the answer because she has a larger body of knowledge than the student, and whose role it therefore is to make that intelligible to the student through lecturing or demonstration or analytic processes or whatever. In contrast to that, we're relating to students as conversationalists. The students tell stories about their own experiences, and our response is a very natural human response to the story. My role as teacher is to keep listening and asking what is the significance of this, and what do you mean by this, and could you amplify this? Students respond as they will and I accept their responses. It is literally a conversation. With me it happens to be a conversation in writing, while with you it's actually a dialogue in which you and your students participate in the classroom.

SA: Yes, that's how it is, and it is also always a question of balance, a question of listening with deep involvement to my students and to myself, and of keeping in mind that I am there not to take power but to share it.

Evaluating Another's Reflection

SA: How do you arrive at a grade for your students?

AO: I look for evidence of reflection, of movement. I also question myself to see if I am placing unwarranted expectations on people so that only those who happen to resonate with my position are the ones who can accomplish anything I can respect.

SA: I have to watch that I don't harm people in my classes by making them feel stupid. It's a question of language for me. I have students in my classes who are wise in life experience, but very limited in their academic experience and often have limited vocabularies. I work with abuse survivors, so I also have to be sensitive to the possibility that what I say may trigger painful memories. All this affects the materials I choose and how I present them. I don't evaluate the students. In the end, they evaluate the class. In contrast to most teachers, I don't have to grade my students.

AO: I have a slightly different set of concerns. To begin with, I bring in materials which have the potential of expanding my students' knowledge of the curriculum field and will enable them to see more deeply into their own practice. For me the emphasis is not so much on people's capacity to understand the language, though in fact that is a concern. Language is a problem with the literature in Curriculum Studies. Some of it is filled with jargon and not very well written and therefore impenetrable. I feel constrained to use the literature because I am teaching a course in curriculum theory, and I feel an obligation to expose people to that literature. As well, in order for my students to be able to move to reflection they need a language. So I ask it of myself to bring materials to them that will help them find the right words at the right time. Now, I *do* have to grade my students, and this idiosyncratic use of materials that I encourage makes assigning grades quite problematic. If each student is truly encouraged to pursue self-understanding, then what criteria can be used to evaluate each member of a class fairly?

SA: Is this also a question of resonance?

AO: Yes, to some extent it is an attempt to create a convergence at the right time and place, a resonance, a feeling of being connected, but I do not prescribe what it is that students must feel connected with. That is up to each individual.

SA: So people's feelings are a definite part of this process?

AO: Perhaps more than anything, it's feeling that situates people so that they are receptive and experience themselves as capable of moving into reflection? Perhaps it happens because we're engaged not so much in judging our students but more in coming to an understanding of things with them? And here is where I think we as teachers have our role to play. The kind of self-awareness we're espousing is not the sort of thing that we can simply advocate only for our students; we have to exemplify it ourselves. We have to be questioning our questions at the same time as we're trying to address those questions. While we are looking at all the possible theoretical frames that may help our students perceive where they are, we have to be willing to look at ourselves through those same frameworks.

SA: So we have to know where we ourselves are coming from and know that we are taking a position?

AO: Yes. That is it. We have to be committed to our position, our orientation, and at the same time hold it tentatively in order to be open to shifting it.

SA: So we proceed, always conscious of how we put our intentions and meanings into language because it's there that our subjectivity is reflected. Hugh also had a question about all of this in his letter to us. He pointed out that in our use of terms like 'resonance', 'convergence' and 'connectedness', terms which simply rolled off our tongues, he found himself up against the same kind of difficulty with jargon that we ourselves discuss with regard to some of the opaque language to be found in the literature in Curriculum Studies. How can we remain clear, I wonder?

AO: I don't know if we always can be clear, especially at the outset. For example, Hugh and I, in our conversation about the first draft of this chapter, arrived at clarity by engaging each other. Hugh said an important thing about this sort of process. He told me that the more he asked me questions, the more my responses helped to show him what he needed to understand about what we were saying. I think that that statement points to how things have to go when we involve ourselves with each other in this way.

Being Oriented

AO: As I teach, the question that guides me is: 'What is being taken for granted here?'

SA: And I ask myself: 'How are we making sense of our experience?'

AO: If assumption and sense-making are what we are trying to unravel, we need to be critical of the processes we are using. I think we need to pay close attention to language.

SA: Are you saying that we have to begin with how we bring to language the things that occur for us as we teach?

AO: Yes. Soeffner (1985) argues that the existence of a language that can be recorded and gives the appearance of a discourse is the precondition for the existence of history, historicity and the possibility of spoken thought. Language itself makes possible certain dimensions of lived experience.

SA: So to say it again, but this time in a different context, our use of language, the words we choose to describe ourselves, our students, our experiences both affect how we experience these and point out our orientation?

AO: Yes, we touched on this earlier in terms of clarity, but it's also important in terms of an ability to be self-reflective. I believe that here, also, we have to be sensitive to how we bring our experiences to language.

SA: The struggle here is with knowing oneself, isn't it? Realizing that I do indeed have a position, an orientation through which I structure my experience, and that it permeates everything I do, including the way I speak about it.

AO: Yes, we all have a window on the world, and that's what I think we both want our students to come to understand, while, at the same time, continually coming to an understanding of our own.

SA: I also want my students to see clearly that their particular window is not the only one, and that it is not a matter of finding the right and best window. In a sense, one could say that that is my intent.

AO: But intent here surely isn't framed as an aim for provable improvement is it?

SA: No, not in an instrumental, measurable sense, but I am looking for a shift in consciousness, a broadening of awareness.

AO: So intention here describes the kinds of experiences students must be put in the way of, the materials and the subject matter, not what the students will learn.

SA: Yes, that's how I see it. I don't believe that I can define what students will learn.

AO: No, neither do I. I believe that what people learn can't be predetermined. In other words, the curriculum cannot be known until after the fact; I can predict only the materials.

SA: Materials are an important influence on what the curriculum becomes, as are the participants in the class. I have a student who has a high anxiety level and doesn't often come to class, but when she is there the curriculum is affected by her presence. For one thing, I teach differently when she is there and when she is not.

AO: Hmm. That raises important questions: 'To what extent is it appropriate to maneuver around a particular person in a class?' 'How do I as a teacher plan an environment, provide materials, devise a route so that students can both work through what they have to personally and also become able to get to the kind of writing I want them to do?'

SA: What do you look to when you're struggling with those questions?

AO: I find van Manen's notions of pedagogical tact and thoughtfulness helpful here. His notion is that in teaching, if I am sensitively attuned to the student with whom I am working, I act in a way that is called for by my being, as we said earlier, a mentor for this student. Looking back thoughtfully on this interaction, I attempt to discern where my response was appropriate and where it was inappropriate, thus contributing to my potential to act more tactfully in the future.

SA: That implies that what is done and how it is done is part and parcel of the person doing it.

AO: Yes, a teacher can only become more thoughtful and more tactful through continual reflection, which is always about something that has passed. I prepare myself for the next step through reflection, but I must look back to understand more deeply and thereby be ready for what is coming. I cannot know what it will be in advance.

SA: Teaching with that kind of an orientation becomes a continuous encounter with the self. It requires a certain flexibility and a willingness to let go. Each step is a moment of recognition and choice and a process that takes place within myself.

AO: In a sense, to understand my teaching I have to be willing to undergo a continuous examination of my self.

SA: Yes, but at the same time, I have to be willing to enter into a relationship with my students and to acknowledge and encourage

their self-understanding. I think the emphasis has to be on the relationship. I believe that people are able to come to terms with and
shift their positions if there is a sense of trust for the teacher. In your
case, trust is created through the private interaction of writing back
and forth. Each student has a private and personal relationship with
you and that builds confidence. It allows students to take risks in their
learning that they might not take in a more public forum.

AO: You know what this does, it totally reverses the premise in the
Canadian Journal of Education forum that writing for the professor is
writing for an inauthentic audience. There it is argued that when
students write assignments for their professors, they use 'superficial,
global and largely opaque' (Gelb and Dippo, 1989, p. 262) language,
presumably in an attempt to restate what they have gleaned from
authoritative texts. Neither the form nor the content is their own.
The writing is produced to please the professor but not to communicate something of importance to them. We, in contrast, are saying
that in our experience writing for the professor is exactly what gives
the writing depth, that having an interested audience who will respond to the substance of the writing, like a partner in a conversation, makes the writing that much more meaningful.

SA: Is writing for the professor the key thing here?

AO: Yes and no. What's key is the relationship between the teacher and
the students and the focus of the writing on students' own practice.
As we said before, it's not that the teacher already possesses a body
of knowledge which the students are expected to master. It's not even
that the students are to emulate the teacher. Instead, the teacher
embodies a reflective orientation in her practice, which is an invitation to students to orient themselves reflectively in their practice.

Epilogue

What do we see when we look back critically on our conversations? What
does the form and content of our discourse reveal? We see a preoccupation
with the practical and a valuing of knowledge gained by direct experience
over knowledge gained from others. We see a concern for our relationship
with and responsibility toward our students. We see a desire to escape the
encapsulation in empirical-analytic language and to move beyond dichoto-
mous thinking and the quest for an absolute. We examine each of these in
turn.

Our concerns in the preceding dialogue have been primarily practical:
How do we behave as reflective teachers? If we are not dispensers of
knowledge or guides to its discovery, what place do we occupy in the
classroom and by what right? How do we presume to evaluate the reflective
activities of our students? To what extent do we belie our own intentions by

our actions in the classroom? As we look back critically on the way we addressed these concerns in our conversations, we see that we are divesting ourselves of the authority of external texts as the only valid source of knowing. We find the knowledge we evolve from our own experiences settles much deeper and lasts much longer than the knowledge we borrow from others. Knowledge originating externally becomes permanently ours only when we appropriate it into our quest for understanding our own experience, that is, when our own interest rather than the structure of the knowledge organizes our understanding.

This way of speaking about knowledge and understanding shows the grounding of our commitment to reflective practice. We believe, as did Heidegger (1962), that much of everyday practice, like everyday life, is unreflected. It moves along, channelled by accustomed patterns, so that it takes the shape of what people in our culture recognize as 'teaching', or 'administration', or 'consulting', or 'advising', or whatever name is given to the professional activities in question. We have become curious about the *meaning* of these activities in the lives of our students and have therefore prompted them to ask the basic Heideggerian question, 'Who are you in your practice?' or, in other words, 'In what mode of *being* (or existence) do you participate when you practise the way you do?' The attempt to answer such questions must inevitably begin with the self and proceed by means of thoughtful reflection.

In the writing of Heidegger and van Manen, the word 'thoughtful' has acquired a special meaning beyond its ordinary usage. For Heidegger (Steiner, 1978) thoughtfulness meant attentiveness to the nature of Being or the 'isness' of existence. It was a quest for the animating life principle that Heidegger believed was overlooked by metaphysical (from Plato) and scientific (from Aristotle) modes of inquiry. For Heidegger, thoughtfulness was required to get at the root and meaning of existence. Van Manen (in press) uses thoughtfulness to signify an attentiveness to other people, parti-cularly of a teacher to a student. Thoughtfulness signifies a capacity to see from the other's point of view, to experience the other's vulnerability, and to act in the best interest of the other.

Thoughtful reflection may go in many directions. We might ask how professionals have shaped themselves through their own personal histories. The wording of this question is important. In contrast to the typical auto-biographical inquiry in which one asks about the forces that have shaped a life, this question implies that people are complicit in shaping their lives. It asks about the agency of teachers in having become the people they are, recognizing that the very act of pursuing the question is another stage in the construction of a life. We might also ask what larger social practices teachers' activities are part of, or what cultural interests their practices serve. Here the question is not the Marxist search for the solution to social injustice that is presumed to stem from the hegemony of the ruling classes, but rather Gadamer's (1975) recommendation to seek out the historically rooted biases and prejudices that inform our understandings. It asks teachers to strive to gain some objectivity on their historical situatedness, to see beyond their accustomed ways of seeing. These last two questions are inspired by the post-structuralist critique of modernism, especially the writings of Foucault (Foucault, 1983; Rajchman, 1985). Many similar questions can be posed. Always, however, the reflections that are constitutive of the most meaningful new understandings are directed by the interests of the individual rather than by any externally originating agenda.

Our respect for the capacity of human beings to generate their own understanding makes us very cautious about assuming the role of teacher. What are we teachers of, if the knowledge we have to offer does not organize students' attempts to understand themselves? What is our role if we cannot offer advice on how to organize the quest? We have called into question every conception of teaching we know. The words themselves, 'teacher' and 'role', carry uncomfortable implications for us, as if we could step into and out of a position that is somehow above or beyond where our students are. We have worried about how to fulfil our institutional responsibilities without jeopardizing the relationships with students we have come to value so highly. The essence of these relationships is in both giving and taking responsibility. We give our students responsibility for their own learning, while we, in turn, take responsibility to create conditions under which they can become thus responsible. This relationship 'works' when students are willing to assume that responsibility and, in turn, acknowledge that we too are taking responsibility not for their learning, but for our own.

The careful balance of this relationship can easily be upset in the process of our evaluating students' efforts. The act of evaluation becomes not only what we make it, but also what students make it. All too easily responsibility is shifted back to the teacher, and all too often we accept it. We notice in the transcripts of our conversations that we question the basis for our judgment and we exhibit a desire to find the 'right' standard. This desire, as Smith (1990) reminds us, comes from the Western tradition of theorizing in which correctness is the goal. Our quest for 'truth' must continually be questioned. Resonance with another's ideas is important not as a criterion for rightness, but as a sign of mutual understanding and of connection through dialogue in which *together* we call into question the assumptions that ground our inquiry. It is not that we have no ground, but rather that the ground is always shifting.

Through the careful analysis of our language, we have become aware of subtle influences on our thinking. When we first read our own words in print, we noted with some surprise and dismay a still lingering tendency to use the language of causes and effects, dichotomies and absolutes. Even as we try to question these modes of reasoning, we are encapsulated by them. We say we believe that meanings are arrived at referentially and relationally, and yet there are remnants of an expectation that there are absolute answers waiting to be found. We have come to realize that the expectation for a resolution of the issues we have raised must remain unsatisfied, that we must learn to live with the tension that arises from the uncertainty of unanswered questions. This is in the nature of reflective practice. And so we must turn our attention back to our own origins and reconsider our words even as we speak them. . . .

References

FOUCAULT, M. (1983) 'Why study power: The question of the subject', in DREYFUSS, H. and RABINOW, R. (Eds) *Beyond Structuralism and Hermeneutics: Michel Foucault*, 2nd ed., Chicago, University of Chicago Press, pp. 208–226.

GADAMER, H.-G. (1986) *Truth and Method* (translation of the second edition, 1965, G. BARDEN and J. CUMMING, Eds) New York, Crossroad, (Original work published 1960).

GELB, S. and DIPPO, D. (1989) 'Audience, empowerment and student writing: A response to Harker', *Canadian Journal of Education*, **14**, pp. 261–264.

HEIDEGGER, M. (1962) *Being and Time*, trans. by J. MACQUARRIE and E. ROBINSON, New York, Harper and Row (Original work published 1927).

OBERG, A.A. (1989) 'Supervision as a creative art', *Journal of Curriculum and Supervision*, **5**, 1, pp. 60–69.

OBERG, A.A. (1990) 'Methods and meanings in action research', *Theory Into Practice*, **29**, 3, pp. 214–221.

OBERG, A.A. and BLADES, C. (1990) 'The sound of silence', *Phenomenology and Pedagogy*, **8**, pp. 161–180.

OBERG, A. and UNDERWOOD, S. (in press) 'Facilitating teacher self-development: reflections on experience', in HARGREAVES, A. (Ed.) *Understanding Teacher Development*, New York, Teachers College Press.

RAJCHMAN, J. (1985) 'The transformation of critique', in RAJCHMAN, J. and FOUCAULT, M. (Eds) *The Freedom of Philosophy*, New York, Columbia University Press, pp. 77–95.

SMITH, D. (1990) *The Hermeneutic Imagination and the Pedagogic Text*, unpublished manuscript, The University of Lethbridge, Lethbridge, Alberta, Canada T1K 3M4.

SOEFFNER, H.-G. (1985) 'Hermeneutic approaches to language', *Sociolinguistics*, **15**, 1, pp. 21–24.

STEINER, G. (1978) *Heidegger*, London, Fontana Press.

VAN MANEN, M. (in press) *Pedagogy and the Tact of Teaching*, New York, State University of New York Press.

WEBSTER'S NEW COLLEGIATE DICTIONARY (1975) Springfield, MA, Merriam.

10 Practitioner Research and Programs of Initial Teacher Education

Jean Rudduck

Giroux and McLaren (1987) remind us that 'one of the great failures of North American education has been its inability seriously to threaten or eventually replace the prevailing paradigm of teacher as a former classroom manager with the more emancipatory model of the teacher as critical theorist' (p. 286). At the same time, they continue, 'teacher education has consistently failed to provide students with the means ... for fashioning a more critical discourse and set of understandings around the goal and purposes of schooling'. And John Wilson (1989) has recently said that 'all practising teachers, right from the beginning, face problems both inside and outside the classroom which are not purely 'practical' and involve serious reflection on educational and social issues' (p. 5).

In this chapter I argue the crucial need, in the present climate, for higher education to work with new and experienced teachers in ways that are intellectually challenging as well as relevant to practice, and I suggest that some form of reflective classroom-based research or, more ambitiously, critical action research, is an appropriate medium.

The Context: Education and Teacher Education Brought under Control

In 1985 Sockett described teacher education in the UK as having had a 'turbulent recent history'. The turbulence has not abated. Concern about teacher education seems to follow in the wake of concern about teaching. The schools, it has been said, have failed to produce the human resources necessary to sustain the country's economic position, and teacher educators have failed to offer appropriate training to school teachers:

> [school leavers] never have the right skills nor the right attitudes. Teachers [are] damned if they do change and damned if they do not

... Teacher educators are also implicated ... Whatever emphasis they give to teacher education courses, it is probably wrong.
(Ball, 1988, p. 290)

The vulnerability of teacher education courses is increased because the
public hammering of teaching, combined with relatively poor pay and conditions of service for teachers, has led to a severe problem of recruitment,
particularly in those subjects which are deemed to be most directly related
to scientific and technological advance. Anxiety about the shortages of
teachers in these subjects — physics, chemistry, mathematics and technology — has opened the way for a populist attack on curriculum content in
schools that also strikes out at teacher education programs (see Hillgate
Group, 1986, 1987).

Some of the criticism (see Booth *et al.*, 1989, p. 29) is based on an
out-dated view of the content of teacher education programs. Anderson
(1988, p. 3), for instance, suggests that higher education tutors offer a
program whose core is 'the theoretical study of teaching' and O'Hear (1988,
p. 17) implies that teacher education promotes learning through 'talking and
thinking abstractly' and he repeatedly returns to an image of the dominance
of theory. O'Hear makes a series of points — some patently untenable in
their logic — which cumulatively point to the need to remove teacher
education from the influence of higher education. Teachers in training need
a solid grounding in the real world, he says (p. 6); there are perfectly good
teachers who have not undergone formal training (p. 7); the results of
teaching are often better in the independent sector than in the maintained
sector where employment is not dependent on qualified teacher status
(p. 10); and practical knowledge is best acquired through experience (p. 17).
Such views have a superficial, popular appeal that makes them particularly
potent. What they offer is a picture of teacher education that will weaken
public confidence in the quality of newly qualified teachers.

As Hargreaves and Reynolds (1989) have suggested, the state has
constructed and then exploited a view of schooling as a crisis of under-
achievement. The same thing is happening in relation to teacher education.
In the face of such a crisis, the state has assumed a mandate for reform.
The reform that O'Hear and fellow writers endorse is school-based, on-the-
job training (see also Warnock, 1988). Acceptance of the idea of on-the-job
training (although not uniformly welcomed by the teacher unions) is made
more palatable by a recognition of the desperate shortage of teachers in
some areas of the country. Its acceptance has also been eased by the
structural and intellectual softening-up that the new accreditation procedures for teacher education courses have, possibly unwittingly, effected.

In the mid-1980s a Council for the Accreditation of Teacher Education
(CATE) was set up by the then Secretary of State for Education. It provided criteria for the judgment of teacher education courses, and part of the

evidence which CATE considered was supplied by teams of Her Majesty's Inspectors (HMI) who would 'visit Departments of Education on an invitational basis (the courtesy language has now been dropped and, in the new consultation document, May 1989, the word 'inspect' is directly used). Teacher educators were wary, and were inclined to protect their own futures by conforming to the CATE criteria — even though many of these criteria were sharply criticized (see, for instance, Sockett, 1985; Rudduck, 1989).

The criteria (DES, circular 3/84) do not, at first glance, seem problematic:

(i) postgraduate certificate in education courses should be at least thirty-six weeks long;

(ii) institutions should develop and run their initial teacher training courses in close partnership with experienced practising schoolteachers;

(iii) teacher trainers should maintain regular and frequent experience of classroom teaching and be released for this purpose;

(iv) teaching practice and school experience together should amount to no less than fifteen weeks in postgraduate courses, and not less than twenty weeks in BEd (Bachelor of Education) or concurrent courses;

(v) taken overall, the higher education and initial training of all intending teachers should include at least two full years of course time devoted to subject studies at higher education level, and courses should include the methodology of teaching the chosen subject specialism or curricular area;

(vi) entrants to courses should have at least grade C in 'O' level maths and English; students going in for secondary teaching should hold an 'A' level appropriate to their intended main subject;

(vii) students should be prepared to teach the full range of pupils they might encounter in an ordinary school, with their diversity of ability, behaviour, social background and ethnic and cultural origins;

(viii) institutions should carefully assess the personal and intellectual qualities of candidates and should involve practising teachers in the selection of students. (Rudduck, 1989, p. 179)

Critical reactions to these criteria focused mainly on two things: the absence of any plans for adequate resourcing of the projected partnership with schools; and the implicit assumptions about control that the paraphernalia of CATE imply, particularly at a time when moves were being made to set up a General Teaching Council which would give more power to the profession itself.

There are other criticisms that, in my view, also merit attention. For example, the logic of the criteria is not persuasive and there is no proper justification for certain items — as I have already pointed out (Rudduck, 1989, p. 183):

> There is an insistence on a thirty-six week PGCE course: ... was it assumed that extending courses by four to six weeks would automatically improve their quality ...? The important question for CATE in scrutinizing PGCE programmes ought not to be 'Are you moving to a thirty-six week course?' but 'How do you propose to use the extra four to six weeks? ...
>
> Another controversial criterion is that teachers be involved in the selection of students for teacher education courses. Again, no systematic research evidence has been offered to justify such an investment of time and energy on both sides. It is not clear that the involvement of practising teachers does significantly modify the judgments of higher education tutors. Indeed, it seems that the agreement between teacher and tutor is generally so close that busy teachers could well argue that this is one part of the process of teacher education that higher education tutors should manage on their own!

Then there is the concern with the personal and intellectual qualities of applicants. Hargreaves (1988, p. 213) comments:

> In the main, exactly which personal qualities are likely to make a good teacher are not discussed, nor is there any discussion of whether those qualities might vary according to the age group being taught, the special requirements of a teacher's subject, or the ethos of the school, for instance. And no advice is forthcoming on how these (largely unstated) qualities might be identified through the selection process either ... all that is recommended is that experienced, practising teachers be increasingly involved in the selection process. It seems then, that in the absence of more objective procedures and criteria, Government is here prepared to place its trust in the process described in a well-known British idiom: 'it takes one to know one'.

McNamara (1986, p. 33) asks two pointed questions:

> If it is claimed that personal qualities are related to teacher effectiveness, is it sensible to make judgments about those qualities when they are manifested in non-teaching contexts such as staff rooms or selection interviews?
>
> If, say, established teachers, the lay public or politicians are given more influence in deciding what sorts of people become

teachers, will this not dispose the school system to greater conservatism and conformity?

Other criticisms focus on the emphasis given to subject studies (an emphasis which O'Hear and his fellow pamphleteers were, later, to defend):

> To reshape teacher education to produce teachers who can only work within a subject-based curriculum, who regard themselves principally as transmitters of a certain body of knowledge, is to turn the clock back and ignore recent developments. (NUT, 1984, p. 19; quoted in Hargreaves, 1988, p. 15)

My overall interpretation of the CATE criteria is that they are, in fact, paving the way for school-based training. They imply, for instance, that higher education tutors will be more credible if they become more like teachers: they are required, illogically, to demonstrate their competence at school teaching rather than at higher education teaching. Moreover, partnership, if its conditions are not clearly worked out, can itself be seen as a strategy for blurring identities in the interests of making higher education tutors more like school teachers — hence CATE's interest in shared appointments and short-term opportunities for job exchanges between higher education and schools.

This homogenization of role which is implicit in the early CATE criteria and reaffirmed in the revised draft criteria (1989) would, in my view, have some unacceptable consequences. We have to recognize that what teachers as partners in the enterprise of training can offer is practice-based knowledge rooted in sustained experience of a particular setting. What higher education tutors can offer is an analytic perspective that is fed by observation in a range of classrooms and sharpened by the evidence of research. Our contribution is different from and complementary to that of the practising teacher. To fulfil our part of the contract, tutors in higher education need:

(a) to understand the problems and achievements of teachers and learners, in different contexts, taking into account social, historical and ideological perspectives;
(b) to be well-informed about changing structures and practices in the school system;
(c) to understand, and to accept responsibility for helping others to understand, the pressures and values that influence such structures and practices.

Concern with classroom practice and with subject knowledge are crucial components of training for teaching, but they are only part of the process whereby an adult becomes a competent, confident and committed teacher, capable of educating young people in a rapidly changing world where jobs are few and inequality abounds. The concerns of the school and the class-room, despite what O'Hear (1988, 1989) and Cox (1989) think, are now the main point of reference for almost all that happens on most training courses. But this is not to say that concern with practice denies concern with the critical analysis of practice — and I suspect that what O'Hear, Cox and others are really worried about is the commitment of higher education tutors to develop 'thinking teachers'. By this I mean teachers who will, through the quality of their work, struggle to lift the status of the profession and to improve the life chances of *all* their pupils. Although some students will, sadly, support the narrow and ultimately disabling view that says you can learn all you need to know about teaching from merely doing it, others disagree and complain, justifiably, if they think that they are entering teaching without frameworks for analysis, evaluation and reflection — which they see as the basis for improving practice and maintaining the personal and communal excitement of teaching.

The power of such frameworks will, according to Hargreaves and Reynolds (1989, p. 192), be weakened by the government's new education policies. They offer the following predictions which could, if the distinctive contribution of universities is not permitted to survive, hold true for teacher education as well as for secondary education:

1   that education will henceforth exercise a 'reproductive' rather than a 'transformative' function, re-enforcing traditional social, ethnic and gender divisions rather than seeking to change them;
2   that education will henceforth reassert academic goals rather than social or personal goals;
3   that opportunities for critique, both within courses of initial and inservice teacher education and in schools, will be diminished or delegitimised.

It is the third point that concerns us most in this paper. There are a number of aspects that need to be unpacked: the status of teaching as a profession and the significance of qualifications to professional status; higher educa-tion's loss of territory within both initial and inservice teacher education programs; and the need for higher education to maintain its commitment to the nurturing of critical thinking in a situation where market forces are becoming increasingly influential.

Critical Thinking Brought under Control

For many years the government endorsed the notion of teachers' autonomy as a basis of professionalism. It was safe to do so, for the government saw the great majority of teachers as conservatively respectable and anxious to be regarded as 'true professionals' whose concerns would be pedagogic, moral and inter-personal but not political (Grace, 1987, p. 208). Several things have happened to challenge the stability of that perception. First, aware that they were not achieving the conditions of service and pay that they believed they merited, some groups of organized teachers broke the professional protocol and started to use their autonomy radically rather than conservatively. Second, the structural reforms of the 1960s (expressed in the move towards comprehensivization) and the curriculum reforms of the 1970s and 1980s, have made teachers more aware of issues of equality of opportunity with consequent threat to the principles of differentiation and competition around which schooling has been organized. Third, many teacher educators have tried to take on board ideals of teacher empowerment, using 'reflection', 'action research' and 'teacher research' (often rather loosely construed) as a framework for critical thinking.

Such trends threaten to turn teachers into 'radicals' and radicals are a threat to the authority of central government. 'The problems', said a conservative politician (referring in fact to only the first of my three trends), 'can be solved by making schools again accountable to some authority outside them. The necessary sanction is either a nationally enforced curriculum or parental choice, or both' (Boyson, 1975, pp. 141–142; in Grace, 1987, p. 217). 'Both' have now happened. Thus, the profession is being brought to heel in terms of its autonomy, and tighter accountability procedures are now in place.

At the same time, the profession's status is being challenged by the erosion of its base in qualifications. Progress towards establishing teaching as an all-graduate profession has been celebrated with a robust pride. But members of the new right have questioned the need for a training qualification (indeed, for a first degree) and there is some danger of our returning to an earlier era when the only qualification for entry to teaching was to be over 18 and vaccinated! There is undoubtedly a recruitment crisis, but to solve it by lowering entry qualifications brings a generalized loss of identity and position:

> Certification requirements provide important psychic benefits . . .
> they make teaching seem more like a profession by guaranteeing
> that not just anyone can become a teacher; in this sense, certifica-
> tion, along with the professional education courses they require,
> serve an important symbolic function. (Silberman, 1970, p. 439)

The claim of the new right that teachers do not need training — that teaching is caught, not taught — seems to be fuelled by a sharp anti-intellectualism which leads them to denounce as worthless the efforts of higher education to encourage a habit of critical reflection on practice. Teachers learn by doing, they say. Teacher educators disagree:

> Practice alone is, of course, not enough; without some coordinating theory, some inter-connected ideas, purely practical subjects can ossify and degenerate into congeries of rules-of-thumb and obsession with technique. Practice without theory can become basely conservative; theory without practice can become arcane, unintelligible or simply trivial. (Goodlad, 1988, p. 54)

In my view, teacher educators are, at the moment, getting the balance about right.

Another link in this chain of attack on the professional and intellectual status of teachers and on the role of higher education in the training of teachers is the curtailment of opportunities for extended professional study. The number of teachers on one-year secondments working for a higher degree has dropped dramatically in the last two years. (In the UK, unlike some other countries, teachers have not traditionally paid their own way in seeking opportunities for full time study). The public justification for this move is that when public funds are limited it is better to give many teachers short bursts of inservice refreshment than to give a small number a whole year of study. There is some reason in this, but what is lost is the opportunity for teachers to commit themselves to sustained and coherent practice-related studies that have a critical and reflective edge. As Hargreaves and Reynolds say (1989, p. 23): '[there is] greater pressure towards productivity, but reduced opportunity to reflect on the worth and rationality of what is being produced'. They go on to say that the structure of current inservice events denies teachers the opportunity to engage in sustained critical questioning. And Carr (1986, p. 6) warns:

> Any approach to teacher education which does not encourage teachers to reflect critically on their own educational views and on the nature of education as it is realised in the institutional setting of schools will be either inherently conservative or dangerously doctrinaire.

'Reflective' Research?

Lawrence Stenhouse once said: 'It is teachers who will, in the end, change the world of the classroom by understanding it'. I believe that it is the responsibility of teacher educators to help teachers do three things: develop a commitment to understanding the world of the classroom; acquire some basic principles of research that will allow them to feed their understanding; have some constructive experience of what reflective research will yield when applied to the everyday problems and dilemmas of teaching and learning in schools. I also believe that it is important to establish such commitment and capacities during programs of initial teacher training.

Given the already crowded agenda of initial teacher education programs, it may be asked why this cannot wait until later. There are a number of possible — and positive — responses to this question. One is to argue that teaching as a career is peculiarly subject to the deadening effects of routinization, for teachers tend to encounter, as Schön (1983) says, the same kinds of situation over and over again. After a while, teachers see what they expect to see and constantly reconstruct the classroom in its own image. Reflective research is a way of helping teachers to sharpen their perceptions of the everyday realities of their work; it helps them to identify worthwhile problems to work on, and through their enquiry to extend their own understanding, insight and command of the situations in which they work. It helps teachers to recognize contradictions of purpose and value, and to monitor the effects of strategies designed to achieve the purposes that they have in mind.

Commitment to such activity is not part of the public agenda of most school staff rooms and the socializing force of schools is such that, if the students are not introduced to the excitement and power of practitioner research during their period of initial training they may not, given the demise of opportunities for sustained inservice study, turn voluntarily and readily to such a way of learning later in their career.

Connelly (in press) summarizes Schön's two recent books (1983, 1987) by saying that 'the idea is that practitioners are essentially self-educated via the pursuit of their ongoing practices and reflection upon them': teaching is perceived as a 'sequence of problem-finding and problem-solving episodes in which teachers' capabilities continually grow as they meet, define and solve practical problems'. This sounds very much as though the extension of capabilities occurs as a natural process, with the recognition and definition of worthwhile problems a constant element in that natural process. Our own experience of working with experienced teachers suggests that capabilities are not automatically subject to growth in this way and that the likelihood of teachers opting to learn from the thoughtful and critical study of their own practice is greater if such activity has been legitimized during initial training.

Critical Action Research?

So far, I have outlined the case made for introducing student teachers to a reflective style of practitioner research, but a reflective approach to teaching is not enough, some would argue: '... the defect of the reflective approach is that it is severely constrained and limited by what it ignores' (Smyth, 1987, p. 159). What it ignores are the wide social and political frameworks, beyond the classroom and the school, that shape the parameters of education in ways that teachers, with their eyes drawn to the minutiae of their own practice, too often fail to see. What is needed is a more full-blooded commitment to critical research. Advocates of this position argue that the responsibilities of teachers have been too narrowly defined and that only by helping teachers to see themselves as bearers of critical knowledge, rules and values, through which they can problematize the fundamental relationships of teaching and learning, can we hope to change the disabling image of teachers as primarily technicians or public servants whose role it is to implement rather than to conceptualize pedagogic practice (Giroux and McLaren, 1987, p. 279).

The critical action research approach enables teachers to exercise the right to question the authority of past practice. Maxine Greene suggests why this is normally so difficult to do: it could be, she says, because 'the processes that go on in (teachers') institutions strike them as so automatic, there seems to be no alternative but to comply. Their schools seem to resemble natural processes: what happens in them appears to have the sanction of natural law and can no more be questioned or resisted than the law of gravity' (1985; in Smyth, 1987, p. 156). Action research is a powerful tool because it helps teachers to problematize what has hitherto been taken for granted.

Aspirations to extend the teacher's sphere of concern in this way are ambitious and may prove to be unrealistic. Their advocates are virtually saying that teachers themselves, much as Willis's lads (1977), are party to the construction of their own limited futures: they are 'learning to labour', committing themselves to a career as deliverers of other people's policies, purveyors of other people's values, puppets moving to strings that are always manipulated by others.

To sum up: I have broadly mentioned two kinds of research that might be introduced and explored in programs of initial teacher education. On the one hand there is the politically ambitious agenda of the advocates of 'vintage' action research (see Carr and Kemmis, 1983), and on the other there is the more modest attempt to encourage teachers to use reflective research as a means of improving their own classroom practice. Adelman and Carr (1988) spell out the weakness of the softer approach: 'By developing primarily as a form of teacher-controlled classroom research, [it] has managed to create for itself the image of a popular 'grassroots' movement which neither threatens, nor is itself threatened....'. Such practitioner research runs the risk of addressing trivial questions, lacks cumulative power, and offers no collective, radical challenge — but, on the other hand, reflective, classroom-focused research is a way of building personal excitement, confidence and insight — and these are important foundations for career-long personal and professional development.

What Do Teachers Want?

Huberman's recent research (1989) offers an account of career 'stages' derived from a detailed analysis of interviews conducted with 160 Swiss teachers selected to form 'experience groups' (5–10 years of experience, 11–19 years, 20–29 years, and 30–39 years). Teachers in the later stages of their career were presented as passing through a period of structural reform (such as many teachers are now facing in the UK) and entering a final phase of 'positive focusing', 'defensive focusing' or 'disenchantment'. Teachers in the 'defensive focusing' group are described as 'specialising; reducing commitments; using seniority to carve out a comfortable schedule; relating only to a small circle of peers'. They are the traditionalists who opposed educational innovation and 'were brought kicking and screaming through'. The 'disenchanted' are those who supported the idea of reform but who became disillusioned because the values had been undermined or confounded, and because administrators failed to carry through their support for the innovation and for the teachers engaged in the innovation. The 'positive focusers' are characterized by a constructive attitude but at the same time they are committed to doing only what they choose to do: 'I've done my share; now leave me alone to do what I want'.

Huberman's data, and his categorization system, lead him to take the 'positive focusers' as his target group for preventive action and he concentrates on finding, in earlier phases, predictors for those who will not, in later career, be among the 'defensive' or 'disenchanted'. His comments are worth quoting in full:

> Put briefly: teachers who steered clear of ... multiple classroom innovation, but who invested consistently in classroom-level experiments — what they call 'tinkering' with new materials, different pupil grouping, small changes in grading systems ... were more likely to be 'satisfied' later on in their career than most others were and FAR more likely to be satisfied than their peers who had been heavily involved in school-wide or district-wide projects. So 'tinkering', together with an early concern for instructional efficiency ('getting it down into a routine, getting the materials right for most situations I run into') was one of the strongest predictors of ultimate satisfaction. Inversely, heavy involvement in school-wide innovation was a fairly strong predictor of 'disenchantment' after 20–25 years of teaching. Tending one's private garden, pedagogically speaking, seems to have more pay-off in the long haul than land reform, although the latter is perceived as stimulating and enriching while it is happening.

Huberman mentions two other factors which were 'predictive of professional satisfaction later in the career cycle': the first was a capacity to make small 'spontaneous role shifts when one began to feel stale' — changes to the grade level of teaching, subject matter, classroom setting, academic stream, or age of pupils being taught. Here, it seems, teachers are exploiting the natural diversity of the situation to 'keep the brain cells from dying off'. The second factor was to do with teachers' recognizing that they were achieving significant results or having significant impact on their pupils.

Huberman's work has some disturbing implications for those interested in more radical forms of teacher research. It seems, according to his data, that teachers are most satisfied by small modifications in the settings in which they work which allow them to take a different perspective on their work. The data might be construed as questioning the appropriateness or feasibility of introducing teachers to critical action research (such as Smyth, 1987; Lawn, 1989, and others are advocating) that reaches out beyond the walls of the classroom in favour of the more contained forms of 'reflective research'. Alternatively, Huberman's work might be construed as emphasizing the need to encourage teachers to think more deeply about fundamental values, such as equality of opportunity, in their work, and to find satisfaction in their progress towards the realization of such values: in short, to commit themselves to more radical change efforts where there is a clear educationally justifiable need for reform.

Introducing Student Teachers to Reflection and Enquiry/Research

In our own teacher education program we have opted to introduce teachers to reflective research, but with an emphasis on collaboration. Huberman's teachers seemed essentially individualistic in their tinkering and small-scale experiments, whereas we believe that some more collaborative efforts might be more powerful and might even increase some teachers' sense of satisfaction. It is the principle of collaborative research that gives coherence to our 36-week Post Graduate Certificate in Education program (the PGCE course).

There are three structural features that provide opportunities for all students to experience the benefits (or distractions) of reflective dialogue and collaborative research. First, during the early period of block teaching practice, students are paired with another student teaching the same subject and, for part of the time, they share the same teaching timetable. This arrangement allows them to observe each other at work, to identify and explore interesting issues and problems, and to learn the value of giving and receiving constructive peer criticism and support. It also challenges the conventional view of 'the teacher as an island' and helps students to be confident about talking through the problems of practice. Second, we have introduced a three day 'analysis' workshop where students choose to work intensively on a topic that interests them (such as cooperative group work, working with children with special needs, understanding the pupil's perspective in learning). Here, the aim is to help students see experience — their own and the documented experience of others — as evidence from which they can deepen their understanding of the complexities of classroom and school life. Third, all students, in the final weeks of the course, form 'collaborative enquiry' groups: each group returns to a school in which one of its members worked during teaching practice, and the group researches a problem which has been identified by the school and which the group members find interesting and worthwhile. Although the majority of these enquiries are subject-based and classroom-based, some explore broader issues like truancy and anti-racism. (For a fuller account, see Rudduck and Wellington, 1989).

In addition to these opportunities, which all students experience as part of the basic structure of the program, tutors will, according to their own confidence and commitment, model reflection-on-action in relation to their own everyday work with their students. For example, they sometimes tape-record their supervisory exchanges with students and use these as a basis for understanding the problem of authority in learning relationships. (For a detailed account of the ways in which one tutor sustains reflection-on-action as the core of his PGCE program, see Lucas, 1988a, b, c).

All tutors involved in the initial training of teachers are themselves engaged in school-based or school-focused research projects, and colleagues are beginning to feel more comfortable now in acknowledging where their weaknesses in research are, where they need help from outsiders, and what kinds of support they can offer each other.

Our program will continue to build its coherence around the idea of the reflective practitioner because we believe that a capacity for reflection offers teachers a means of sustaining the excitement of teaching and allows them to continue to learn in cooperative but self-critical company. Our approach is also so close to the daily demands of teaching and learning that students, even on a relatively short course of training, do not dismiss it as unrelated to practice.

Conclusion and Summary

If policy-makers were to be guided by the views of such writers as O'Hear, then 'teacher training would become a simple apprenticeship, exclusively the concern of the schools, with novice teachers trying to pick up what craft knowledge they can. Each school would operate its own system of induction, many no doubt taking the line that the best way to learn to teach is to get on and do it. The resulting situation could lead to further disillusionment and defections from the profession' (Booth *et al.*, 1989, p. 30). What higher education can distinctively offer to teacher training is a capacity for reflection on practice as a basis for the improvement of practice or, more contentiously, a commitment to the kind of action research that is both reflective and emancipatory. The present move towards partnership in training is resulting 'in some of the most radical and exciting developments in teacher training seen this century' (Booth *et al.*, 1989, p. 29) and the commitment to reflective practice is increasingly a hallmark of such developments. Such a commitment lies, in my view, at the heart of teacher professionalism, and I do not want to see it disappear.

There is a danger, in the present climate, of two distinct issues — that of the role of higher education in initial teacher education and that of the teacher recruitment crisis — being conflated. Let us not confuse the two issues. On the one hand we should recognize the strengths of current practice in teacher education programs, and on the other we should think constructively about ways of dealing, in the short term and in the longer term, with the problems that lie behind the crisis in recruitment.

References

ADELMAN, C. and CARR, W. (1988) *Whatever Happened to Action Research?*, paper presented at the annual meeting of the British Educational Research Association, Norwich,University of East Anglia, August.

ANDERSON, D. (1988) 'Summary and preface', in O'HEAR, A. (Ed.) *Who Teaches the Teachers?*, Research Report 10, London, Social Affairs Unit, pp. 3–4.

BALL, S. (1988) 'Staff relations during the teacher's industrial action: Context, conflict and proletarianisation', *British Journal of Sociology of Education*, **9**, 3, pp. 289–306.

BOOTH, M.B., FURLONG, J., HARGREAVES, D.H., REISS, M.J. and ROTHVEN, K. (1989) *Teacher Supply and Teacher Quality: Solving the Coming Crisis*, Department of Education, University of Cambridge.

BOYSON, R. (1975) *The Crisis in Education*, London, Woburn Press.

CARR, W. (1986) *Recent Developments in Teacher Education*, paper presented at the Conference on Teacher Research and INSET, University of Ulster.

CARR, W. and KEMMIS, S. (1983) *Becoming Critical: Knowing Through Action Research*, Geelong, Deakin University Press; reprinted by Falmer Press, 1987.

CONNELLY, F.M. (in press) 'Teacher evaluation: A critical review and a plea for supervised reflective practice', in FARRELL, J. (Ed.) *Teacher Development*, Washington, DC, World Bank, originally presented at a workshop for the World Bank Seminar on Teachers' Costs and Effectiveness, Washington, DC, April, 1987.

COX, C.B. (1989) 'Unqualified Approval', *Times Educational Supplement*, 6 January.

GIROUX, H.A. and McLAREN, P. (1987) 'Teacher education as a counter public sphere: Notes towards a redefinition', in POPKEWITZ, T.S. (Ed.) *Critical Studies in Teacher Education*, London, Falmer Press, pp. 266–297.

GOODLAD, S. (1988) 'Four forms of heresy in higher education: Aspects of academic freedom in education for the professions', in TIGHT, M. (Ed.) *Academic Freedom and Responsibility*, Milton Keynes, SRHE and Open University Press, pp. 49–65.

GRACE, G. (1987) 'Teachers and the state in Britain: A changing relation', in LAWN, M. and GRACE, G. (Eds) *Teachers: The Culture and Politics of Work*, London, Falmer Press, pp. 193–228.

GREENE, M. (1985) 'Teacher as project: Choice, perspective and the public space', unpublished manuscript cited in SMYTH, J. (1987) 'Transforming teaching through intellectualizing the work of teachers', in SMYTH, J. (Ed.) *Educating Teachers*, London, Falmer Press, pp. 155–168.

HARGREAVES, A. (1988) 'Teaching quality: A sociological analysis', *Journal of Curriculum Studies*, **20**, 3, pp. 211–231.

HARGREAVES, A. and REYNOLDS, D. (Eds) (1989) *Education Policies: Controversies and Critiques*, London, Falmer Press; see the chapters 'Decomprehensivization' and 'Better schools?', pp. 1–32, 191–212.

HILLGATE GROUP (1986) *Whose Schools? A Radical Manifesto*, London, The Hillgate Press.

HILLGATE GROUP (1987) *The Reform of British Education*, London, The Claridge Press.

HUBERMAN, M. (1989) *Teacher Development and Instructional Mastery*, unpublished paper presented at the international conference on Teacher Development: Policies, Practices and Research, Toronto, Ontario Institute for Studies in Education, February.

LAWN, M. (1989) 'Being caught in schoolwork: The possibilities of research in teachers' work', in CARR, W. (Ed.) *Quality in Teaching: Arguments for a Reflective Profession*, London, Falmer Press.

LUCAS, P. (1988a) 'An approach to research-based teacher education through collaborative inquiry', *Journal of Education for Teaching*, **14**, 1, pp. 55–73.

LUCAS, P. (1988b) 'Teaching practice placement: Laying the foundations for a reflective training community', *British Journal of In-Service Education*, **14**, 2, pp. 92–99.

LUCAS, P. (1988c) 'Approaching research-based teacher education: Questions for a reflective method assignment programme in initial training', *Cambridge Journal of Education*, **18**, 3, pp. 405–420.

McNAMARA, D. (1986) 'The personal qualities of the teacher and educational policy: A critique', *Journal of Curriculum Studies*, **12**, 1, pp. 29–36.

O'HEAR, A. (1988) *Who Teaches the Teachers?*, Research Report 10, London, Social Affairs Unit.

O'HEAR, A. (1989) 'Teachers can become qualified in practice', *Guardian*, 24 January.

RUDDUCK, J. (1989) 'Accrediting teacher education courses: The new criteria', in HARGREAVES, A. and REYNOLDS, D. (Eds) *Education Policies: Controversies and Critiques*, London, Falmer Press, pp. 178–190.

RUDDUCK, J. and WELLINGTON, J. (1989) 'Encouraging the spirit of enquiry in initial teacher training', *Forum*, **31**, 2, Spring, pp. 50–57.

SCHÖN, D.A. (1983) *The Reflective Practitioner*, London, Temple Smith.

SCHÖN, D.A. (1987) *Educating the Reflective Practitioner*, San Francisco, Jossey Bass.

SILBERMAN, C.E. (1970) *Crisis in the Classroom: the Remaking of American Education*, New York, Vintage Books.

SMYTH, I. (Ed.) (1987) *Educating Teachers*, London, Falmer Press.

SOCKETT, H. (1985) 'What is a school of education?', *Cambridge Journal of Education*, **15**, 3, pp. 123–127.

WARNOCK, M. (1988) *A Common Policy for Education*, Milton Keynes, Open University Press.

WILLIS, P. (1977) *Learning to Labour*, Farnborough, Saxon House.

WILSON, J. (1989) 'Authority, teacher education and educational studies', *Cambridge Journal of Education*, **19**, pp. 5–12.

11 The Content of Student Teachers' Reflections within Different Structures for Facilitating the Reflective Process

Anna E. Richert

Preparing teachers to teach thoughtfully, to consider carefully the consequences of their work, involves creating opportunities for beginning teachers to learn the skills and attitudes required for reflective practice. While there are many teacher education programs that are constructed to promote reflective thinking, little or no attention has been given to the impact of specific program structures on the processes or content of beginning teachers' reflections. One conclusion that might be drawn from this lack of attention is that the structures of such programs are seen as unimportant or insignificant in determining the outcomes in the reflective practice of beginning teachers. The research reported here addresses the question of the relationship between structures designed to promote reflection in beginning teachers and the subsequent reflections of those teachers. This moves the spotlight of research on reflection in teacher education from a consideration of levels of reflectivity to the structural conditions employed to facilitate the process.

Recently, the focus on reflection in teacher education has centered on the types of questions or problems that confront teachers or the 'level' at which they are required to engage in reflective decision-making. Van Manen's (1977) three-tiered typology is useful in understanding the range of issues and problems that teachers face. At the first level are the practical or technical questions. The conception of reflection guiding the work of Cruickshank and colleagues (1981, 1986) represents preparing teachers for reflective practice at this level, because the focus is on how to prepare teachers to be technically competent in selecting from among alternative teaching techniques for any given classroom interaction. Zeichner's (1981–82) work, which is drawn from Dewey's (1933) conception of reflective teaching, attends to preparing teachers to function at Van Manen's second and third levels of reflectivity: social/political and moral/ethical. Reflective teachers, according to this conceptualization, need to develop both the attitudes and skills required for thinking through and responding to the purposes and consequences of their actions in classrooms. For Zeichner and others who share this orientation to reflection in teaching, the ends as well as the means of teaching practice are central in their relevance to the scrutiny of practising teachers (Feiman-Nemser, 1979; Buchmann, 1983; Tom, 1985; Wedman and Mahlios, 1985; Russell and Spafford, 1986).

Shulman (1986) identifies reflection as one stage in a model of pedagogical reasoning. During this stage teachers look back on the teaching and learning that has occurred as a means of making sense of their actions and learning from their experiences. In the study reported here, the process of 'looking back' is conceptualized as one of reenactment: rather than looking back to recall what occurred in any particular teaching episode, reflection is seen as a process of reconstructing classroom enactments, including both cognitive and affective dimensions (Richert, 1987). And this reconstruction occurs in consecutive iterations. Each stage of the process is different from preceding stages as the teachers use additional information and knowledge gained during earlier iterations.

In this view, facilitating reflection involves creating conditions under which reenactment or reconstruction can occur. These conditions exist as frames for the process and are seen as potentially influential. The conditions that were isolated for this study were drawn from practical and theoretical research on teaching reflection to beginning teachers, as well as from those efforts in other professions to facilitate reflective practice. Two broad approaches were apparent: the social (here operationalized as working with a partner), and the artifactual (here operationalized in the creation and use of a teaching portfolio).

In this study the social and artifactual conditions of reflection were examined for their influence on the *content* of reflection. Research on teaching in the last decade has moved its focus from a consideration of what teachers *do* to a new set of observations and considerations about how teachers *think* (Clark and Yinger, 1977; Shavelson and Stern, 1981; Clark and Peterson, 1986). More recent research in teacher thinking focuses on what teachers think about and what they know. When teachers think, they think about something; when they reflect, they reflect about something as well. The present study investigated how the programmatic structural conditions under which reflection occurred in one program of teacher education influenced the content of what the teachers thought about when they reflected about their work in classrooms.

The assumption that teachers need to learn to become reflective, and the belief that teacher education programs should be instrumental in this development provoke the question: 'What conditions can we create in our programs to cultivate reflective practice?' Though teacher educators have been employing methods for promoting reflection for years, the teacher education research literature offers little systematic analysis of differences achieved in the reflective content and process of beginning teachers under different structural conditions.

Design and Method

I used a parallel case study design to study four conditions for reflection and their differential influence upon the reflection of twelve beginning teachers enrolled in a program of teacher education. The four conditions were drawn from approaches commonly used in preparing professionals: working jointly with a colleague (in this case, with a partner), and keeping a tangible record of work accomplished (in this case, a teaching portfolio). The two facilitating factors — a partner (social) and a portfolio (artifactual) — were crossed to create four conditions:

Condition I   No partner and no portfolio
Condition II   A portfolio but no partner
Condition III A partner but no portfolio
Condition IV   A partner and a portfolio.

Each of the twelve beginning teachers reflected under two of the four conditions, resulting in six participants reflecting under each of the four conditions. For each condition, I asked the teachers to reflect about one week of their teaching. The data consisted of the reflections themselves (journals for Condition I, forty-five minute 'freewrites' for Condition II, and forty-five minute reflection interviews for Conditions III and IV), as well as self-reports about the reflections that occurred in each case after the earlier reflection. Additionally, the portfolios created by the teachers in Conditions II and IV and the reflection 'freewrites' for Conditions III and IV were gathered as supplementary evidence, along with questionnaires about the process of Condition I.

A coding system was developed for preliminary treatment of the entire data set. The coding categories, initially drawn from Schwab's (1973) four commonplaces — the teacher, the student, the curriculum and the context — evolved to include the knowledge categories in the conceptualization of the knowledge base of teaching developed as part of the 'Knowledge Growth in Teaching' project (Shulman, 1986). This evolution of the coding system resulted from the preliminary study of the data: it was evident that in addition to reflecting on aspects of classroom events represented by Schwab's four categories, the teachers reflected about the interactions *among* the factors. For example, there was reflection on student-teacher interaction, as well as on student and teacher independently. So the coding scheme that emerged incorporated indicators of the interactions among the four commonplaces as well as the commonplaces themselves. A simple

Table 11.1   Content of reflection by structures for reflection

CONTENT OF REFLECTION	STRUCTURE	I	II	III	IV
Personal		38%	25%	10%	4%
Teacher		3%	0%	0%	0%
Student		11%	9%	11%	12%
Content		4%	19%	9%	7%
Context		6%	5%	4%	3%
General pedagogy		14%	15%	37%	17%
Content specific pedagogy		24%	26%	28%	57%

numerical content analysis was conducted to show the percentage of the seven content categories of reflection identified in each of the four conditions as a percentage of the total content. The results appear in Table 11.1.

The principal and qualitative analysis of the data proceeded on three levels. The first level of contrast was the within-case level, in which the cases were analyzed individually across the two conditions. The second level was the cross-case-within-condition level, in which the six individual cases within each condition were analyzed for similarities and differences. For the third level of analysis, the cases were aggregated across conditions to examine the central contrasts built into the study — reflection with a partner and reflection with a portfolio.

The initial analysis of the individual cases showed *significant similarity in content* across the four conditions for the twelve teachers. The developmental literature might lead us to predict that beginning teachers would focus their thinking primarily on matters of management and survival (Fuller and Bown, 1975). The teachers in this study thought about all facets of their work. In addition to management and survival, they were concerned about general teaching and learning, their professional identities as teachers, the students as individuals and as groups, subject matter content and curriculum, the context, their teacher education experiences, and even the research in which they were participating. The reflections contained expressions of feelings, assessments (of themselves, their students, the curriculum, the content, contextual factors), ponderings, reportings and pleas for help. As the data were analyzed condition by condition across the four conditions, and analyzed by condition across individuals, the general similarities among the reflections faded and *significant differences emerged in the content of the reflections under the four conditions*. The next four sections of this chapter provide descriptions and illustrations of the reflections under each of the four structural conditions.

Pondering the Personal: Condition I — No Partner/No Portfolio

For Condition I, the teachers reflected on their own by writing in a journal. There was neither partner nor portfolio to facilitate the process. What distinguishes the reflections under this condition is the amount of personal content they contain. As shown in Table 11.1, the reflections for Condition I contained a higher percentage of personal content (38 per cent) than did those for any of the other three conditions (25 per cent, 10 per cent and 4 per cent, respectively). The teachers' personal responses to the world of teaching dominate the reflections under Condition I.

The requirement to reflect alone provided unencumbered time and space for the six teachers to contemplate, as one teacher said, 'whatever was on my mind at the moment'. While the range of content included the full spectrum of teaching issues and concerns, what was 'on their minds at the moment' was very often a *personal* response to factors in their teaching lives, such as their own worth as a teacher, the frustrations they felt about students, and uncertainties they have had about teaching.

> I feel I need to find my own voice in this class — it's hard to step in and take over. Teaching is so personal — it's so honest. You can't hide your personality or your being, unless you're a talented and clever actress. (Glynda I, Journal entry, March 31)

> Underlying the difficult planning process is my fear of presenting boring lessons that elicit little response from the students. I *hate* being the catalyst of a lesson or presentation that is boring to the kids. So when I plan, I am not only concerned with organizing content and figuring out what to teach, but I am constantly thinking about how to reach the kids in my presentation of the material, how to create a situation where the kids are doing some real learning and thinking. (John I, Journal entry, March 30)

> Today I was not as prepared as I like to be and I had to 'wing it'. It was not a total disaster, but I was not pleased at all. Whenever I am less than adequately prepared, I feel as though my students know. It is this that is most uncomfortable. Although probably not true, it is this feeling that I detest. This is my biggest incentive to be well prepared, I really can't wing it. I just don't know the subject area that well.
> Very, very frustrating. (Alex I, Journal entry, April 1)

In each of these cases the teacher is 'pondering the personal' or responding in a personal way to the experience of teaching. In the following statement Jill demonstrates the construction of the reflection in personal terms. While she thinks about the students, she is thinking primarily in terms of her response to the students and how she should act in relation to that response.

> [When I'm thinking alone] I think about myself in terms of my reactions to kids. I think about the kids, but when I think about

Raymond, I think about how I am going to deal with Raymond or
how did I deal with Raymond that was right or wrong and how am I
going to do it differently tomorrow sort of thing'. (Jill IV, AR
Interview 8:13)

The Condition I reflections are characterized by the generation and expression of personal responses to teaching, in particular to those factors that have
captured their attention most immediately for any particular day. Since
there were no externally imposed guidelines (guiding questions, predetermined expectations) to focus the reflections nor any external person to
whom they had to respond, the teachers found this situation an open
opportunity to explore their work in a deeply personal way. Reflecting alone
provides a particular kind of safety and openness to think about things that,
as the teachers indicated in the self-reports about the reflection, they might
not think about if someone else were sharing in the endeavor. This resulted
in more expression of personal response than is evidenced in the reflections
in the other conditions that included a partner, a portfolio, or a combination
of the two. Glynda compares the Condition I journal reflection with the
reflection she did late with a partner:

If I were writing in my journal I'd probably be more open and
would include things that I wouldn't include in my discussion with
TC, like my feelings about different students and different days and
things like that. Like I was sick one day and one day I was incred-
ibly tired, I could barely, I was really tired and I thought, 'I'm never
going to be this tired and teach again'. It was horrible. Unless it was
on an informal basis I might feel dumb telling somebody else. It
wasn't all that important. (Glynda III, AR Interview, 6:6)

Feelings and Mood in Condition I

While there is substantial expression of feeling throughout the reflections in
all four conditions, the impact of feelings or mood is most readily evidenced
in the Condition I data. Reflecting on one's own by responding to their work
at a personal level resulted in significant expression of feelings.

Usually I consider certain aspects which stand out during the day —
key feelings. I wrote these entries on an emotional level mostly.
(Glynda I, Quest. 3)

The feelings about which the teachers write influence both the teaching (at
least as they describe it) and recollections they have of the teaching.

> When I'm feeling good, I'm more likely to delve more deeply into curricular and creative problem solving [in my reflections]. When I'm depressed, I focus on negatives and don't think in general terms. (Glynda, Quest. 5)

> Today the lesson was good, but I felt so bad it didn't really matter. I'm glad it is Friday so I can relax and recuperate. I don't want to get sick now or my teaching will really suffer. (Alex I, Journal entry, April 4)

> It's amazing to me how much my own mood can affect the presentation of my lesson and the entire goings-on in the classroom. Today, for example, I was in a down mood because of some emotional turmoil in my life, and I simply couldn't get too excited about teaching. As a result, my presentation was pretty flat, and my lethargy seemed contagious. (John I, Journal entry, April 1)

It is interesting to note that, in the Condition I reflections, the initial expression was often about feelings, even though there was much more than feelings on the minds of the teachers as they thought about their work. It is possible, at least for these six beginning teachers, that feelings need to be expressed before any substantive analysis of the teaching can be done. Reflecting alone provides the opportunity for that expression of feelings.

The reconstruction of classroom events that is self-generated, highly personal and expressive of feelings, as were the Condition I reflections, often takes the form of an internal dialogue about the teaching. Importantly, this form did not appear in the reflections under the other three conditions. By definition of the condition parameters, an internal dialogue is unlikely and not discernible for Conditions III and IV, which consisted of partner conversations. However, in Condition II, where there was no partner, there was little evidence of the internal dialogue (such as the questioning of one's self and general pondering) that is common in Condition I. As beginning teachers 'talk to themselves' about their teaching, they respond to the perplexities of teaching in a personal way by questioning themselves and pondering their teaching actions and reactions.

> Sometimes I wonder if I ask 'the obvious' too often, but there are always kids who don't get what the fastest kids pick up. (Glynda I, Journal entry, March 3)

> I must admit I was in shock. This young woman [16] is my top student and is very attractive. How could she think that she was overweight? What has society done to our youth? I spend an hour every day with this student. How could I have been so unobservant?

How many of my other students are suffering from this disease? (Sally I, Journal entry, April 2)

It is important to reiterate that there is a broad range of topics that these beginning teachers reflect about when they reflect on their own without a partner or a portfolio. In the quotations above, for example, how to deal with particular students, how to ask questions, how to assess the limits of one's professional responsibility, and how to assess one's teaching decisions, are all represented in the content. What is different is not the content of what beginning teachers think about, but rather how the content is understood and expressed in personally referenced, emotion-laden ways.

Considering the Content: Condition II — Portfolio/No Partner

To prepare for the Condition II reflection the teachers assembled a portfolio of materials representing one week's work in the classroom. The portfolio was to be a collection of a variety of materials from the week: lesson plans, handouts, overhead transparencies, examples of student work, examples of their responses to student work, text materials, and so on. At the time of the reflection, the portfolio was with them; they could use it or not as they wished.

The introduction of a portfolio of materials resulted in a greater focus on *content* than was true for the reflections in Condition I. As shown in Table 11.1, 19 per cent of the reflections for Condition II focused on the content of instruction, in contrast to only 4 per cent for Condition I. Even though there were no instructions to use the portfolio materials in any particular way (or necessarily to use them at all), both the reflections themselves and the teachers' self reports about the reflections demonstrated that the teachers interpreted the portfolio as an opportunity to think about the content of their teaching, or possibly as a directive to do so. Phil, for example, discussed the expectation and focus that the portfolio provided him. Keeping a portfolio similar to the one he did for this reflection exercise as a matter of course in his teaching resulted in his using the portfolio as he typically does. To him the portfolio meant planning, and planning meant content.

> [Without a portfolio] I would have done less. I would have had less of this style and more of what I felt about it, what the students said, and things like that because I wouldn't have this [portfolio] to refer to. Since I use it for planning, I just slipped into that mode of thinking. (Phil II, Interview 7:1)
>
> I did leave out some details, some emotions about the teaching that I did. What I wrote about was especially related to planning. In creating this [portfolio] and using it, that just turned out to be the

emphasis of what I was thinking when I wrote. (Phil II, Interview 6:9–11)

For Lucy, the portfolio also meant content; having a portfolio available communicated to her an expectation that her reflection would be content-related. Lucy found this distracting, explaining that what was on her mind and what she wanted to think about was her students, not the content of her instruction. When she thinks about her students, she says, 'I don't use props' (Lucy II, Interview). To Lucy, 'reflecting' about her teaching means thinking about students. The other thinking she does, which orients her more towards the content of her instruction (and which she does not call 'reflection'), requires 'props' of some sort — a gradebook, the text, her plans.

> When I'm usually thinking about my teaching I'm either grading some students' papers or tests, or I'm thinking about what I'm going to do and what I've done which is why I have the book. So when I'm thinking about them, I usually have them around me. When I'm out on my own and I'm doing dishes and I'm thinking, I don't have that and that's when I do more individual student thinking. You know, how can I deal with this person? (Lucy II, Interview 8:4)

For Lucy, the 'props' (or the portfolio) signalled content.

'Considering the content' for these teachers caused them, as Phil indicated, to try to 'leave out emotions' or to reflect without expressing feelings — a second distinction that the teachers made between reflecting with and without a portfolio. The portfolio focuses the reflection on the materials and what they represent, and away from the teachers themselves as the center, or so they perceive it as they talk about the reflection experience in retrospect.

> I think in collecting the materials I think more specifically about what is happening in the classroom and I think more from my head and less from my heart. When I'm looking at the materials I'll say to myself, 'Well, what specifically went wrong and what went right?' Whereas when I'm just reflecting I do tend to go over these bigger questions — Are they learning anything? Am I benefitting my students? — and a lot more about feelings than about actual class-work'. (Jill IV, AR Interview, 11:7)

As stated in the summary of the Condition I findings, feelings were significant in all four conditions. Although for five of the six teachers, the primary focus of the reflections for Condition II was not on feelings, it is interesting to note that four of the six teachers began their reflections indicating some general emotional state. This finding again suggests that expressing feelings may take immediate precedence in the reflections of beginning teachers. Meghann began by expressing anger over the final visit of her university supervisor; Alex began by expressing discouragement over the imbalance of demands and rewards in teaching; Sally began by expressing frustration with her teaching which she attributed to low subject matter knowledge for the unit she was teaching; and Jill began by expressing a general malaise that pervaded her experience of the week.

The power of feelings in determining reflection content, especially when there is no intervening factor, is substantiated by looking at the two teachers who did not use their portfolios during the reflection. These two teachers focused more on feelings throughout the reflection than did the other four. One focused primarily on students and her reactions to students; the other reflected entirely about her feelings about being a teacher and how uncertain she was about that career choice.

The focus on feelings in a way that resembles the Condition I reflections raises an important point in distinguishing the effects of Conditions I and II. When the portfolio was NOT used for Condition II, the condition became closer in structure to Condition I. We can look for evidence to support this claim in the reflection content of the two teachers who did not use their portfolio for the Condition II reflections. For both of these teachers the amount of 'personal' content in their reflections (50 per cent and 22 per cent) was greater than the amount of 'content' content (0 per cent and 9 per cent respectively). Though the structure of Condition II was closer to that of Condition I when the portfolio was not used, there remained an important distinction in the structure of the two conditions about which the teachers spoke in the post-reflection interview. The distinction comes in the *creation* of the portfolio. Whether or not the teachers actually used the portfolios, having to create them influenced the reflection by forcing the teachers to think about their content and, subsequently, about the content of their instruction.

For the remaining four teachers, the focus that emerged from their reflections was on the content of the instruction itself, or on how that content is taught (content-specific pedagogy), including questions they had about content instruction. The statements below demonstrate the content orientation of the reflections.

> I am sure that I cleared up the ideas about catalase digestion, enzyme function, protein derivation, etc. for some kids. Most of the kids had the correct knowledge and application of it by the close of the lesson. (Meghann II, Freewrite, p. 3)

> Doing this helps to eliminate an overburden of memorization for my students. Instead of memorizing all the kingdoms, phylums, classes, orders, etc. of plants, I have tried to emphasize the essential structures of the plant and their function. (Sally II, Freewrite, p. 3)

> This week I taught the main bulk of a chapter dealing with polynomial equations. It is one of the better parts of the book but I'm still not in love with my math book. The first lesson was synthetic division, then remainder and factor theorems, then integral roots. (Lucy II, Freewrite, p. 1)

In summary, after an initial expression of feelings, the focus of the Condition II reflection was on content and the pedagogy of that content, for four of the six teachers. Two central reasons for this focus emerged in the post-reflection interviews: the presence of the portfolio materials reminded the teachers of the content of their instruction and issues related to that content, and the teachers interpreted the task — by virtue of the requirement of the portfolio in the first place — as thinking about the materials and the content of the materials represented.

The Condition II data raise an additional issue. Looking back over the content of instruction for the purpose of understanding classroom events concerning that content may not be common for beginning teachers. Although these teachers create records of their work by saving lesson plans and handouts, they do so primarily for the purpose of future use, rather than for reconstructing the past to understand it more fully and to learn from those experiences. In the two instances where the portfolio was not used in the reflection, and content was not the focus, both teachers indicated that they remembered what went on in class, and that 'going back over it', therefore, was not particularly necessary or important. Instead, they focused on what was most immediately important to them, and this, like the reflection for Condition I, included their personal responses to various factors in their week of teaching, their feelings about themselves, and their work of that week. For the remaining four, there was a sense that they should look at the materials in the portfolio but there was no general framework for doing so, other than to report the contents, assess the materials representing that content or, in some instances, use the materials as a guide for planning subsequent lessons. Having a portfolio focused the reflection on the content of instruction.

Puzzling over Pedagogy: Condition III — Partner/No Portfolio

For the third condition, the teachers reflected about their week of teaching in the presence of a partner who had observed the teaching once during the week. There was no portfolio of materials present for the reflection. A focus on matters of *general pedagogy* distinguished the content of the reflection under this condition. In contrast to the artifactual-content focus of Condition II, working with a partner focused the reflections more towards the social elements of teaching, the complex interactions between teachers and learners. As shown in Table 11.1, the percentage of content that was focused on general pedagogy (37 per cent) was more than twice as great as for any of the other three conditions.

The predominant concerns were about teaching in general: how to lecture more effectively; how to ask questions; how to give directions; how to organize materials for effective presentations; how to prepare relevant lessons. The issues raised about learners were also framed in terms of pedagogy: how to engage learners, how to reach learners of different abilities, how to motivate slow students, how to change attitudes about learning in both high and low ability students, and so on. The reflective conversations most often took one of two forms: assessment by the teachers of themselves as teachers and of their work in classrooms (including asking for validation from the partner who had been there) or problem solving with the partner about what occurred in the teaching, what might have occurred if things had been handled differently, and what could occur in subsequent attempts.

The presence of a partner offers the reflecting teachers an opportunity to receive feedback on their work. They are assisted in the reflective reconstruction of the classroom events by talking with someone who has seen the class and who can help them picture what occurred. With a focus on how to teach better and on general techniques for doing so — this was the central concern of each of the six teachers in this condition — the teacher is able to describe what he or she did (often with some assessment of it) as an opening for the reflective conversation. The following examples from the reflective conversations of John, James and Jeff with their partners demonstrate how the initial focus on general pedagogy, incorporating some self-assessment, leads into discussion of pedagogical concerns.

> Before the filmstrip I've got to present it better, introduce it better so the kids understand why they are watching and why I think it's important. And what I found I did, I showed the filmstrip and then I got angry at them for not paying as much attention to it and then explained to them why it was important and they should have watched it and paid attention to it. So I would have reversed the order of what I did in the classroom there. (John III, MS Interview, 3:4)

> As soon as I hear someone make the correct response, even if there are three other wrong ones, I go, 'OK, that's right. You've got it'. And I shouldn't do that because I'm only allowing one person to get it right. But then there are times when I try, if I call on a particular person, someone else will answer, which annoys me no end because I really want to see if that person has it. So I don't know, I guess I've done something that just gets them in that mode. As soon as I ask a question, they'll try and answer it. And sometimes I get bored too which is probably what happened the day you

were there because I had shown the same example the day before. (Jeff III, RT Interview, 7:1)

The self-assessment that occurred so frequently in the reflections of these beginning teachers usually focused on how well they performed in the classroom. How well they performed depended to some extent on what they knew. While knowledge is not a sufficient condition, it is a necessary condition for good teaching; it is also a necessary condition for reflection in teaching. The form of knowledge that surfaced most frequently in the reflections of the teachers in Condition III was general pedagogical knowledge — general or generic knowledge of teaching across content areas. General pedagogical knowledge is often directly translated by beginners into concerns of teaching techniques because the demands of performing well are both immediate and numerous. What works and what doesn't work, or simply how to do things better, are the kinds of issues that are prevalent in these conversations. In the following examples, the techniques of varying the routine, asking good questions, and having students teach one another are raised by the teachers as they reflect on their work.

> I haven't found any other way to structure the class so that we can do something different. I sort of burned them out on group work because we did that last unit every day — every group did their homework together. So I said, okay, time to give that a rest. I think consciously about varying the routine as much as I can. (Jeff III, RT Interview, 4:2)

> One of my concerns is how I can question better. I don't feel like I am a very effective questioner at this point — or not the most effective. (Charlene III, AR Interview, 9:3)

Implicit in these beginning teachers' reflections about teaching and teaching techniques is a concern for the *learner*. They are concerned with how to teach particular learners who present them with one problem or another or, alternatively, how to teach some particular content to learners. The following statements illustrate comments cast in terms of teaching particular learners.

> I think that as eighth graders, too, they just need to make random interpretations. And it is so hard for one student to understand what another student is saying. So I almost have to allow them to hear one another. But if they don't directly respond to one another with direct sentences, saying, 'Well, I agree with what Scott is saying', I have to at least allow them to carry on the conversation. (James III, SW Interview, 3:3)

One of the problems was that they weren't prepared, which is
the problem I have with this class all the time — with group work,
with anything — is that they have a really hard time doing anything
as a group — in little groups, in big groups, in teams — because so
many of the kids don't do the work. (Vanessa III, CH Interview,
2:1)

Data from Condition III show that the beginning teachers like to talk about
their teaching, which they think about 'all the time'. They are concerned
with what they do in their classrooms, and how they should do it better.
Glynda expresses the common sentiment: 'It's crazy, it's the first year and
you want to be the greatest teacher in the whole world' (Glynda III, AR
Interview, 9:6). The opportunity to talk about their work was viewed as
vitally important to the participants. Provided with very few formal occasions for reflective conversations with their colleagues, the beginners reported that they spent a lot of time in informal conversations with friends in
their teacher education program. The informal conversations are different
from the more formal type of reflection that they experienced in this research, they explain. The structural factors that define this formal situation,
such as the partner observing the class and the time guideline of 45 minutes
or longer for the reflection conversation, were cited as examples of why the
formal setting made the reflection 'deeper', 'more thorough', and 'clearer'.
While the content focus of the reflections — on teaching and learning or
general pedagogy — is the same for the informal and formal conversations,
the quality of the conversations is different.

In summary, the opportunity for conversation with a colleague who had
observed the teaching is important in considering the reflection that occurred under Condition III. All reflection involves a conversation of some sort,
either a conversation with oneself or a conversation with others. When they
reflected alone, the teachers' focus was often deeply personal. With a
partner, they shifted the focus to the more social aspects of teaching, to the
issues of general pedagogy and the complex interaction between teacher and
learners in the classroom. With a partner who has seen the class, the teacher
is able to think back on what occurred in the teaching and reconstruct those
events with the assistance of someone who has experienced the class from a
different vantage point. The opportunity to talk with a partner who has seen
the class orients the teacher to an examination of the general aspects of
teaching and learning.

Contemplating Content Pedagogy:
Condition IV — Partner and Portfolio

Condition IV combines the features of the partner and the portfolio. The
teachers were asked to create a portfolio of materials that represented their

week of teaching and to bring the portfolio to a reflection interview that was held at the end of the week with a colleague who had observed the class once during that week. The condition permitted study of the combined and interactive effects of the partner and portfolio on the content of the reflection.

Of the six teachers in this condition, three used the portfolio extensively during the reflection interview. The remaining three did not appear to base their reflections on the portfolio, though they did refer to it from time to time. The findings reported here, then, are based primarily on the three cases where the portfolio and the partner were both part of an interactive process (including the process of using a portfolio to reconstruct the events of the week in an effort to understand them).

The content of the reflection for Condition IV mirrors the process in which teacher, partner and portfolio interact. As might have been predicted by combining the content focus (characterizing Condition II) and the general pedagogy focus (characterizing Condition III), the focus of reflections in Condition IV is on the intersection of pedagogy and content, recently termed 'content-specific pedagogy' (Shulman, 1986). As shown in Table 11.1, 57 per cent of the content of the Condition IV reflections were on content-specific pedagogy, double the percentages for the other conditions.

Content-specific pedagogy refers to matters of teaching and learning that are unique to particular subject-matter content. The knowledge that undergirds content-specific pedagogy is knowledge that distinguishes the student of a discipline from the teacher of that discipline.

> It represents the blending of content and pedagogy into an under-standing of how particular topics, problems, or issues are organized, represented, and adapted to the diverse interests and abilities of learners, and presented for instruction. (Shulman, 1987, p. 8)

For Condition IV, the teachers reflected with their partners by reenacting classroom events just as they did for Condition III. This involved reliving the events and emphasizing the pedagogical concerns that framed their thinking at the time of the original teaching experience. By rehearsing the event with someone who experienced it and who could validate the rehearsal, the teachers were able to understand their teaching in new ways. At the same time, the portfolio stimulated a focus on the subject matter content of the teaching: In the presence of those materials that represent the classroom instruction, the teachers were more likely than they were under Condition III to focus their attention on the particular content of the week of instruction. Unlike the reflection of Condition III in which the teachers and their partners talked primarily about teaching in general, the portfolio seemed to orient the teachers to a discussion of *teaching subject matter in particular*.

In the cases where the portfolio was used extensively by the teachers and partners, the teachers began most frequently by reporting what they were teaching, citing the lesson that the partner observed to orient the partner to particulars of the instruction they were discussing. The dialogue that ensued most often involved a discussion about the content-specific pedagogical issues.

> It's kind of like magnetism, but it's electrical — electrostatic fields are charging things and getting things to move with these kind of mysterious charges. You don't touch them. We were talking about some of that, why this happened when you rubbed these things together. And they seemed to be interested in it because it started out talking about walking across the room on a dry day and getting an electric shock when you touch something. That's something they're all familiar with, so they could see what was going on there. So that seemed to work pretty well. It took all period to do that. (Phil IV, MS Interview, 3:1)

The interactive process that focuses on content-specific pedagogy involves the active participation of the partner who, in combination with the teacher, is drawn towards the content by the portfolio and by the teacher's raising of content issues of importance. In the cases of Phil and Jeff, both partners facilitated the conversation by providing feedback, validation and general questions about the lesson and the particular subject-specific content that was part of that lesson. Here Phil's partner responds to the examples Phil used.

> I find the examples that you use are great. Toward the end of the lesson you were talking about magnets and tapes and how you can, you know, magnetic field and actually taping something and radio waves and AM and FM and that is — I mean, those are, they're so practical and realistic for these kids. Everyday they're dealing with those things. It's as if you picked something and I could actually see that the kids were paying [attention]. (MS in Phil IV, MS Interview, 5:5)

Under Condition IV, when the teachers were asked to reflect with the assistance of both a partner and a portfolio, they focused their attention on the interactive aspects of teaching and learning the content that was represented in the portfolio materials. As with Condition II, the portfolio of Condition IV focused the reflection on matters concerning the content of instruction. However, with the presence of a partner — the Condition III characteristic that resulted in a focus on the interactive aspects of teaching — the combined partner/portfolio factors of Condition IV focused the reflection on the interactive aspects of teaching particular content. The presence of the portfolio provided the teacher with a way to recall content in detail, and perhaps an expectation that the focus should be on the materials and content they represented. The presence of a partner — one who had attended the class — facilitated an interactive exchange as well as a focus on the interactive aspects of teaching and learning. With the partner and teacher both using the portfolio of materials as a stimulus for remembering classroom events, the content of the reflection focused on how that content was taught.

Summary of the Content Analysis

The content of the reflections for the beginning teachers clearly varied according to the conditions under which the reflection occurred. When the teachers reflected without the aid of either partner or portfolio, the focus of their reflection was personal — their personal responses to both teaching and learning to teach. For Condition II, when a portfolio was introduced to facilitate the reflection process, the focus shifted towards the content of instruction as represented by the materials contained in the portfolio. When a partner was introduced in Condition III, the teachers reflected more frequently about the social or interactive aspects of teaching and learning. Here the focus was on matters of general pedagogy — teaching and learning issues that are common across all the subject domains. The specificity of the reflections regarding subject matter and pedagogy shifted again in Condition IV, when the teachers had both a partner and a portfolio to facilitate the process. For Condition IV the focus of the reflection was on content-specific pedagogy.

The data show that beginning teachers focus on different aspects of their work when they reflect within different structures. Likewise, the data indicate that they think about their teaching differently — in greater depth, with greater clarity, with more or less openness to exploration — depending on the structural circumstances under which the reflection occurs. This shows that if we want beginning teachers to think about the full spectrum of issues in their work, we must offer them a broad range of opportunities to do so. If we want them to focus on content, or general pedagogy, or the goals of instruction, we must create structures known to promote the desired reflection. The data presented here suggest that reflection on content, for example, or the teaching of that content, would be enhanced by having the teachers establish an 'audit trail' (Guba and Lincoln, 1985, p. 319) of their classroom experiences similar to the kind of audit trail a series of architectural tracings would provide an architect, or case records would provide an attorney. Such an audit trail for beginning teachers, which might take the form of a teaching portfolio such as the one employed in this research, would not only help teachers remember what occurred in the flurry of classroom action, but would also focus their thinking by 'grounding' their ideas to the content issues represented by the portfolio materials.

The existence and significance of feelings in the reflections of the

Anna E. Richert

beginning teachers is obvious in the data, and it appears that teachers need to express those feelings before other types of reflection can occur. Learning to teach is an emotional experience. The move from experienced learner to beginning teacher frequently causes uncertainty, self-doubt, frustration and fatigue; the process generates many feelings that need expression. The data reported here suggest that, while feelings dominate their initial reflections, there is much more that beginning teachers think about when they think about their work. What the findings indicate, therefore, is that opportunities for the expression and validation of feelings are an important component of teacher education. If beginning teachers have an opportunity to respond to the emotional content of their work by articulating it and sharing it with others, they are more likely to move to other areas or levels of analysis as they contemplate their experiences in classrooms. Regardless of the particular structure of the reflection opportunity, that is, whether the structure is created to facilitate reflection about matters of general pedagogy, subject-specific pedagogy, the moral and ethical dimensions of schooling, or whatever, the provision of time and space for the expression of feelings is necessary as we move beginning practitioners to new levels of analysis about their work. In so doing we facilitate their growth as professionals.

Reflection in teaching is difficult in many ways. Some research has suggested that many teachers are not reflective in their practice (Wehlage, 1981; MacKay and Marland, 1978; Lortie, 1975; Jackson, 1968; Zeichner, 1981–82), and it is easy but misleading to criticize teachers for this finding. Reflection is inhibited by many structural features, including the prescriptive nature of curricula and the structure of schools that isolates teachers from one another (Lortie, 1975; Sarason, 1971; Jackson, 1968). The structures of teacher education likewise inhibit reflection (Richert, 1987). In addition to the structural barriers to reflection, research shows us that there are also cognitive barriers. Looking back at one's work and learning from one's experiences can be extremely problematic (Nisbett and Wilson, 1977; Nisbett and Ross, 1980; Tversky and Kahneman, 1974; Feiman-Nemser and Buchmann, 1985).

While the barriers to reflection confront all teachers, beginning teachers are particularly thwarted by the complexity of the task. One participant offered a clear description.

I've been thinking recently about just how difficult it is to be a reflective teacher. Even given that I'm only teaching two classes a day, and have the opportunity to think about my teaching within the context of my university classes, I still often feel like I don't have enough time to step back and evaluate how effective my teaching is. By the time I finish one lesson, I usually feel like there is still the next day's mountain to climb. Another thing about reflection — it's hard. It's hard because one must analyze what's transpired and to some degree make a value judgment about it. And if the reflection is honest, it can mean that a teacher may have to alter his/her style or completely chuck something that he/she had worked hard to develop. It seems to be much safer and more secure not to reflect, because one doesn't have to change that which he/she doesn't see as being wrong. (John 1, Journal entry 4:4)

Overwhelmed with the demands of the job and fearful of failure and vulnerability, beginning teachers seem reluctant to look back on their work with a critical eye. Even when the conditions are 'right', and when they have the time and a space that is safe for them to do so, they often don't know how to think about their work in productive ways. They are caught at the level of feelings and cannot move beyond, around, or through them to the substance about which those feelings are generated. They remain at the level of 'reporting' what occurred, rather than moving to a level of analyzing, which requires skills they lack or have not developed fully. They focus on one area of their pedagogy, such as how to control a particular group of unruly students, rather than responding to any broader set of teaching concerns. By highlighting the immediate or 'pressing' matters that face them moment-to-moment, they proceed without giving adequate consideration to the goals of their practice. In short, they have not developed the skills of reflective practice.

To facilitate reflection in beginning teachers, teacher educators may wish to create programs that offer opportunities for students of the profession to learn the knowledge and skills of reflective practice. Understanding the conditions that promote reflection in beginning teachers is fundamental to creating such programs. This study is a starting point for developing that understanding.

Acknowledgment

An earlier version of this chapter was presented at the annual meeting of the American Educational Research Association, Washington, DC, April 1987.

References

BUCHMANN, M. (1983) *Justification in Teacher Thinking: An Analysis of Interview Data*, Research Series No. 124, East Lansing, MI, Institute for Research on Teaching, Michigan State University.

CLARK, C.M. and PETERSON, P.L. (1986) 'Teachers' thought processes', in WITTROCK, M. (Ed.) *Handbook of Research on Teaching*, 3rd ed., New York, Macmillan, pp. 255–296.

CLARK, C.M. and YINGER, R.J. (1977) 'Research on teacher thinking', *Curriculum Inquiry*, **7**, pp. 279–394.

CRUICKSHANK, D.R. and ARMALINE, W.D. (1986) 'Field experiences in teacher education: Considerations and recommendations', *Journal of Teacher Education*, **37**, 3, pp. 34–40.

CRUICKSHANK, D.R., KENNEDY, J.J., WILLIAMS, E.J., HOLTON, J. and FAY, D.E. (1981) 'Evaluation of reflective teaching outcomes', *Journal of Educational Research*, **75**, pp. 26–32.

DEWEY, J. (1933) *How We Think: A Restatement of the Relation of Reflective Thinking to the Educative Process*, Chicago, Henry Regnery Co.

FEIMAN-NEMSER, S. (1979) 'Technique and inquiry in teacher education: A curricular case study', *Curriculum Inquiry*, **9**, pp. 63–79.

FEIMAN-NEMSER, S. and BUCHMANN, M. (1985) 'Pitfalls of experience in teacher preparation', *Teachers' College Record*, **87**, pp. 53–65.

FULLER, F. and BOWN, O. (1975) 'Becoming a teacher', in RYAN, K. (Ed.) *Teacher Education*, Seventy-fourth Yearbook of the National Society for the Study of Education, Part 2, Chicago, University of Chicago Press, pp. 25–52.

GUBA, Y.S. and LINCOLN, E.G. (1985) *Naturalistic Inquiry*, Beverly Hills, CA, Sage.

JACKSON, P. (1968) *Life in Classrooms*, New York, Holt, Rinehart and Winston.

LORTIE, D. (1975) *Schoolteacher: A Sociological Study*, Chicago, University of Chicago Press.

MacKAY, D. and MARLAND, P. (1978) *Thought Processes of Teachers*, paper presented at the annual meeting of the American Educational Research Association, Toronto.

NISBETT, R.E. and ROSS, L. (1980) *Human Inference: Strategies and Shortcomings of Social Judgement*, Englewood Cliffs, NJ, Prentice Hall.

NISBETT, R.E. and WILSON, T.D. (1977) 'Telling more than we can know: Verbal reports on mental processes', *Psychological Review*, **84**, 3, pp. 231–259.

RICHERT, A.E. (1987) *Reflex to Reflection: Facilitating Reflection in Novice Teachers*, unpublished doctoral dissertation, Stanford University.

RUSSELL, T.L. and SPAFFORD, C. (1986) *Teachers as Reflective Practitioners in Peer Clinical Supervision*, paper presented at the annual meeting of the American Educational Research Association, San Francisco, ERIC Document Reproduction No. ED 270 410.

SARASON, S. (1971) *The Culture of the School and the Problem of Change*, Boston, Allyn and Bacon.

SCHWAB, J.J. (1973) 'The practical 3: Translation into curriculum', *School Review*, **81**, pp. 501–522.

SHAVELSON, R.J. and STERN, P. (1981) 'Research on teachers' pedagogical thoughts, judgments, decisions and behavior', *Review of Educational Research*, **51**, pp. 455–498.

SHULMAN, L.S. (1986) 'Those who understand: Knowledge growth in teaching', *Educational Researcher*, **15**, 2, pp. 4–14.

SHULMAN, L.S. (1987) 'Knowledge and teaching: Foundations of the new reform', *Harvard Educational Review*, **57**, pp. 1–22.

TOM, A. (1985) 'Inquiry into inquiry-oriented teacher education', *Journal of Teacher Education*, **36**, 5, pp. 35–44.

TVERSKY, A. and KAHNEMAN, D. (1974) 'Judgement under uncertainty: Heuristics and biases', *Science*, **185**, pp. 1124–1131.

VAN MANEN, M. (1977) 'Linking ways of knowing with ways of being practical', *Curriculum Inquiry*, **6**, pp. 205–228.

WEDMAN, J. and MAHLIOS, M. (1985) *Addressing the Development of Reflectivity through the Study of Journal Writing, Conferencing and Teacher Routines*, paper presented at the annual meeting of the Midwestern Educational Research Association, Chicago.

WEHLAGE, G.G. (1981) 'Can teachers be more reflective about their work? A commentary on some research about teachers', in TABACHNICK, B.R., POPKEWITZ, T.S. and SZEKELY, B.B. (Eds) *Studying Teaching and Learning*, New York, Praeger, pp. 101–113.

ZEICHNER, K.M. (1981–82) 'Reflective Teaching and Field-based Experiences in Teacher Education', *Interchange*, **12**, 4, pp. 1–22.

12 The Roles of Reflective Practice and Foundational Disciplines in Teacher Education

Allan MacKinnon and Gaalen Erickson

In educational circles of the 1980s the term 'reflection' has been used frequently with reference to teaching practices (Erickson, 1987; Kilbourn, 1988; MacKinnon, 1987, 1989b; Munby, 1986; Roberts and Chastko, 1990; Russell, 1987; Shulman, 1987), in part as a result of the provocative ideas of Schön (1983, 1987, 1988). This body of work opened a new forum of discussion by advancing a new image of the nature of professional knowledge and how it is acquired. Much discussion has followed, giving rise to diverse meanings of the term reflection in teacher education literature (Grimmett, 1989; Grimmett, MacKinnon, Erickson and Riecken, 1990; Clift, Houston and Pugach, 1990). More fundamental than the differences in how the term 'reflection' is used is how teacher education programs might be structured so that they meet this image of how professional knowledge is acquired. At the heart of program discussion lies the perennially awkward problem of determining what is foundational to teacher education.

One point of difficulty in designing teacher education for reflective practice concerns the place of 'foundations courses', such as the history and philosophy of education, educational psychology, sociology and ethics. With the recent proliferation of 'school-based' teacher education programs that seem to emanate from ideas about reflective practice, it is crucial that we address questions such as the following: What are the foundational disciplines and what areas of study should be included? What is the nature of a program based upon courses offered in the foundation areas and, at the same time, reflective practice in schools? Is this possible? How should these foundational disciplines and their relationship to the program at large be conceptualized? Is it, for example, meaningful to talk about 'integrating' the foundations with other parts of the program? All are questions that should be, and indeed are being raised in faculties of education. These questions are equally poignant to those who support either 'reflective practice' or 'the foundations' as principal orienting frameworks for thinking about teacher education. Although it is not clear that the 'foundations' and 'reflective practice' positions stand in opposition to each other, the ongoing debate in faculties of education seems to be based on an artificial dichotomy.

The aim of this chapter is to show that the institutional separation of foundations courses from reflective practice in teacher education programs is problematic; the intellectual dichotomy seems to have developed from a misreading of John Dewey's work. First, we review the historical context for understanding the concept of reflection by asking why we need such a construct in dealing with matters of teaching and teacher education. We use this approach to try to establish a reciprocal relationship between 'foundations' and 'reflective practice'. We begin by revisiting some of the writings of Dewey and then proceed to analyses of reflection in the work of Harold Rugg, and of Gordon Hullfish and Philip Smith. We show that thought about reflection from the 1940s to the 1960s followed the tradition of Dewey for the most part, but nevertheless changed the concept of reflection in subtle yet significant ways.

Later interpretations of 'foundations' as *distinct from* 'reflection' created a division or 'rift' within teacher education programs, but ultimately set the stage for Schön's work and its return to Dewey. Our journey continues by reviewing this work, especially in terms of how Schön's analysis may help to repair the institutional-programmatic 'rift' in teacher education. As we proceed through this brief history of the concept of 'reflection', we give our interpretation of the common ground shared by all of these scholars, although ultimately we intend to show where we think Schön has ventured into new terrain and what this means for conceptualizing a teacher education program. The latter half of the chapter presents data collected in our research program investigating science teacher education. These data provide a context for analyzing and illustrating a typology of foundational knowledge that is evident in the reflections of student teachers.

Why Reflection?

Dewey's work provides a useful starting point for talking about reflection, not simply because it provides insight into Schön's intellectual roots, but also in order to understand the development of thought about reflective teaching in this century. In *The Sources of a Science of Education*, Dewey (1929) began by asking two questions: Is there a science of education? Can there be a science of education? The very phrasing of these questions raises many difficulties because of the variety of ways in which we use the word 'science'. As Dewey noted, the term might suggest the activities of mathematics and physics, excluding activities belonging to the disciplines of geology or psychology, for example, on the grounds that the latter are relatively descriptive, inexact, or lacking in rigorous methods of demonstration. Dewey rephrased the questions as follows:

> What are the ways by means of which the function of education in
> all its branches and phases ... can be conducted with systematic
> increase of intelligent control and understanding? What are the
> materials on which we may — and should — draw in order that
> educational activities may become in less degree products of routine
> tradition, accident and transitory accidental influences? (Dewey,
> 1929, p. 9)

Dewey viewed disciplines such as psychology, sociology or biology, as
sources of a science of education. These sources were seen to provide
'intellectual instrumentalities' for *widening our range of attention to particular detail in practice situations*; they were *not* to be viewed as sources of
'rules of practice'. Dewey was well aware of the hazardous intellectual
connections from theory, to middleman interpreter, to practitioner, to instruction itself. He preferred to think that educational science 'had no
content of its own', that is, there were no 'rules' for the art of teaching.
Rather, Dewey chose to think of educational science residing in the inquiries of practitioners.

> It is often assumed, in effect if not in words, that classroom teachers
> have not themselves the training which will enable them to give
> effective intelligent cooperation to disciplined inquiry in practice.
> The objection proves too much, so much so that it is almost fatal to
> the idea of a workable scientific content in education. For these
> teachers are the ones through whom the results of scientific findings
> finally reach students. They are the channels through which the
> consequences of educational theory come into the lives of those at
> school. I suspect that if these teachers are mainly channels of recep-
> tion and transmission, the conclusions of science will be badly
> deflected and distorted before they get into the minds of pupils. I
> am inclined to believe that this state of affairs is a chief cause for the
> tendency ... to convert scientific findings into recipes to be fol-
> lowed. The human desire to be an 'authority' and to control the
> activities of others does not, alas, disappear when a man becomes a
> scientist. (Dewey, 1929, p. 47)

Thus we have in Dewey's writings the same objection to what Schön (1983)
later referred to as technical rationality, 'the view that ... professional
activity consists in instrumental problem solving made rigorous by the application of scientific theory and technique' (p. 21). The meaning of technical rationality is also apparent in the context of teacher education. As a case
in point, methods courses might characterize teaching in terms of methodo-
logies and techniques that have been shown to correlate positively with
student achievement, possibly drawing on the so-called 'effective teaching'
research literature. Thus students of education may be taught about the

'principles of teaching'. For instance, they may learn about the concept of 'wait-time' — the time elapsing between a question and its answer and then be told that student achievement is optimized when a teacher waits three to five seconds after asking a question. The idea here is that pupils need time to think about what a question means before formulating an answer. As a guide for teaching, the concept of wait-time has merit; no doubt, it may serve to prevent some beginning teachers from moving too quickly from one student to another in search of the right answer. But two aspects of the handling of this concept make it an 'element' of technical rationality, generally due to the expectation that the proposition of wait-time is a rule that can be readily transferred to most instructional contexts. First, it is tested rigorously under experimental conditions in order to make a technical claim, such as 'optimal wait-time' falls within the three to five second range. Second, having achieved the status of a 'scientific finding', the three to five seconds of waiting becomes a principle for practice. This is a case in point of a general tendency to divide the activity of teaching into technical components, to deliver these components as an integral part of a teacher education curriculum that frequently takes the form of 'what research says' to the teacher, to expect that the meaning of these components can then be construed *from words* in lieu of experience in the practice setting and, finally, to expect students of education to construct their practice from these construed meanings that are supposed to describe the technical building blocks of teaching. In short, technical rationality is the view that the principles of teaching can be 'delivered' during the on-campus component of a teacher education program, and then applied by candidates in their practice teaching. The primary source of valid and reliable knowledge is taken to be rigorous scientific experimentation.

Dewey concluded that 'the final reality of educational science is not found in books, nor in experimental laboratories, nor in the classrooms where it is taught, but in the *minds* of those engaged in directing educational activities' (Dewey, 1929, p. 32). Thus his ideal was that the 'intellectual tools' afforded by science could be used by teachers *as* inquirers, investigators examining their own practices. To provide the substantive features of this type of 'inquiry in practice', Dewey turned to the notion of reflection.

From Dewey to Schön

In *How We Think* (1909, second edition, 1933) Dewey distinguished reflective thinking from other forms of thought by two characteristics: a state of doubt or hesitation in which thinking originates in the practice situation, and an act of inquiring to find material that will resolve the doubt and dispose of the perplexity. These features were seen by Dewey to arise in the course of practice much like the occasional fork in the path we travel:

> In the suspense of uncertainty, we metaphorically climb a tree, we try to find some standpoint from which we may survey additional facts and, getting a more commanding view of the situation, decide how the facts stand related to one another.... Thinking is not a case of spontaneous combustion; it does not occur just on 'general principles'. There is something that occasions or evokes it. (Dewey, 1909/1933, pp. 14–15)

As reflection arises from a directly experienced situation that puzzles or surprises us, so it aims to produce a situation that is clear, coherent, settled, harmonious. However, the conclusion arrived at is tentative and subject to further examination by

> the active, persistent, and careful consideration of any belief or supposed form of knowledge in light of the grounds that support it and the further conclusions to which it tends.... once begun, it includes a conscious and voluntary effort to establish belief upon a firm basis of evidence and rationality. (Dewey, 1909/1933, p. 9)

Dewey noted that the data at hand in a situation of doubt or perplexity cannot, in any straightforward manner, supply the solution to the practical problem at hand; they can only suggest it. 'What, then', he asked, 'are the sources of the suggestion'?

> Clearly, past experience and a fund of relevant knowledge at one's command. If the person has had some acquaintance with similar situations, if he has dealt with material of the same sort before, suggestions more or less apt and helpful will arise. But unless there has been some analogous experience, confusion remains mere confusion. (Dewey, 1909/1933, pp. 15–16)

Dewey advanced the idea that the basic intellectual content for teacher education should come from established sciences outside of the family of educational research disciplines. He pointed to physiology, biology, psychology and sociology as likely sources, and proposed that 'conceptualists' would translate these to primary concepts for educational application. But the application would take the form of 'reflective inquiry', with the tools of the intellect enabling the broadening of perception, rather than a 'recipe-style' form of practice. Grounded in the practitioner's knowledge and experience, reflective thinking originates in directly experienced situations that are puzzling and uncertain, and proceeds through observation, inference, suggestion, intellectualization and the subsequent testing of hypotheses in practice.

In this light, Dewey can be considered as one of the 'founding parents' of ideas about 'reflective practice' and about the 'sources' of educational thought. Here we can begin to see the path that Dewey's thinking took in subsequent writings until it became likened to some kind of 'scientific method'. Dewey's view on these 'sources' led to the 'Foundations of Education' movement, beginning in the 1930s, in which the focus of teacher education was on the fundamental concepts and theory essential for understanding and improving practice. In *Foundations for American Education*, Harold Rugg (1947) agreed with Dewey about the nature of the sources for the intellectual content of educational thought, although Rugg included aesthetics and morality as additional sources from which a science might be developed. The foundations of education shifted from the established sciences to the psychological, social, aesthetic and ethical foundations of civilization and education. Like Dewey, Rugg regarded education as a subject of study that would naturally emerge from the intellectual interest and concern of practitioners. For Rugg, teacher education institutions would have to move away from their traditional 'trade school temper' and, by means of the foundations program, become centers for the synthesis of information and creative expression pertinent to the invention of a sound theory of society, of the nature, behaviour and expression of man. Rugg's analysis of reflection was much like Dewey's:

> *First*: We recognize the problem; we confront it directly. Dewey calls it the 'felt-difficulty' ... the 'forked-road situation'. It has become a problem — impulsive, habitual behavior will no longer serve. We confront *alternatives*: hence we must choose. The situation is tense; we must confront it directly in *head-on-collision*.
>
> *Second*: We meet it in a rapid process of calling up suggestions ... ways of behaving ... from our past experience. In imagination we bring to consciousness things that we might do, find factors that may fit the situation.
>
> *Third*: We try them, comparing and appraising, rejecting one or other.
>
> *Fourth*: We accept one and act upon it.
>
> In this analysis the process has been broken down into a series of enumerated steps. Actually they are fairly concurrent, flashing up in swift succession, shot through with the mood, feeling, and emotion of the moment, tangled with meanings, desires, or fears. (Rugg, 1947, pp. 114–115)

Although Rugg departed somewhat from Dewey on what the 'foundations' or 'sources' for educational thought should be, Dewey's portrayal of reflective thinking remained largely unchanged in Rugg's work. In the main, reflection was seen as a conscious, deliberative move away from habitual ways of responding to situations in practice.

Hullfish and Smith (1961) offered a different analysis of reflection in their book, *Reflective Thinking: The Method of Education*. Although they began with a similar set of 'phases' for reflective activity, their idea was that 'reflection' involves the reconstruction of experience.

1. The presence (and recognition) of a problem situation....
2. Clarification of the problem....
3. Hypotheses formed, tested, and modified. Hypotheses, which may also be called hunches, guesses, ideas, or insights, lead us to cast predictive statements in the form of 'if-then' propositions. Such hypothetical propositions account for or explain the facts already observed or stumbled upon and, in addition, serve to direct further observation or fact finding ...
4. Action taken on the basis of the best-supported hypothesis....
(Hullfish and Smith, 1961, pp. 43–44)

The notion of reflection as the 'reconstruction of experience' is to be contrasted with Dewey's notion of reflection as 'practical deliberation' in a situation. The idea of 'reconstruction' entails more than broadening one's range of attention to particular detail. As the term 'reconstruction' denotes, it is a complete alteration of the situation. We submit that this is much more than 'deliberation' about a 'given' problem; the 'problem' may change significantly when the situation is reconstructed.

> This new development doesn't fit the basic structure of patterns already accepted. Consequently, there is a *feeling* of incongruency. This *feeling* frequently occurs with immediacy, apart from reflection, and thus may precede by a considerable time any intellectualization of the difficulty. This lack of coherence, of course, makes further reflective activity necessary; and, at this point, the patterns of knowledge held must be *reconstructed* if the new experience is to be accounted for. (Hullfish and Smith, 1961, p. 54)

The view of reflection as the reconstruction of experience follows, in part, the idea that knowledge is never a matter of direct disclosure. According to this view, we can never completely know the world as it is independent of our ways of *apprehending* it.

> When it is said that knowledge is mediated, never immediate, reference is thus made to the necessary role of meaning or cues.... So long as activity goes forward in terms of recognition ... there is no need to exercise conscious control over it. No problems are confronted. But when recognition fails, even momentarily, the situation calls forth feelings of uncertainty and doubt. This is the ground from which reflective activity (often designated in a more limited and

limiting way as 'problem solving') arises. And it is a ground, we should note, which intermingles emotional involvement and reflective activity. Thinking is not the work of an impersonal logical machine. (Hullfish and Smith, 1961, pp. 34–35)

This development of the concept of reflection focuses on the matter of breaking habitual ways of recognizing and dealing with situations. Thought about reflection has grown out of the problematic distinction between 'science' and 'art', 'theory' and 'practice', the 'general' and the 'particular'. Having their roots in Dewey's classic works, modern ideas about reflective thinking have included the notion that reflection involves the reconstruction of experience, which we believe is much more than 'deliberation' about a given problem. Our contention is that in the course of this development, the familiar theory-practice dichotomy has been relaxed for the most part, such that the two are inextricably bound together in the way people attend to and perceive their practice.

Thus we have the foundation on which Schön's analysis of reflection rests — the idea of inquiry and experiment *in* practice as the basis for the development of professional knowledge. But Schön has added two fundamental ideas to Dewey's notions about inquiry and experiment in practice. First, some of our knowledge (or ability) is held 'tacitly' by practitioners, hence Schön's need for the constructs of knowing-in-action and reflection-in-action. When we carry out the activity of ordinary life, much of our knowledge is 'implicit in our actions'; when we are asked to say what we know, we are sometimes at a loss for words. Second, we construct our representations of practice in action on the basis of the 'frames' available to us from past experience and from our existing knowledge. *Construction* of a practice is quite different from *deliberation* about it. For example, construction of a practice does not carry the instrumental separation of 'theory' from 'practice'; conceptions and perceptions of practice situations are inseparable from the 'appreciative systems', or ways of 'seeing' available to practitioners, the context of their world, the way they recognize dimensions of their students' worlds. These appreciative systems are acquired through experiencing classrooms in a new way — learning to pay attention to particular events in particular ways while at the same time acquiring a *feel* for situations of practice. It is useful to recall Schwab's (1970, 1971) analysis of deliberation in his classic treatment of the 'practical arts of the eclectic'. Deliberating on a practical problem, according to Schwab, involves examining the problem from a variety of theoretical 'lenses', and comparing and contrasting the consequences of taking action according to various views. It is not clear that Schwab's 'deliberation' would allow the problem to be reshaped to the extent that Schön is referring to with his notion of 'reframing'. A practitioner could deliberate on a problem without necessarily reframing it. A new frame would open up new territory for deliberative inquiry to proceed.

The Premises of a Teacher Education Program

It remains possible to interpret all that has been said thus far in two quite different directions for conceptualizing a teacher education program. On Dewey's view that the foundations of education are paramount in the development of teachers, we would concern ourselves primarily with the *sources* of an educational science. Granted, this never occurs in isolation from other aspects of a program, but in this endeavor we would continue in the lecture halls, 'shaping' the minds of prospective teachers with the historical, psychological, sociological and moral foundations of civilization and education. In this effort, we would construe a 'program' as a set of courses that would prepare the mind to interpret, make judgments about, and act in the wide and varied world of practice. We would continue to treat these foundation courses as *forms of knowledge*, pure and good in their own right; and there would be a tendency to separate the sources from the practice in much the same way as the courses are separated from the practicum.

Following Schön's view, we would concern ourselves with the provision of candidates' *experience* in schools. We would talk about a teacher education program as a forum for nurturing an appreciation of school life, including particular dispositions for inquiry, ways of seeing, critiquing and acting in classrooms. We would regard programming much like a conversation of practice (Yinger, 1990), something that comes together in our students' mindful and improvisational performances. Thus we would orchestrate occasions on which prospective teachers could display for us what they are already able to do in teaching, what they already understand teaching to be, how they recognize learning when it happens in front of them, and so on. These would be the building blocks of competent practice among students of teaching.

Resolution of these different ways of thinking about programming in teacher education is an extremely difficult matter. In our view, neither direction for conceptualizing a program is sufficient on its own, although we advocate the idea that a program should provide a forum for *nurturing particular dispositions* for inquiry, ways of seeing, critiquing and acting in classrooms. In order to elaborate and illustrate what we mean by this, we turn to a description of our recent research activities and we present some of the case material that has shaped our thinking.

Development Occurs in the Context of Reflective Practice

We approach the problem of nurturing and enhancing professional growth in the practice of teaching by investigating specific cases of experienced teachers working with student teachers in a practicum setting (MacKinnon and Erickson, 1988). These experienced teachers have created a collaborative research team with university personnel for the purpose of developing a systematic approach for teaching science using a 'constructivist perspective' (see Erickson, 1986, 1988 for an extended description of this project). Although our work focuses on the teaching of science, we believe that the methods we have employed and the findings we have reported tell a great deal about how one acquires the knowledge and dispositions that lead to competent professional practice.

The early work of this project was aimed at translating a general 'constructivist' perspective on learning into a set of practical activities for classroom use. This constructivist perspective on the acquisition of knowledge is informed by thinking in the philosophy of science, cognitive psychology, the sociology of knowledge and ethics. Briefly stated, it portrays learners as being purposeful sense-makers, constantly engaged in the task of *constructing* ideas to make sense out of the situations and events they encounter. Particular attention is placed on the existing knowledge and prior experiences that learners bring to the classroom, and the ways in which these interact with their current observations and interpretations.

The 'constructivist perspective' that guided our study serves as an example of an orienting framework that guides pedagogy and has its roots in 'the foundations'. One might expect that this framework could be monitored rather easily by examining its use by practitioners in interpreting situations encountered in their work. Yet at the outset of our research project we faced two problems. First, much of the literature on the nature of students' conceptions of science topics was based on clinical interviews and seemed to have limited direct application to the context of a classroom, where ideas are expressed through sharing and, in some cases, argument. Second, the theoretical frames and analytic schemes used to represent students' knowledge varied widely. The group had to distil from a diverse literature a general orienting frame that would help teachers develop a functional repertoire of materials and strategies for working in classrooms. A further consideration in the development of this frame was the need to establish a 'working language' that would enable us to interpret and analyze the characteristic features we associate with constructivist approaches to teaching science and also permit us to communicate that understanding to others. After numerous meetings and discussions over a period of a year, an orienting frame for analyzing practice gradually emerged. As the year progressed, the practical classroom problems encountered by the teachers became framed more frequently in terms of the insights and language drawn from selected articles read by the teachers in our group. Two distinct bodies of literature were drawn upon: a group of articles on constructivist approaches, outlining the nature of students' intuitions about science concepts and the pedagogical implications of this approach (e.g., Driver, Tiberghien and Guesne, 1985), and a second group of readings focusing on the nature and growth of professional knowledge — in particular, Schön (1983, 1987) and Shulman (1987).

As our research proceeded, we turned our attention to the matter of communicating our perspective to other experienced teachers and to beginning teachers in preservice preparation programs. We have found the preservice program and its practicum in particular to be especially informative, and it is our work in this latter setting that forms the basis for the case material presented below.

The task of communicating an interpretive framework for 'seeing' and analyzing classrooms is complicated. Our work with one student teacher, 'Rosie' (MacKinnon, 1989a; Erickson and MacKinnon, 1991), made this abundantly clear. In the early weeks of her practicum, Rosie displayed an 'extended teacher elaboration' pattern in her dialogue with students, in which she would constantly explain classroom phenomena for them. Rosie's performance in the classroom was telling of her view that *she* was the arbiter of knowledge, and the activity of teaching was to display her knowledge for the students. We have found this extended teacher elaboration pattern to be common among beginning science teachers, and we think it occurs for several reasons. First, we have observed that many preservice science teachers tend to have a 'naive inductivist' or 'positivistic' view of scientific knowledge (Aguirre, Haggerty and Linder, 1990; Kilbourn, 1990; Geddis, 1985). Second, this type of verbal domination is a more secure form of 'managing' instruction where teachers can control the classroom discourse. Finally, and perhaps most important, many preservice teachers appear to have a view of teaching and learning as a form of transfer or 'transmission' of knowledge from the teacher's mind to that of the student.

In his critique of her teaching, Rosie's supervising teacher, Colin, framed this particular issue in terms of a practical principle that he stated as 'giving over more responsibility for learning to the students'. However, it was not sufficient for Colin to simply *tell* Rosie about the elaboration pattern. Nor did it suffice to tell Rosie the importance he attached to giving over more responsibility for learning to the students. In the next several weeks of practicum, Colin had to revert to numerous 'showing' moves where he modelled for Rosie, in a variety of contexts, how a teacher might relinquish some of the usual control mechanisms found in classroom organization and hence might give students more responsibility for their own learning. Rosie's difficulty in understanding Colin's critique seemed rooted in her conception of what it means to teach. When he pointed out that she did much of the explaining of things herself, Rosie responded, 'Well, isn't that what teachers do? Isn't that a part of it?'

Rosie's case presents a challenge familiar to those involved in teacher education. Her own view of teaching as transmission, probably originating in her own experiences, may limit attempts to foster a disposition for her to inquire into her work with children so that her thinking about teaching is not fettered by rules. In our research, we have attempted to meet this challenge by returning to Dewey's ideas of foundations and by exploring the idea of *unifying the foundations* in experiences designed to promote reflective practice.

The notion of unifying the foundations of education with experiences designed to promote reflective practice is probably what Dewey had in mind when he wrote *The Sources of a Science of Education*. Yet there are few documented cases that illustrate what it looks like when a beginning teacher reflects on practice or what it means to bring foundational knowledge to life in the inquiries of practitioners. Our investigations show that this means particularizing the efforts of research in teacher education in terms of *this* beginning teacher, working with *these* students, dealing with *this* subject matter, using *these* materials, and so on. Another case from our research is illustrative:

Kevin, 24 years old with a first degree in engineering science, was a student teacher who claimed he always wanted to be a teacher. Much of his twelve-week practicum was spent teaching science at the Grade 9 level, working first through a unit on 'heat and temperature', then turning to a short unit dealing with the solar system. Shortly after his practicum began, it became evident that Kevin had a desire to inquire into his teaching, particularly in terms of how students were understanding the subject matter. During his initial lessons, Kevin discovered that several students failed to grasp the distinction between heat and temperature. In one lesson, he heated up a large bolt and a small nail until both were red-hot. This led students to suggest that the temperature of the two objects was roughly the same. The bolt and nail were then immersed in separate beakers with equal volumes of water to show that the heat from the bolt caused a greater increase in water temperature than that from the nail. This demonstration was used to help to establish the difference between the concept 'heat' (the amount of thermal energy transferred from one body to another) and the concept 'temperature' (a measure of the average kinetic energy). The students were to understand that heat is proportional to mass, whereas temperature is not. The following excerpt from the end of the lesson illustrates the difficulty students had with this idea.

Kevin: Everyone seemed to come up with the idea that the bolt caused a larger rise in temperature so it had more heat. It had the same temperature, but a higher heat. The only thing that was different was the mass. That's good. That's what I want to leave you with this lesson. I want you to realize that things can have the same temperature, but different amounts of heat. And the basic difference is mass. Because the larger bolt ... you're not really sure about that Jeni?

Jeni: I don't understand what you're talking ... what you just said. How is it that something can have the same ...

Kevin: Temperature . . .
Jeni: Yeah.
Kevin: . . . but different heat?
Jeni: I didn't understand that.

Later, Kevin discussed this episode from the lesson with his supervising teacher, Gary:

Kevin: The reason that I sometimes feel down after a lesson is that I'm not sure afterwards whether we have a lot of concrete things to show for it. It's so hard to gauge exactly what they've learned or whether they've understood the concepts that we've been discussing.
Gary: You feel disappointed sometimes when you get a little bit of feedback that seems to suggest that not everybody got it.
Kevin: Yeah.
Gary: I asked the kids, when I did this lesson, to develop analogies of heat and temperature.
Kevin: Actually, Mark [another student] gave me an analogy. He said, 'Well, I'm just starting to think about it like this . . .' And, you know, that's an excellent way.
Gary: One kid said, 'Think about two piles of dollar bills, one with only a few bills in it, one with hundreds of bills. The average value of each bill is the same in both piles'. Equivalent to the average kinetic energy . . . two things of the same temperature being the same.
Kevin: Yeah.
Gary: 'But there's more money in that pile than this pile'. That's an analogy of more heat.

This exchange provides an example of the sort of discourse that characterized Kevin and Gary's work together. On the one hand, Kevin showed a rather well developed disposition to inquire into what students understood in his lessons. On the other hand, Gary supplied the right kind of information to sustain a reflective stance in his conferences with Kevin. In thinking about the type of knowledge base we see developing within this general reflective framework, we have found it useful to draw upon Shulman's (1987) notion of 'pedagogical content knowledge'. Gary's 'money-pile' analogy that he uses to help students understand the distinction between heat and temperature illustrates the kind of knowledge we are referring to: pedagogical content knowledge develops with *reflective* experience in dealing with particular subject matter in particular ways, given certain students' approaches and understandings.

Kevin used similar analogies with the class as a whole and with the individual students who continued to have difficulty with the distinction between heat and temperature. However, the class performance on the test at the end of the unit gave rise to further inquiry, much of which had to do with the following question on the test:

> If you have a large ice cube and a small ice cube in water, the small ice cube will melt first. Are both ice cubes the same temperature? Do you think both ice cubes need the same amount of heat to melt them? Explain your answers.

Several students answered, 'Yes, the ice cubes are the same temperature because they are both frozen', and 'Yes, they will need the same amount of heat to melt'. This was quite perplexing for Kevin, who by now had spent considerable time on the concepts of heat and temperature. Kevin asked four students to stay after class to discuss their answers to the test question shown above. Two students had written that the ice cubes would require the same amount of heat to melt, and the other two said that the larger ice cube would require more heat. As the discussion proceeded, Kevin determined that these students seemed to be using two different conceptions of heat. Those who suggested the ice cubes required the same amount of heat to melt seemed to be thinking of heat as the *level of hotness* of the water, or temperature. They said once the water was a certain temperature, both ice cubes would begin to melt, though the larger one would take longer. In that sense, both would require the same amount of heat. The other two students argued that the larger ice cube would take more heat to melt, since it had a greater mass. The former conception of heat, Kevin thought, was consistent with the everyday use of the word. For example, Kevin noted that we talk about how hot it is outside, but we mean temperature. The latter conception of heat is consistent with the scientific concept of heat, namely, the amount of thermal energy transferred from one body to another. Once the students were able to see their different uses of language, they seemed to understand that both answers to the question were reasonable, but only one was 'correct' according to the scientific concept of heat.

Kevin's disposition to inquire into the ways students make sense of science was striking. After the episode involving students' understandings of heat and temperature, he commented on how he felt better prepared to teach, now that he had extended his own conceptual repertoire for understanding students' ideas. The vignette tells something of the idiosyncratic nature of the knowledge base required for competent practice, the nature of inquiry *in* practice, and the features of Kevin's program that allow this inquiry to flourish, and, subsequently, his knowledge base to develop. However, it is not yet clear how 'foundational disciplines' in education relate to these matters. To help elucidate the connection, we turn now to one final vignette from Kevin's practicum.

Kevin concluded his practicum with a short Grade 9 unit on the solar system. During one lesson, a student asked if the moon is a star. Another student suggested that stars give off their own light, but the moon reflects light from the sun. The following discussion occurred:

Kevin: Is the moon like a star? Does it give off light, or does it reflect light? Elise?

Elise: It reflects light.

Kevin: Does everyone feel comfortable with that?

Carol: Well, if it wasn't reflecting light, it probably wouldn't show the faces of the moon.

Grace: If it wasn't reflecting light, it would be so bright you'd just see ... all the color.

Kevin: Shadows?

Karen: You wouldn't see the shadows.

Carol: Well, that s because of the craters.

Karen: Yeah, there are shadows on the craters.

Kevin: If it were generating light, you wouldn't see those shadows.

Kevin discussed the episode with Gary as follows:

Kevin: A couple of kids offered some really good evidence to suggest that the moon isn't a star. And I didn't carry that at all.

Gary: Evidence that it is a star?

Kevin: Evidence that it isn't a star.

Gary: ... that it isn't. OK.

Kevin: I think some of the ideas they offered were really profound, and I don't think I really appreciated some of the things they were saying. One girl said, 'Well, if it wasn't reflecting, like, it wouldn't show the *faces* of the moon'. Later, I wondered if she said the *phases* of the moon.

Gary: Yes.

Kevin: Or maybe she was thinking of faces, which would imply shadows. I would have felt a lot better had I asked her to elaborate on that.

Gary: Yeah.

Kevin: We seem to be getting a lot of short answers out of people and I think, in order to get the gist of what they mean and what they really comprehend, I would have liked a bit more explanation on some of these things.

Kevin acknowledged that reference to either the moon's faces or its phases would count as evidence for the claim that it is not a star. By definition, a star gives off its own light. If the moon did give off its own light, neither its faces (the shadows of craters) nor its phases (new moon, half moon, etc.) would be visible. Kevin recognized that though he thought Carol referred to the moon's faces, she could have said 'phases'. He wondered what she did say, for if it had been phases, then his mention of shadows may have been inappropriate and he would have missed the point she was making.

Such stories were characteristic of the case of Kevin's practicum. We have drawn from these cases of student teachers working with experienced teachers in practicum because we believe that it is in this setting that we will learn something of the knowledge base required for competent teaching practice and how this knowledge is acquired. We have mentioned already that we feel that much of the knowledge base of teaching is idiosyncratic, meaning that it pertains to particular students working with particular subject matter, using particular materials, and so on. We believe, as Dewey did, that the 'science' of education is to be found in the *inquiries* of practitioners, and it is in these inquiries that knowledge about teaching takes on this idiosyncratic character.

However, there is also something of the 'foundations' to be found in the inquiries of practitioners. Inherent in the examples we have presented is foundational knowledge about the character of science as a way of interpreting and explaining nature on a firm footing of evidence. This is true not only of the established sciences but also of the thinking done by students of science. Kevin's recognition of this fact is manifest in his concern to honor the rationality of his students. When he inquires into whether Carol referred to the faces or the phases of the moon as evidence for the claim that it does not produce its own light, and is therefore not a star, he honors the conditions called forth to support a particular claim. In other words, he honors the scientific thinking of his student, relying on foundational knowledge of the nature of the discipline, science.

There is also an ethical component to Kevin's inquiries that can be said to emanate from foundational knowledge. Indeed, this ethical component may stem from a philosophical appreciation of the nature of knowledge itself, coming to fruition in a deep respect for students' existing knowledge of heat, temperature or the solar system, for example, and the subsequent ways they understand the business of the classroom. In other words, to disregard students' existing knowledge would be unethical.

The upshot of our argument is that the foundations of education derive contextual meaning *within* the reflective inquiries of practitioners. These inquiries take place in actual situations and they depend on the particular subject matter at hand, the previous knowledge, interests and purposes of students, as well as the materials and strategies used by the teacher. The foundational knowledge that is evident in the inquiries of the student teachers in our research includes the person's conception of what it means to teach, his or her understanding of the nature of the discipline of science, and the particular dispositions held about honoring (or not honoring) the rationality of students. Thus we have drawn from our work with beginning science teachers to illustrate the intertwining of Dewey's inquiry, his sources of knowledge, and Rugg's moral dimensions.

Repairing the Institutional 'Rift'

We began this chapter by drawing attention to questions raised in faculties of education about the place of 'foundation courses' in teacher education programs designed to promote reflective practice. We showed in Dewey's early work the interdependency of his 'sources of a science of education' and 'reflective inquiry'. Drawing from cases in our research with beginning science teachers, we illustrated how foundational knowledge comes to life in practitioners' inquiries. The point of the chapter, then, is to argue that it is a mistake to divide the world of teacher education into two extremes, with 'reflective practice' contrasting sharply with 'foundations'.

Perhaps the tendency to contrast reflective practice and foundational knowledge arises from the tradition of our thinking about education as a field of study that draws upon the established disciplines. We have traditionally held 'theory' apart from 'practice', for example. A related factor, which may be at the heart of the problem, is our institutional separation of 'foundations departments' from 'curriculum and instruction'. Perhaps we have lost sight of what Dewey was saying and have institutionally driven a wedge between reflection and foundations, where Rugg and Dewey saw them as inseparable.

In our work with beginning and experienced science teachers, we have begun to describe the knowledge base required for competent teaching practice. Certainly, knowledge of the subject matter is essential. We believe that an understanding of the nature of science is equally important. A third type of knowledge that seems essential is 'pedagogical content knowledge' (Shulman, 1987) — how to handle particular subject matter, with particular students, given a deep appreciation of how they understand the material.

A crucial question remains: Can these forms of foundational knowledge actually be learned in a meaningful way independent of experience in classrooms? In our work with beginning teachers we have observed that the knowledge base for teaching develops gradually and continually. With the prerequisite attitude toward inquiry, it is likely that this knowledge base develops throughout the career of a teacher. We think that dialogue with other teachers enhances this development when it takes the form of sustained 'constructive feedback' (Kilbourn, 1990). Further, we believe that an important aspect of a teacher education program is the provision of structures that allow this form of dialogue to occur, and that will allow us to see how the foundations of educational thought inform practice. Much work remains to be done on how such structures can be conceptualized and operationalized so that they can begin in preservice teacher development, be sustained by inservice professional development, and enhanced by graduate programs in education. Central to this continuum of teacher development is the fundamental premise that development occurs in the context of *reflective practice in educational situations*.

The 'forms' of knowledge we have mentioned do not in themselves provide an exhaustive list for the foundations of education. While we have not commented on the psychological foundations of educational thought, an appreciation of how students learn presupposes some awareness of psychological theories of learning. Nor have we commented extensively on how these forms subsume the various dispositions and capacities, such as intellectual empathy and caring, that are important to nurture among candidates in teacher education programs. Our observations and analyses foreshadow the need to embed foundational knowledge in reflective practice in schools. To the extent that the latter has become an acceptable construct for designing teacher education programs, we are encouraged. However, we do not see that the foundations program stands in opposition to this movement. We think there is great promise in repairing institutional 'rifts' and moving toward the design of teacher education programs that will allow us to analyze how foundational knowledge informs reflective practice.

References

AGUIRRE, J., HAGGERTY, S. and LINDER, C. (1990) 'Student-teachers' conceptions of science, teaching, and learning: A case study in preservice science education', *International Journal of Science Education*, **12**, pp. 381–390.

CLIFT, R.T., HOUSTON, W.R. and PUGACH, M.C. (Eds) (1990) *Encouraging Reflective Practice in Education: An Analysis of Issues and Programs*, New York, Teachers College Press.

DEWEY, J. (1909/1933) *How We Think*, New York, Heath and Company.

DEWEY, J. (1929) *The Sources of a Science of Education*, New York, Horace Liveright.

DRIVER, R., TIBERGHIEN, A. and GUESNE, E. (1985) *Children's Ideas in Science*, Milton Keynes, Open University Press.

ERICKSON, G.L. (1986) *Development of an Instructional Approach Based on a Cognitive Perspective*, Final Report 410-85-0611 to the Social Science and Humanities Research Council of Canada, Ottawa.

ERICKSON, G.L. (1987) *Constructivist Epistemology and the Professional Development of Teachers*, Paper presented at the Meeting of the American Educational Research Association, Washington, DC.

ERICKSON, G.L. (1988) *Processes and Products from the (SI)2 Project: Anatomy of a Collaborative Approach*, paper presented at the meeting of the Canadian Society for the Study of Education, Windsor, Ontario.

ERICKSON, G.L. and MACKINNON, A.M. (1991) 'Seeing classrooms in new ways: On becoming a science teacher', in SCHÖN, D.A. (Ed.) *The Reflective Turn: Case Studies in and on Educational Practice*, New York, Teachers College Press, pp. 15–36.

GEDDIS, A. (1985) *Perspectives on Knowledge in the Classroom: A Case Study in Science Teaching*, unpublished doctoral dissertation, University of Toronto, Toronto.

GRIMMETT, P.P. (1989) 'A commentary on Schön's view of reflection', *Journal of Curriculum and Supervision*, **5**, 1, pp. 19–28.

GRIMMETT, P.P., MacKINNON, A.M., ERICKSON, G.L. and RIECKEN, T.J. (1990) 'Reflective practice in teacher education', in CLIFT, R.T., HOUSTON, W.R. and PUGACH, M.C. (Eds), *Encouraging Reflective Practice in Education: An Analysis of Issues and Programs*, New York, Teachers College Press, pp. 20–38.

HULLFISH, H.G. and SMITH, P.G. (1961) *Reflective Thinking: The Method of Education*, New York, Dodd, Mead and Company.

KILBOURN, B. (1988) 'Reflecting on vignettes of teaching', in GRIMMETT, P.P. and ERICKSON, G.L. (Eds) *Reflection in Teacher Education*, Vancouver, Pacific Educational Press and New York, Teachers' College Press, pp. 99–111.

KILBOURN, B. (1990) *Constructive Feedback: Learning the Art*, Toronto, OISE Press.

MacKINNON, A.M. (1987) 'Detecting reflection-in-action among preservice elementary science teachers', *Teaching and Teacher Education*, **3**, 2, pp. 135–155.

MacKINNON, A.M. (1989a) *Conceptualizing a Reflective Practicum in Constructivist Science Teaching*, unpublished doctoral dissertation, University of British Columbia, Vancouver.

MacKINNON, A.M. (1989b) 'Conceptualizing a "Hall of Mirrors" in a science-teaching practicum', *Journal of Curriculum and Supervision*, **5**, 1, pp. 41–59.

MacKINNON, A.M. and ERICKSON, G.L. (1988) 'Taking Schön's ideas to a science teaching practicum', in GRIMMETT, P.P. and ERICKSON, G.L. (Eds) *Reflection in Teacher Education*, Vancouver, Pacific Educational Press and New York, Teachers College Press, pp. 113–137.

MUNBY, H. (1986) 'Metaphor in the thinking of teachers: An exploratory study', *Journal of Curriculum Studies*, **18**, 2, pp. 197–209.

ROBERTS, D.A. and CHASTKO, A.M. (1990) 'Absorption, refraction, reflection: An exploration of beginning science teacher thinking', *Science Education*, **74**, 2, pp. 197–224.

RUGG, H. (1947) *Foundations for American Education*, New York, World Book Company.

RUSSELL, T. (1987) 'Reframing the theory-practice relationship in inservice teacher education', in NEWTON, L.J., FULLAN, M. and MacDONALD, J.W. (Eds) *Rethinking Teacher Education: Exploring the Link between Research, Practice and Policy*, Toronto, Joint Council on Education, University of Toronto/OISE, pp. 125–134.

SCHÖN, D. (1983) *The Reflective Practitioner: How Professionals Think in Action*, New York, Basic Books.

SCHÖN, D. (1987) *Educating the Reflective Practitioner: Toward a New Design for Teaching and Learning in the Professions*, San Francisco, Jossey-Bass.

SCHÖN, D. (1988) 'Coaching reflective teaching', in GRIMMETT, P.P. and ERICKSON, G.L. (Eds) *Reflection in Teacher Education*, Vancouver, Pacific Educational Press and New York, Teachers College Press, pp. 19–29.

SCHWAB, J. (1970) *The Practical: A Language for Curriculum*, Washington, DC, National Education Association.

SCHWAB, J. (1971) 'The practical: Arts of the eclectic', *School Review*, **79**, 4, pp. 493–542.

SHULMAN, L.S. (1987) 'Knowledge and teaching: Foundations of the new reform', *Harvard Educational Review*, **57**, 1, pp. 114–135.

YINGER, R.J. (1990) 'The conversation of practice', in CLIFT, R.T., HOUSTON, W.R. and PUGACH, M.C. (Eds) *Encouraging Reflective Practice in Education: An Analysis of Issues and Programs*, New York, Teachers College Press, pp. 73–94.

Notes on Contributors

Sibylle Artz is a communications teacher and counsellor at the Bridges Project in Victoria, British Columbia. The project is a second stage program for women survivors of abuse. At the master's level, her inquiry focused on how ways of knowing affect life changes. Her doctoral research interests focus on teaching as a reflective praxis.

John R. Baird is Senior Lecturer at the Institute of Education, University of Melbourne, where he has responsibilities for staff development and lectures in science education. For four years (1987–1990) he was Senior Research Fellow in the Faculty of Education at Monash University, where he directed two major research projects that aimed to enhance the quality of teaching and learning in science classrooms. His recent publications relate to secondary-tertiary collaborative research, improvement of practice through enhanced metacognition, and staff development and school improvement.

Douglas Barnes was Reader in Education at the University of Leeds until his retirement in 1989. His publications have been in the areas of language for learning and curriculum studies: *From Communication to Curriculum*, *Practical Curriculum Study*, and (as co-author) *Language, the Learner and the School* and *Versions of English*. He has more recently published a short monograph on 'active learning' that arose from the evaluation of the Technical and Vocational Education Initiative.

Mary Louise Bellamy is Education Director of the National Association of Biology Teachers and author of the 'Biology Discovery Activities Kit', a supplementary laboratory manual for high school biology teachers. She completed her PhD in science education at the University of Maryland at College Park, with dissertation research focused on how teachers' knowledge of Mendelian genetics is translated into classroom teaching and related to students' understanding in high school biology.

Hilda Borko was Associate Professor at The University of Maryland, College Park. Her current research is in the areas of teacher cognition and learning to teach, and she is co-director of a longitudinal study of learning to teach middle school mathematics, funded in part by the National Science Foundation. She is editor of the 'Teaching, Learning, and Human Development' section of the *American Educational Research Journal*. In August 1991 she has accepted an appointment at the University of Colorado at Boulder.

Kathy Carter is Associate Professor in Teaching and Teacher Education at the University of Arizona. She is Advisory Editor of the Elementary School Journal and the American Educational Research Journal. She currently serves as Vice President of Division K of the American Educational Research Association. Her publications have appeared in the *Journal of Teacher Education, Teaching and Teacher Education, Elementary School Journal, Curriculum Inquiry, Journal of Education for Teaching* and *Journal of Curriculum Studies*. Her current work is focused on studies of teachers' knowledge and learning to teach and on the development of a case literature for teacher education.

D. Jean Clandinin is Associate Professor at the University of Alberta. Her research involves collaboration with teachers, using personal practical knowledge and story and narrative as ways of giving accounts of teachers' practice. She is the author of two books and many articles and chapters that explore issues in narrative inquiry, and she has published widely with F. Michael Connelly. Her forthcoming book *Learning to Teach: Teaching to Learn* is co-authored with teachers and student teachers who participated in a collaborative study of teacher education.

Gaalen Erickson is Associate Professor in the Department of Mathematics and Science Education at the University of British Columbia. He also serves as Acting Director of the Centre for the Study of Teacher Education at UBC. He has studied children's understandings in science with an active research group at UBC for fifteen years. While this research continues, his attention has turned to professional preparation and teacher education as well.

Brent Kilbourn is Associate Professor in the Joint Centre for Teacher Development and the Department of Curriculum at the Ontario Institute for Studies in Education. His contribution to this collection is one in a series of explorations of the nature of various school subjects in the context of the particulars of classroom interaction, reflection, self-monitoring, feedback and the improvement of teaching. His recent book, *Constructive Feedback: Learning the Art* (OISE Press, Brookline Books) is a detailed case-study of feedback as professional development in science teaching.

Allan MacKinnon is Assistant Professor in the Faculty of Education at Simon Fraser University, where he teaches in the area of science education. He is co-investigator in a study of science teacher development in which the focus is on analyzing the factors in teacher education programs that seem to enhance reflective processes among novice teachers. He is collaborating with teachers and school districts in British Columbia in the design of school-based teacher education programs.

Hugh Munby is Professor of Education in the Faculty of Education at Queen's University, Kingston, Ontario. He teaches graduate courses in research methods and curriculum studies, and works with preservice teachers in uses of computers. His research interests include science education and the role of metaphor in teachers' thinking about their practice. Since 1985, he has collaborated with Tom Russell in a series of studies of teachers' professional knowledge in which they have combined their interests in metaphor and reflection to develop case studies of preservice, beginning and experienced teachers. He also coaches sabre with the Queen's University Fencing Team.

Antoinette A. Oberg is Associate Professor in the Faculty of Education at the University of Victoria, British Columbia. Since 1978, she has worked with experienced educators in the Curriculum Studies Graduate Program, which is also the site for her research into reflection on practice. Accounts of her work have been published in *Theory into Practice, Phenomenology and Pedagogy* and the *Journal of Curriculum and Supervision*.

Anna E. Richert is Assistant Professor of Education at Mills College in Oakland, California. In both her teaching and her research she is examining notions of reflective practice. She places her research on teacher reflection into nested frames of teacher learning at one level, and the moral and ethical imperatives of teacher decision-making and knowledge construction at the next. Her current work focuses on the use of case methods in teacher education to enhance teacher reflection and teacher empowerment. In 1989 she received a research award from the Association of Colleges and Schools of Education in State Universities and Land Grant Colleges for her research on the use of case methods to enhance teacher reflection.

Jean Rudduck is Professor of Education and Director of the Qualitative and Quantitative Studies in Education Research Group at the University of Sheffield. She is currently working with David Gillborn and Jon Nixon on a series of studies of the positive ways in which schools are responding to issues of gender, race and discipline. She has recently published *Innovation and Change* (Open University Press, 1990) and four books on cooperative group work in schools (with Helen Cowie, BP Publications, 1988, 1991).

Tom Russell is Professor of Education in the Faculty of Education at Queen's University, Kingston, Ontario. He teaches in the areas of science education and curriculum studies, with special interests in the improvement of teaching; he works with preservice teachers in the area of physics. Since 1985, he has collaborated with Hugh Munby on a series of studies of teachers' professional knowledge, with special interest in how reflection can lead to new frames for practice and to new practices. He is co-editor of *Science Education in Canadian Schools: Cases Studies of Science Teaching* (Science Council of Canada, 1984).

Linda Sanders works in undergraduate and graduate teacher education programs at Christopher Newport College in Newport News, Virginia. Her research interests are in the areas of teacher knowledge and beliefs and their development in preservice and inservice teachers. She completed her Ph.D. degree in science education at the University of Maryland at College Park, where her dissertation study examined the planning, interactive teaching and reflections of experienced secondary teachers.

Name Index

Subject Index

'A' level, 158

Backtalk, 101, 106
Biography, 119
Bullock
    Committee, 27
    Report, 28–9

Case method, 109, 112–121 study, 6
Chemistry, 90, 96, 102–3, 107, 157
Classroom
    management, 92, 99, 103
    understanding, 75 –6, 87, 89
Cognitive
    skill, 49–50, 54, 68
    structure, 67,
Collaborative reflection, 33
    research, 128
Constructivism, 36, 201
Content, 97
    analysis, 174
    specific pedagogy, 185–7
    see also Knowledge
Conversation of instruction, 72–3, 75,
    79–80, 82, 85, 89
Council for the Accreditation of Teacher
    Education, 7, 157–60
Critical action research, 164–5
Curriculum
    development, 4, 9, 12, 18
    studies, 145, 149

Dilemma, 10, 15, 17, 163
    see also Teaching
Disciplinary knowledge, 111

Education, science of, 2, 193–4, 203
Expert, 5, 49, 50, 52, 54–5, 62, 66–8

Feedback, 101, 106
Foundational disciplines, 192–3, 205
Foundations, 7, 192–3, 200–3, 207–8
Foundations of Education Movement,
    197
Frame, 4, 9–10, 15–21, 24–7, 29–31, 98,
    103, 104, 106, 199
    see also Reframing

Gender bias, 86

Hegemony, 153
Hermeneutics, 141
Higher education, 157–8, 160
Historical inquiry, 74, 80, 82, 86–7
History, 71–3

Knowing-in-action, 4, 40, 199
    see also Reflection-in-Action
Knowledge
    content, 102, 106, 120
    pedagogical, 6
    pedagogical content, 50–1, 65–6, 71,
        90–1, 204
    personal, 111, 129
    personal practical, 125, 128
    professional, 90, 101, 118, 192
    structures, 50–1, 66, 68
    teacher, 16, 49, 109, 110–119, 125

Language Across the Curriculum, 4, 28–
    9
London Association for the Teaching of
    English, 4, 11–12, 27

Management, 49, 52
Mentor, 144

218